What they said about
The Truth of ...

'The merit of this book is the accumulation of detail—facts not really secret but unknown to the public at large—that makes a very formidable indictment against Kerr.'

Graham Freudenberg

'Who to believe. Sir John or Mr Whitlam? Mr Whitlam's account, in my view, is more believable than Sir John's.'

Peter Bowers, *Sydney Morning Herald*

'...makes some powerful points, both as to the political happenings during the troubled years of 1975 and in regard to Whitlam's relationship with Sir John Kerr, points which undoubtedly put some very large question marks after some of Kerr's assertions in his book *Matters For Judgment*.'

Alan Reid, *Bulletin*

'The last chapter of Mr Whitlam's book is entitled "Towards the Republic". It is also the best chapter...With characteristic freshness he points out that under the Statute of Westminster, which he would like repealed, Australia and Canada are less independent monarchies than Papua New Guinea...'

Peter Hastings, *Sydney Morning Herald*

Gough

Whitlam

The Truth of the Matter

MELBOURNE
UNIVERSITY
PRESS

MELBOURNE UNIVERSITY PRESS
An imprint of Melbourne University Publishing Ltd
187 Grattan Street, Carlton, Victoria 3053, Australia
mup-info@unimelb.edu.au
www.mup.com.au

First published by Penguin Books Australia 1979
Second Edition by Penguin Books Australia 1983
Text © Gough Whitlam 1979, 2005
Design and typography © Melbourne University Publishing Ltd 2005

Designed by Guy Mirabella
Typeset in Granjon by J&M Typesetting
Printed in Australia by McPherson's Printing Group

National Library of Australia Cataloguing-in-Publication entry:
Whitlam, Gough, 1916– .
The truth of the matter.

3rd edn.
Bibliography.
Includes index.
ISBN 0 522 85216 5.

ISBN 0 522 85212 2 (pbk).

1. Australia – Politics and government – 1972–1975. I.
Title.

994.062

To strive, to seek, to find, and not to yield.
Tennyson, *Ulysses*

To the Federal Parliamentary Labor Party 1972–75

CONTENTS

INTRODUCTION TO THE THIRD EDITION

'MAINTAIN YOUR RAGE AND YOUR ENTHUSIASM
FOR THE ELECTION NOW TO BE HELD . . .'

I republish *The Truth of the Matter* as a tribute to the men and women of Australia who uphold the spirit of the second and more important of my injunctions on the steps of Parliament House on 11 November 1975—to those of all parties who maintain their enthusiasm for Australian parliamentary democracy, despite the grievous blow it suffered on that momentous day thirty years ago. The youngest voters in 1975 are now forty-eight; and I am grateful to Melbourne University Publishing for the opportunity to present to the new generations the enduring principles at stake in the crisis, as relevant as ever to Australia's future.

I offer this edition unrevised since 1979. In the second Penguin edition of 1983 I was able to say:

The revelations of the past four years have reinforced the central themes of this book: that the crisis of 1975 was essentially not only a *constitutional* crisis but also a *political* crisis; that the action of the Governor-General can be understood only in political terms, not in constitutional terms at all; and that his action represented not only a gross perversion of the Constitution and its conventions but a gross misreading of the political realities. The Governor-General had no right whatsoever to make a political assessment even if it had been correct. There was a political crisis entirely capable of a political solution. Although the constitutional anomalies would remain, the political resolution was imminent.

Since then, a mass of new material has accumulated in the shape of histories, biographies and autobiographies, personal reminiscences, television interviews, documentaries and scholarly writings on the law and the Constitution. My Government's Cabinet papers are now open to the public. No episode in our political history has been so thoroughly traversed. Overwhelmingly, the new material confirms the central arguments and assertions of this book.

Yet illuminating and conclusive as the additional matter may be, it can at best only supplement what is already known from the contemporary public record. In the writing and understanding of history, there is no substitute for *the document*. In the case of Australia's political and constitutional crisis of October–November 1975, we have always had available the greatest public document of all—the Hansard, the record of debates and proceedings in the Australian Parliament. In no other publication is the true nature of the crisis in its political and constitutional aspects more thoroughly exposed, explored and explained. Even in its more farcical aspects, Fred Daly's hilarious account to Parliament of the visit of Tirath Khemlani to Canberra tells more about the so-called loan affair than all the other outpourings put together.

The real story revealed in Hansard is a tale of two crises; one conducted openly, frankly, robustly in the full light of day before Parliament and the public; the other conceived in secrecy and deceit. One was the authentic crisis from 15 October to the morning of 11 November. By definition, Hansard is silent on the ambush. Yet knowing what we now know, that silence itself speaks volumes; and again, a careful reading of the available documents, such as Sir John Kerr's Statement and Sir Garfield Barwick's Opinion, can provide fresh insights in the light of the later knowledge.

If I were rewriting this book the only change would be to emphasise the parliamentary record as the primary source of the truth of the matter for the new generations. I take the opportunity of this new introduction to make the point by way of five references to Hansard.

(1) Even after thirty years, it is breathtaking to read the actual terms of the Senate resolutions against my Government and to realise the arrogance of the demand which a mere half of the Senate was making on the House of Representatives. The breaches of constitutional convention which had created this 'tainted Senate' are described in Chapter 5 of this book. Thus, on 15 October the coalition Opposition was able to muster the numbers for a resolution: 'This Bill (the Loan Bill 1975) be not proceeded with until the Government agrees to submit itself to the judgement of the people . . .'.

The Senate was claiming the unilateral power to terminate the House of Representatives, elected only seventeen months earlier, without itself going to an election. Further, it was claiming to exercise this power, not by a vote to reject the Budget or refuse Supply—it never dared to do so from the beginning to the end of the crisis—but by the mere expression of its political opinion. This is what I called the Senate's act of aggression. My colleagues and I were determined to resist it because we were duty bound to resist it. As I said in the House of Representatives on 21 October (p. 2306):

> The Government—any elected government—based upon the majority in the House of Representatives, must be able to govern. This is an issue not just for this present Government or for me; it is a principle of fundamental importance for all future governments and Prime Ministers and for Australia. This must be emphasised: In this grave constitutional crisis, this crucial dispute between the two Houses, none of the electoral options available are in any way relevant to the issue at stake. The fact, for example, that there are grounds extant for a double dissolution does not solve the problem—it compounds it. There can be no double dissolution on this issue—on the grounds of Senate deferral or even rejection of the Budget. The grounds for a double dissolution on this issue do not exist. They could not exist for at least another 3 months—until after the Senate had twice rejected the Appropriation Bills.
>
> To seek a double dissolution now on other grounds, however sound in themselves, would simply concede the right of the Senate to send the House of Representatives to an election any time the Senate chose. It would concede the

very principle at stake. It would be surrender to the
unconstitutional pretensions of the Senate to make or break
governments formed in the House of Representatives. To
concede that right now, to surrender that principle now,
would be to establish a spurious right, a non-existent power
to the Senate for all time. We will not sell out the
constitutional rights of this House. We will not barter
away the future of this House.

That was the whole issue at stake throughout the entire
crisis, until the moment of Sir John Kerr's coup.

(2) Far from denying the existence in the Constitution of a
Senate power to *reject* money Bills, I never ceased to challenge
Mr Fraser to bring it to the test. In answer after answer and
speech after speech, Hansard shows that our standing challenge
to him was to allow his followers to stop stalling and vote directly to reject the Appropriation Bills. Everyone in the House knew
that such a vote would end the crisis once and for all. I knew
and he knew that there were honourable senators who would
never break the fundamental convention of our parliamentary
democracy. Just one changed vote would have been enough.

Hansard discloses a decisive change in the atmosphere in
Parliament from Tuesday 28 October. Two things had happened
during the weekend. The published opinion polls showed that
70 per cent of the people wanted the Senate to pass the Budget.
On the Saturday night, on the ABC's *Four Corners*, Senator Eric
Bessell (Liberal, Tasmania) said that he would not vote for
rejection and 'I would think that there would be a good many
others who would feel the same as I do on the question of
rejection'. In other words, Senator Bessell would never have

been party to the ultimate breach of parliamentary government—the rejection of Supply by an Upper House. In the
original edition of this book, Chapter 6, entitled 'The Senate on
Strike', I was able to provide indirect evidence of 'the good
many others' who shared his principled view; and after its
publication, Senators Neville Bonner (Queensland) and Don
Jessop (South Australia) identified themselves. But the great
significance of Senator Bessell's statement was that it placed on
the public record, as an absolute certainty, that the Budget Bills
would pass as soon as the Senate could be brought to vote on
them. From that moment it was no longer a question of 'if', but
only a question of 'when'. Senator Bessell had clearly pointed the
way to an end of the crisis. I read his statement to Parliament on
28 October. Sir John Kerr must have known about it.

(3) Hansard explodes the many myths about my attitude to
Sir John Kerr. Indeed, the most remarkable feature of the
parliamentary record of the crisis is the almost total absence of
discussion of the Governor-General or his role. For my part, the
one substantial reference was on Tuesday 21 October when I said:

> There have been those long months of conditioning by the
> political, the business and media interests who have never
> been prepared to accept the legitimacy of an Australian
> Labor government. Now we are seeing a fresh phase in this
> exercise. Now we have the headlines: 'Will Sir John Kerr
> act?' and 'Fraser says Kerr must sack PM'. Where will this
> intimidation stop?

In Chapter 7 of this book, entitled 'The Governor-General
Consults', I give the context of this reference (pp. 125–7). I

included it in my speech in response to, and in sympathy with, a complaint about the 'intimidation' by Sir John Kerr himself!

Mr Fraser made almost as many speeches as I did during those four weeks. Yet in Hansard you will find only one reference to the role of the Governor-General. Almost literally at the eleventh hour of the eleventh day of the eleventh month, in his last speech before my dismissal, when he was privy to what was about to happen, he said:

> He has not said that he would accept the Governor-General's decision taken in accordance with his constitutional prerogative. There are circumstances, as I have said repeatedly, when a Governor-General may have to act as the ultimate protector of the Constitution. He ignores that prerogative.

And that's it. Whatever Mr Fraser might have said outside about the Governor-General's 'prerogative', he never discussed it openly in Parliament. There it could have been debated seriously and disposed of completely. But that would have given the game away.

(4) The only notable exception to the general parliamentary silence about the Governor-General was a speech by Robert Ellicott, also on 21 October. In his speech Mr Ellicott repeated his notions of the Governor-General's 'prerogative' which he had already communicated to Sir John Kerr, at least by way of press release, on 16 October, the first full day of the crisis. On the very day Mr Ellicott made his speech, Sir John Kerr telephoned me at Parliament House to say: 'This Ellicott thing ... it's all bullshit, isn't it.' The full story of the Ellicott memorandum, and its 6000-word rebuttal by the Crown law officers, is set out in the

book on pages 113–16. I need, however, quote only one sentence from Mr Ellicott's statement: 'The Prime Minister is treating the Governor-General as a mere automaton with no public will of his own, sitting at Yarralumla waiting to do his bidding.' Note the date—16 October, less than twenty-four hours into the crisis!

The more sinister implications of Mr Ellicott's speech in Parliament surfaced only months later when he had become Attorney-General in the Fraser Government. Vowing to leave 'no stone unturned', he referred to a petition he had presented earlier that afternoon after it 'just happened to come in the mail'. The petition was in fact from the Sydney solicitor Danny Sankey, seeking Hansard documents in order to prosecute me, Rex Connor, Jim Cairns and Lionel Murphy under the Commonwealth Crimes Act in relation to the Executive Council's authority to borrow US\$4000 million in December 1974. I describe the so-called loan affair, which was used to ignite the crisis, in Chapter 4, entitled 'Resource Developments'. The Sankey prosecution, as it stood at the end of 1978, is dealt with in Chapter 10, entitled 'Breach of Faith'; the end of this expensive farce is described in the third item in Extended Biographies in this edition.

(5) Hansard utterly refutes Mr Ellicott's claims about my attitude to the Governor-General. Assuredly, I asserted the fundamental principle of Westminster parliamentary democracy: that the monarch or the viceroy must act only with and upon the advice of the Prime Minister having the confidence of the people's House, in Britain the House of Commons, in Australia the House of Representatives. On 11 November Sir John Kerr, in collusion with the Chief Justice, Sir Garfield

Barwick, turned this basic principle on its head. Barwick invented the monstrous doctrine that a Prime Minister must have the confidence of both Houses; that, he later said, was a condition of a government's legitimacy. Thus, according to the Barwick doctrine, the Howard Government was illegitimate from 1996 to 2005. In essence, Sir John Kerr dismissed the Prime Minister who had the undefeated confidence of the House of Representatives but who would not give him the advice he wanted and installed a Prime Minister who would. The House of Representatives immediately voted no-confidence in the new Prime Minister by a majority of ten. The House requested Speaker Gordon Scholes to inform the Governor-General of its vote. Kerr refused to receive the Speaker until after the Parliament had been dissolved, the ultimate act of contempt for the House of Representatives.

The spurious nature of the advice Mr Fraser purported to give the Governor-General is revealed in his first and last speech as Prime Minister to the 29th Parliament, when he said:

> Under the terms of the double dissolution the Bills that are
> in a double dissolution position will all be cited in that
> double dissolution and honourable members will have in
> mind the significance of that.

He had been commissioned to form government on condition that he advise the Governor-General to dissolve both Houses on the grounds that the Senate had twice rejected twenty-one Bills. If Sir John Kerr had believed for a minute that this rejection was a genuine ground for a double dissolution, he would have insisted that Mr Fraser undertake that, if he won the election, he would reintroduce and support the twenty-one Bills.

If he had been in the least competent, he would also have submitted the Constitutional Alteration (Simultaneous Elections) proposal to the electors on the same date as the elections were held.

In this retrospect, I have stressed the importance of the parliamentary record because I believe it contains the most coherent and comprehensive account of the crisis and the issues at stake—right up to the morning of 11 November. We then move into a murkier sphere, from the openness of Parliament to the secrecy and duplicity of Yarralumla. Herein lies the importance of publications and revelations since the first edition of 1979 and the second edition of 1983. From the mass of material I select a few of the most illuminating.

(i)   Sir Clarrie Harders, Secretary of the Attorney-General's Department (1970–79), has condemned Kerr's conduct in a comprehensive interview for the Oral History Collection at the National Library of Australia (December 1996–January 1997):

Peremptorily handing Mr Whitlam a letter [of dismissal] but giving at the very least a broad hint that things would be okay pretty soon for Mr Fraser . . . was not excusable. Sir John should have taken his courage in his hands and had it out with Mr Whitlam before 11 November.

(ii) In *Things You Learn Along the Way* (David Lovell Publishing, 1999) John Menadue, who was the Secretary of the Prime Minister's Department from August 1974 to November 1976, wrote:

The Palace was not amused by what Kerr had done. I learned of this later from a note from Tim McDonald, the

Official Secretary at Australia House, London, who relayed to me a discussion he had had with Sir Martin Charteris, who was personal secretary and political adviser to the Queen at the time. The discussion that McDonald had with Charteris was within a few weeks of the dismissal. Commenting on the Whitlam dismissal, Charteris said to McDonald that 'the Palace shared the view that Kerr acted prematurely. If faced with a constitutional crisis which appeared likely to involve the Head of State, my advice would have been that [the Queen] should only intervene when a clear sense of inevitability had developed in the public that she must act. This had been Kerr's mistake.' A clear sense of inevitability had not been arrived at.

(iii) Sir John Kerr purported to dismiss my Government under what he called the 'reserve powers'. Despite the 6000 words in the memorandum by the Solicitor-General Sir Maurice Byers, endorsed by the Attorney-General Kep Enderby, he said in his statement of 11 November: 'I should be surprised if the Law Officers expressed the view that there is no reserve power for the Governor-General to dismiss a Ministry.'

Sir Maurice Byers condemned Kerr's plea of 'reserve powers' in a powerful interview published in *Millennium Dilemma* (University of Wollongong, 2000):

I would say now, having a long life of reflection, that the reserve powers are a fiction. They don't exist. I've refrained from saying so in the advice I gave to the Governor-General at Gough Whitlam's suggestion in 1975. But it seems to me that the reason why the reserve powers can't exist is that you

can't have an autocratic power which is destructive of the
granted authority to the people. They just can't coexist.
Therefore you can't have a reserve power because you are
saying 'the Governor-General can override the people's
choice'. That is really what you're saying. And that's
nonsense. I should have been more explicit and said
'reserve powers are nonsense'.

(iv) In his balanced account *November 1975* (Allen & Unwin,
      1995), published for the twentieth anniversary of the
      Dismissal, Paul Kelly quotes an interview he had with
      Sir Roden Cutler VC, who, as Governor of New South
      Wales, would have been Administrator had Kerr
      proceeded with his proposed overseas trip in November.

I thought it was wrong for the Governor-General to dismiss
Whitlam when he had a majority in Parliament. I thought
that the Parliament had created the problem and the
Parliament should solve it . . . My view was that he did not
have to act at that time . . . My impression is that Kerr acted
from a sense of *folie de grandeur*. I think that Kerr liked
being in the job and did not want to leave it. In one sense
I think he welcomed the opportunity to be the political
dictator of Australia. (p. 298)

Further, in a *Four Corners* program on 6 March 1995, Sir Roden
said:

I think a Governor-General should never be worried about
the security of his job. I think that it is always on the line

and I think Sir John Kerr was not prepared to put it on the
line. I think he intentionally meant to deceive Whitlam.

I had readily agreed to Kerr's request that he be allowed to
discuss the Supply crisis with the Leader of the Opposition. Paul
Kelly wrote (p. 160):

Whitlam let Kerr see Fraser because he trusted Kerr.

That trust, more than anything else, was based on my respect
for the office, whoever held it. Writers and commentators
continue to assert that my great mistake was to take Kerr for
granted. The only thing I took for granted was that he would act
honourably and openly with the Prime Minister. Kerr himself
has said: 'I can hardly be blamed for the fact that they misread
my character. If they were deceived they deceived themselves.'
And Malcolm Fraser told SBS television that he was a better
judge of Kerr's psychology than I was. I reject the notion that
my job was to assess Kerr's character or to psychoanalyse him. If
there was any assessment to be made, it was about the character,
duties and responsibilities of our respective offices under the
Constitution, on the same basis of mutual trust and respect
which I enjoyed with his predecessor, Sir Paul Hasluck.

*   *   *

In December 1974 Hasluck prepared five groups of records for
the National Archives. The records were to remain sealed until
they approached the open period. They included his notes of
conversations with Prime Ministers and ministers, including his

conversations with me about his retirement as Governor-General and the appointment of his successor. These records were at last released on 5 May 2005.

Hasluck took office as Governor-General on 30 April 1969. The Queen commissioned him to be Governor-General 'during Our Pleasure'. There is a tradition that Governors-General should hold office for five years but their commissions do not state periods or dates. Quite soon after I was elected I had asked him if he would stay in office for a further two years after April 1974 and he had said that he would consider it but, having regard to the attitude of his wife, he doubted whether he could do so. In June 1973 I again raised the possibility with him. He told me that since I had taken office he had had more conversations with me in six months than he had had in the full term of my predecessors. He said that in order to be of possible help to me he had jotted down some names to be considered as examples of various classes of persons to be considered rather than as nominations: Ministerial, Crean and Beazley; Judiciary, John Kerr; Academic, David Derham and Kenneth Wheare; Big Business, Vincent Fairfax and Kenneth Myer; and Trade Unions, H. J. Souter. It is reasonable to speculate why Hasluck could have confidential and fruitful conversations with me and why Kerr could not. There was not the slightest reason, at least on my part, why Sir John Kerr could not have had the same frank and open relationship. It was his for the choosing. He chose otherwise.

I am profoundly, almost preternaturally, reluctant to use the term 'conspiracy', whether referring to collusion between Kerr, Barwick and Fraser or to allegations of possible CIA involvement. In the light of later revelations, however, there is one aspect of those events which is seldom noticed but which

Confidential

GOVERNMENT HOUSE
CANBERRA

for P. M

Hon Frank Crean
Hon K. E. Beazley
David Derham
John Kerr
Sir Kenneth Wheare
Sir Vincent Fairfax
mr - Kenneth Myer
H. J. Souter.

Sir Paul Hasluck's list of types of possible successors

might justify the term. I refer to the question of a half-Senate election. On page 135 of this book I deal with Kerr's failure to take the many opportunities to be open with me, such as our relaxed conversation at Kirribilli House after the visit there by Princess Margaret late in the afternoon of Sunday 2 November. On page 37 of my book *Abiding Interests* (University of Queensland Press, 1997) I was able to give an account of another event that same afternoon, the meeting at Treasury Place, Melbourne, between Fraser, Lynch and Anthony and Premiers Hamer (Victoria), Lewis (NSW) and Bjelke-Petersen (Queensland). At that meeting the Premiers decided that they would advise the State Governors to disregard any request by the Governor-General to issue writs for a Senate election. There could scarcely be a more flagrant breach of the conventions of the Constitution. Fraser's staff telephoned this information to Kerr's Official Secretary, David Iser Smith, at Admiralty House. At no time did Kerr discuss this with me. With the authority of the Labor Caucus I had gone to Government House to advise such an election; instead he handed me his letter of dismissal. I later learnt that a few days after 2 November, in the critical first sitting week in November, the President of the Senate, Justin O'Byrne, happened to walk round to the office of the Clerk of the Senate, James Rowland Odgers, who was notoriously involved in giving tactical advice to the Opposition. O'Byrne found Odgers closeted with Smith. One is entitled to ask why the Official Secretary of the Governor-General was consulting the Clerk of the Senate without informing the President of the Senate. From such improprieties, piled one upon the other, the coup of 11 November 1975 was manufactured.

Kerr's conduct towards me would be unimportant today except that its result was a blow to the authority of the House of Representatives from which it has never really recovered. A House of Parliament whose Speaker, metaphorically and almost expressly, was kept waiting outside the gates of Government House, was lowered immensely in public esteem. I was the last Prime Minister of Australia to defend and protect the rights and authority of the House of Representatives. The constitutional right of the House of Representatives to run the term for which it was elected is basic to its authority, just as this right was not only at the heart of the crisis of October–November 1975 but also at the heart of the crisis of April 1974. As the leader of the coalition in the Senate, Reg Withers, confessed: 'From March 1973 we set upon a course to bring about an election for the House of Representatives.' Until 1955 the House of Representatives ran its term except for the double dissolutions of 1914 and 1951 and the government defeats in the House in 1929 and 1931. Sir Robert Menzies held premature and opportunistic elections in 1955 and 1963; but even he felt obliged to cite exceptional circumstances to justify his advice to the Governor-General. Since 1975 it has become routine, accepted apparently without demur, for my successors to advise elections at any time to maximise their Party's advantage. Especially since 1996, nothing has done more to undermine the effectiveness of the House of Representatives as a legislative body than the way in which the Prime Minister has kept its members in almost permanent election mode.

In 1979 I concluded this book by a commitment to an Australian republic. In the preface to the 1983 edition I stressed the necessity to amend the Constitution to synchronise the elections and terms of members of both Houses and to counter the capricious conduct of Prime Ministers. I concluded:

> The uncertainty of election dates remains the most serious problem of Australian politics. Its resolution is the most urgent task for the Federal Parliament, whichever party or coalition has a majority in it.

Since then I have constantly urged Federal and State parliamentarians to move to the US system of holding simultaneous Federal and State elections on fixed dates. Since the double dissolution election on 13 December 1975 there have been eleven elections for the Senate and the House of Representatives (four in March, one in July, three in October, one in November and two in December), ten elections for the Assembly in Queensland, nine elections for the Assemblies and Councils in NSW, Victoria and WA and the Assembly in Tasmania and eight elections for the Assembly and Council in SA. (Some of Tasmania's Legislative Councillors are elected every May.) States held simultaneous elections only once; WA's two Houses and Tasmania's Assembly were both elected on 8 February 1986.

Australia and the USA have two-party systems. In Australia both sides of politics at Federal elections blame the State Governments for health, educational and transport short-comings and at State elections both sides blame the Federal Government for those shortcomings. In the USA each side presents a co-ordinated and co-operative program at simultaneous Federal and State elections.

In Australia since 1918 a Federal law has prevented State elections being held on the day of a Federal election or by-election or referendum; it should be repealed. The permanent electioneering associated with the multiplicity of election dates comes at an unacceptable cost: the lack of respect for parliaments and politicians, the buck-passing of responsibility for finances and functions between the parliaments and the risk of political corruption in the political parties.

In Australia the multiplicity of State and Federal elections, far from strengthening parliamentary democracy, weakens it. It is the major reason for the growing ascendancy of the party machines over parliamentarians and candidates. It facilitates the systematic corruption of democracy perpetrated by the expenditure of vast sums of public money on propaganda masquerading as government advertising on television. Democracy! What crimes are committed in thy name!

During the crisis of 1975 the debate hinged upon the meaning of the constitutional term 'responsible government'. It revived the question which dominated the great Constitutional Conventions from 1891 to 1898: 'Will Federation kill responsible government or will responsible government kill the Federation?' Next year the Parliaments of NSW, Victoria, South Australia and Tasmania will celebrate 150 years of responsible government. Parliamentarians of all parties could make no greater contribution to restoring the health and strength of responsible government, in both its constitutional and common usage, than to celebrate 2006 by working towards simultaneous Federal and State elections on fixed dates. It would transform our parliamentary democracy. It would transform and re-energise our Federation. Not least, it would make impossible a repetition of 11 November 1975.

PREFACE TO THE FIRST EDITION (1979)

OVER THE PAST YEAR I have been gathering material for an account of the aspirations and achievements of the Labor Government which was elected by the Australian people on 2 December 1972 and again on 18 May 1974 but which was dismissed by the Governor-General, Sir John Kerr, on 11 November 1975.

Late in November the Australian metropolitan dailies serialised Sir John's book, *Matters for Judgment*. It was published in December. I decided to set the record straight immediately on the personal, political and constitutional issues raised in that book.

Gough Whitlam
Australian National University
Canberra
January 1979

1

THE SENATE V. THE PEOPLE

'WE EMBARKED ON A COURSE SOME TWELVE MONTHS
AGO—I AM NOT TRYING TO BE PROVOCATIVE—TO BRING
ABOUT A HOUSE OF REPRESENTATIVES ELECTION.'
Senator Reginald Withers, 10 April 1974

On 10 November 1975 the Chief Justice of Australia, Sir Garfield Barwick, visited Admiralty House, the Governor-General's official residence in Sydney, at Sir John Kerr's request. Sir John's invitation was made without the knowledge or consent of his constitutional advisers, of whom I, as Prime Minister, was then chief. Rather, I had specifically advised against such a course as improper. Writing to the Governor-General that day, to confirm that in his opinion 'the course upon which Your Excellency has determined is consistent with your constitutional authority and duty', Sir Garfield asserted: 'A government having the confidence of the House of Representatives but not that of the Senate, both elected Houses, cannot secure Supply to the Crown.'

I shall, in its appropriate place, examine the merits of Sir Garfield's assertion—and his action. At this stage, it is enough to point out that, in a single sentence, he purported to settle the whole range of issues, political as well as constitutional, which had been the subject of the most intense and intensive debate of its kind Australia has ever known.

It must be emphasised that the crisis of October–November 1975 was essentially a political crisis, capable of solution by political means. Sir Garfield's assertion is in fact not a description of the Australian Constitution at all but a description of the Australian political situation as he claimed to see it on 10 November 1975. I propose to show that it was, at best, an inadequate description; there was, neither on 10 November nor on 11 November, justification for anybody to assert baldly that my Government '*cannot* secure' Supply. Again, I emphasise that such a judgement, in the circumstances of October–November 1975, was political not constitutional. Of all the principal persons involved in the crisis, the Chief Justice of Australia was the least fit or fitted to make it. When judges make pronouncements *sub rosa* and *ex parte,* they are no wiser than lesser breeds without the law.

Australian conservatives have since attempted to erect Sir Garfield's dictum into a doctrine. That is why it is so dangerous and why I have chosen to introduce my account by referring to it. If indeed, as Sir Garfield asserts, a government must have the confidence of both Houses of the Australian Parliament to secure Supply, he has written a prescription for permanent instability and for the paralysis of responsible government. In a two-party parliamentary system, such as ours essentially is, the 'confidence' of both Houses would require a majority in both Houses. Such a requirement overturns the fundamental principle of responsible government: that governments are made and unmade in the Lower House—in Australia, the House of Representatives.

Between 1949, the first election using the proportional system of voting for the Senate, and the 1975 double dissolution, the parties controlling the House of Representatives had had a majority in the Senate for only eight years. The Liberal and Country Parties never had a majority in the Senate under Prime Ministers Holt, Gorton and McMahon and had a majority for less than half the time under Prime Minister Menzies. They did not have a majority in the Senate for over two of the five years that Sir Garfield was Attorney-General.

In 1963 Sir Robert Menzies successfully asked the Governor-General, Lord De L'Isle, to dissolve the House of Representatives a year ahead of due time. The senators at that time had begun their six-year terms of service on 1 July 1959 and 1 July 1962. The Constitution allows an election to fill vacant places in the Senate within one year before the places are to become vacant. Therefore there could not be a Senate election before July 1964. As a result, Australia had an election for half the Senate in 1964, a House of Representatives election in 1966, another half-Senate election in 1967, a House of Representatives election in 1969, yet another half-Senate election in 1970 and a House of Representatives election in 1972. For a decade, therefore, the two Houses of Parliament lacked contemporaneity; they were chosen at different times, on different issues. The two Houses were neither co-equal nor coeval. Above all, in none of the separate elections for half the Senate, in 1964, 1967 or 1970, was the fate of the government involved.

In May 1977, 62.2 per cent of Australia's electors voted to correct the disruptive consequences caused by Sir Robert Menzies' decision of 1963. They then supported a referendum which they had rejected in 1974, to ensure that elections for the House of Representatives and half the Senate should be held simultaneously and terms of both Houses should be synchronised. The majority view still did not prevail because the proposal was beaten narrowly in Queensland, Western Australia and Tasmania. Had the proposal for simultaneous elections applied in 1972, the course of events in 1974 and 1975 would have been vastly different.

Even this reform, however, would not and could not guarantee that the party gaining a majority in the House of Representatives would possess control of the Senate. The Barwick 'doctrine' remains a potentially disastrous interpretation of responsible government under the Australian Constitution.

The Barwick 'doctrine' of 10 November 1975 was no more than a single-sentence summary of the entire case put in Parliament and the press by the Leader of the Opposition, Malcolm Fraser, and his supporters throughout October and November 1975. It was no more correct then than it had been at any time in the preceding three years. For the fundamental fact is that my Government, twice elected with a clear majority in the House of Representatives in 1972 and 1974, never enjoyed the 'confidence' of both Houses. At no time in those three years did we have a majority in the Senate. And in our first truncated term, between December 1972 and April 1974, there was just no possibility of having such a majority. The reason is simple and absolute: the election of 2 December 1972 was for the House of Representatives alone; there could be no election for the Senate that year. Thus it can be seen with hindsight that the seeds of destruction of the Labor Government in 1975 took ground in December 1972.

Yet it must be stressed that the crisis of October–November 1975 was unthinkable in 1972. We still lived in an age if not exactly of innocence, yet of decent regard to constitutional conventions. The Barwick 'doctrine' was unknown to most Australians, if not, as most of us would have believed at the time, unknown to the Constitution itself. The Australian voters took it for granted that what they were doing on 2 December 1972 was electing a government for a normal parliamentary term of three years. It was certainly on this basis that both the Prime Minister, William McMahon, and I campaigned. I cannot recall the fact that a successful Labor Party would inevitably face a hostile Senate ever being mentioned by either side throughout the campaign or by press commentators in its immediate aftermath. I did not use it as an alibi against reform; Mr McMahon did not use it as a reason for the return of his Government. As late as 10 November 1975, on the eve of my dismissal, two elections later, I was able, with complete empathy on the part of my audience, to recall the prevailing atmosphere and attitudes of 1972 in an address to the Melbourne Press Club:

> It's like Churchill explaining in his war memoirs why he failed to make any inquiry at all about whether the great guns at the Singapore Naval Base could shoot north as well as south—landward as well as seaward. He didn't raise the question because it never occurred to him: 'It no more occurred to me to ask that question than to ask if a battleship were launched with a bottom'—to quote him.

The comment has since been made, with some justice, that the Churchillian analogy is even more pertinent to my attitude to Sir John Kerr before 11 November 1975.

The Senate as it existed at the end of 1972 comprised twenty-six senators from the Australian Labor Party, twenty-seven from the Liberal and Country Parties,[1] five from the Democratic Labor Party (DLP) and two Independents, a practical majority of four for the new Opposition. This Senate comprised senators who had been elected on 25 November 1967 and 21 November 1970. Except in the case of a double dissolution for all members of both Houses, there could be no new intake of senators before 1 July 1974, when the senators replacing that half elected in 1967 and seated in July 1968 would begin their terms. Thus, the new Labor Government, returning after twenty-three years in opposition, faced from the beginning a hostile Senate which we knew we must live with for at least a year and a half. Neither we nor the people who had returned us 'so handsomely', to quote Sir Robert Menzies' message of congratulations to me, had any choice in the matter.

We approached the prospect with equanimity and our task with enthusiasm. Certainly, we recognised that our inherited position in the Senate would ensure that life would not be easy; but then whoever thought that it was meant to be? We accepted that there could be serious challenges to our legislative program. None of this, however, was deemed as a serious threat to our completion of a full term of three years. If, in 1972, there was serious consideration given to the possibility that the 28th Parliament would not last the distance, it was in the context of advice I might feel obliged to give the Governor-General for a double dissolution, should a major part of our program be twice rejected by the Senate. That choice would, of course, according to the conventions of the time, be my prerogative as head of a government with an unchallengeable majority in the House of Representatives.

---

1   The Country Party changed its name to the National Country Party in May 1975 and the National Party of Australia in October 1982.

Those with long memories recalled the obstruction by the Senate against the Scullin Labor Government elected in the great landslide of 1929. Yet even that Senate had not rejected Supply; the Scullin Government fell in 1931 not because it lacked a majority in or the 'confidence' of the Senate but because it was defeated in the House of Representatives. No Senate had refused Supply since Federation, though many governments lacked a Senate majority. In the twenty years between 1913 and 1975 during which the governing party did not have a majority there, the Senate passed a total of 139 money Bills. The question of the Senate's power to block Supply was, of course, to be at the heart of the crisis of 1975. In 1972, a power which had never been used since Federation scarcely seemed a serious threat to our very existence.

The overwhelming reason, however, why the state of the Senate was not in the forefront of our concerns in the early days of our Government was political not constitutional. We had a fresh and very clear mandate. Even if it were to be conceded that the Senate, to which the 200 000 voters in Tasmania had sent their ten senators two and five years earlier as had the 2 250 000 voters in New South Wales, ever had a popular mandate at all, it was exhausted and superseded by 1972.

Further, and most importantly, the mandate of 1972 was the most positive and precise ever sought and ever received by an elected government in Australian history. The program was the most comprehensive, its promulgation and popularisation the most intensive and extensive in our political history. Its central elements had been developed not in the three weeks of an election campaign or even the three years preceding the campaign but over a period of half a decade and more. Three successive conferences of the Labor Party, in 1967, 1969 and

1971, had rewritten two-thirds of the Party's platform. The program's crucial reforms in the three great areas of schools, hospitals and cities had been presented to the people not once but four times, at elections in 1967, 1969, 1970 and 1972, each time more precisely, each time more successfully, until their unequivocal endorsement on 2 December 1972. I deliberately ignore in this context our equally clear mandate on matters related to international affairs—the ending of the Australian commitment in Viet Nam, our recognition of the People's Republic as the sole government of China, the interment of the already moribund South East Asia Collective Defense Treaty organisation (SEATO), the independence of Papua New Guinea and the ending of conscription for military service in Viet Nam or anywhere else. All of these were administrative decisions and as such not subject to the veto of, or even debate by, the Senate we had inherited.

We believed that the precision of the program reinforced the strength of the mandate and that so strong a mandate would meet with no more than token resistance from a Senate which had no mandate at all. We were grievously wrong. The strongest resistance came on the very matters upon which we were most entitled to believe our mandate to be the most explicit. These matters were education and health—equality of opportunity in schools, equality of treatment in hospitals.

The proposal 'to establish an Australian Schools Com- mission to examine and determine the needs of students in government and non-government primary, secondary and technical schools' may now sound prosaic enough. Behind it lay more than a century of sectarian strife and bitterness over the so- called State Aid issue. The acceptance of the proposal at the Labor Party Conference in Melbourne in 1969 signalled the end of a deeply divisive debate in the Labor Party. Mr Fraser had been my principal antagonist in the public debate on the matter in the late 1960s and early 1970s. Scarcely an aspect of our national life had not been diminished by this sectarian wrangle; every aspect of our national life stood to gain by the adoption of my proposal.

Equally, our proposals for health care and hospital funding were fundamental. No subject had been so thoroughly canvassed, before so many audiences, in public debates, in private discussions, for so long. The issue had been the most important domestic issue during the 1969 campaign and, I believe, of all the specific issues then engaging public attention, had contributed most to the great gains made by the Labor Party, paving the way for the victory of 1972. Yet it was against our reforms in education and health that the strongest and most vehement challenges were mounted against the new Government in 1973.

As leader of a reform government, I placed the strongest interpretation on the meaning of the mandate given at an election by the majority of the people. Conservatives naturally prefer its restricted interpretation—that an election win confers a mandate to govern but is not an instruction to implement an election manifesto to its last detail. The weaker interpretation is not, I believe, acceptable for a party and government of reform. Our minority position in the Senate confirmed my determination to interpret the mandate in the strongest sense.

After the initial shock of their defeat passed, it became clear that our opponents were willing to accept our mandate in neither sense, not in its general sense as a mandate to govern for three years, nor in its specific sense as a mandate to implement a program. The Opposition leader in the Senate, Reg Withers, expressed their innermost convictions when he spoke of the December result as 'a temporary aberration'. And it was Senator Withers who first articulated the strategy by which my Government would ultimately be destroyed. In 1974 he boasted that the Opposition had a year earlier set upon a course to bring about an election for the House of Representatives.

The new Leader of the Liberal Party and Leader of the Opposition, Billy Snedden, seemed disposed, at least in the early months, to accept the common view that the Labor Party had indeed been given a mandate to govern for a normal term of three years. He established a range of policy committees and research units which were required to make interim reports 'within six months' and stated that their work would be 'deepened and extended during the next two years'. Mr Snedden allowed himself to be sidetracked from his three-year timetable. It proved to be a costly mistake. There is every possibility that he could have become Prime Minister at the end of 1975 if he had stuck to his original course. The diversion of the double dissolution of 1974 did great damage not least, as I shall show, to the Australian economy. No one was more greatly harmed by it than Mr Snedden.

The first sign that the Opposition in the Senate intended to carve out a new role for itself, inconceivable under Menzies, was given as early as 20 December 1972. Having elected Mr Snedden as its leader and Phillip Lynch as his deputy, the Parliamentary Liberal Party agreed to allow its senators to choose their own leader. Hitherto this appointment was the prerogative of the Liberal Party leader, a prerogative which Mr Fraser has since reclaimed. The Liberal senators chose a Western Australian, Senator Withers, who had not been a member of the McMahon Ministry, above Sir Kenneth Anderson, Reg Wright, Bob

Cotton and Ivor Greenwood, who had. He was nicknamed 'the Toe-Cutter', as was a Sydney gangster of the Menzies era whose method of enforcement was digital amputation.

Senator Withers, whose services to Mr Fraser were to be of decisive importance at the most decisive times, was himself dismissed from the Fraser Ministry in August 1978. Thenceforward, in a series of off-the-record briefings with selected members of the Parliamentary Press Gallery, he has added substantially to our store of knowledge about the events of October–November 1975. As far as I can assess from the fragmented and fragmentary accounts of these briefings so far published, they add up to full substantiation of the political assumptions upon which I acted in the political crisis of 1975.

Senator Withers' press secretary during these years, Russell Schneider, has published some of his recollections. Mr Schneider asserts that Senator Withers set out in detail the strategy to bring about the dismissal of the Labor Government in a memorandum to his leader, Mr Snedden, in October 1973. According to Mr Schneider, the memorandum stressed that the key element in the strategy was to *defer* a vote on Supply, rather than *reject* it; this would have the dual effect of keeping the Appropriation Bills under the Opposition's control while the whole process of delay could bring increasing pressure on the Governor-General to resolve the deadlock. This, of course, is exactly what happened two years later.

But, as I shall later show, a strategy which was workable in October 1973, when Senator Withers first envisaged it, was not possible in the Senate which the people elected in May 1974. The Senate we inherited in 1972 was an anti-Labor Senate elected in 1967 and 1970; the Senate which the people elected in May 1974 gave us equality of numbers; the Senate which refused Supply in

November 1975 was a different Senate altogether from that which the people elected eighteen months previously.

The first attempt to force the House of Representatives election was by no means as subtle as Senator Withers planned. Very largely at the impassioned urging of Mr Fraser, who seemed to bury the shadow minister for education, Peter Rae, the Opposition decided to resist the Schools Commission legislation in November 1973. It was an issue on which my Government would have been perfectly prepared to go to the people. Central to our proposal was that the vastly increased funding we proposed to grant to both government and non-government schools should be distributed on the basis of needs. Mr Fraser was the chief advocate of the contrary principle, that grants should be made on a per capita basis, irrespective of needs. Wiser counsels than his prevailed in the coalition. The Country Party in particular saw the political folly of forcing an election on such an issue at such a time.

The Country Party, however, played a crucial role in the Opposition's decision to bring about a double dissolution in April 1974. The Country Party's abiding fear is that an electoral redistribution should ever be made on the basis of equal electorates. Under legislation introduced by my Minister for Services, Fred Daly, this had at last become a possibility. His Commonwealth Electoral Bill set a limit of 10 per cent instead of 20 per cent, as had hitherto applied, on the extent to which the number of electors in any electorate in a State could diverge from the quota of electors for the electorates in that State. Long afterwards, Mr Snedden admitted to a member of my personal staff that pressure from the Country Party, determined to prevent a redistribution on the basis of one vote one value, was the major factor in his decision to take the course which led to the double dissolution in April 1974.

On 21 March 1974 I informed the House that the Governor-General had accepted my advice to communicate with the State Governors, proposing that they issue writs for an election on 18 May of the senators whose terms of service were to begin on 1 July. I also advised the House that the Governor-General had accepted my advice that referendums be held concurrently with the Senate election on the four Constitution Alteration Bills which had been twice passed by the House but rejected by the Senate.

In the course of the next few days the Father of the Senate, Justin O'Byrne, learned from Queensland senator Vince Gair, whom the DLP senators had deposed as their leader on 10 October 1973, that he did not propose to see out his term due to end in June 1977. Senator O'Byrne told Lionel Murphy, the Leader of the Government in the Senate, who told me. We thought it more appropriate for Senator Gair's successor to be elected by the electors of Queensland at the forthcoming Senate election than chosen by the Parliament of Queensland a little later. We offered him and he accepted the ambassadorship to Ireland.

The Opposition was incensed at such a wicked political appointment. After all, in 1964 the Menzies Government had sent a Country Party minister as ambassador to Ireland and in 1968 the Gorton Government had sent the New South Wales President of the Liberal Party to succeed him. These appointments, however, were no more political than those of six Liberal ministers as high commissioners, three Liberal ministers and two backbenchers as ambassadors, a Liberal minister and a backbencher as consuls-general and a Liberal minister and two backbenchers as administrators of territories at various times in the 1950s and 1960s.

The Opposition now announced moves to have the Senate, half of whose members were soon to end their terms, block the Supply Bills. These Bills are always passed in the autumn session to cover expenditure during the months of July to November pending the passage of the Budget Bills, which are usually introduced in August.[2]

I countered by advising the Governor-General on 10 April to dissolve both Houses and to have an election for the whole Parliament and not just half the Senate on 18 May. He was able to do this under section 57 of the Constitution, which sets out a procedure for resolving a disagreement between the Houses. If the House passes a Bill and the Senate rejects it and after an interval of three months the House again passes it and the Senate rejects it, the Governor-General may dissolve both Houses simultaneously. (Such a dissolution cannot take place more than two and a half years after the House first meets.) There were, I advised the Governor-General, six Bills justifying the double dissolution: the Commonwealth Electoral Bill and two other electoral Bills covering representation of the Australian Capital Territory and the Northern Territory in both Houses, two health insurance Bills to establish Medibank and a Bill to establish a Petroleum and Minerals Authority.

The 1974 election result was remarkable in many ways. The DLP was reduced from five senators to none and was destroyed for all time as a political force after two decades of very real power and importance. The Labor Party lost Hume (Cowra, Cootamundra), Riverina (Deniliquin, Griffith) and Wide Bay (Bundaberg, Maryborough) as well as Mitchell on the outskirts of

---

2   Since 1944 the Budget Bills have been introduced in May and passed before 30 June. The autumn Supply Bills are no longer required.

Sydney and Lilley in the Brisbane metropolitan area; it won Isaacs and Henty in the Melbourne metropolitan area and the new seats of Fraser in the ACT and Tangney in Western Australia.

In a chamber of sixty senators, the Labor Party won twenty-nine seats and the Liberal and Country Parties won twenty-nine seats. Michael Townley, standing as an Independent, won a Tasmanian seat. He speedily rejoined the Liberal Party. A former Liberal Premier of South Australia, Steele Hall, was elected under the banner of the Liberal Movement, which he had created. Senator Hall was to prove one of the most eloquent opponents of the use of the Senate to block Supply.

Thus the Senate which the people elected on 18 May 1974 was one in which a resolution to reject or defer Supply could not have succeeded. As the Australian Constitution puts it, 'when the votes are equal the question shall pass in the negative'. Only the subsequent corruption of the Senate elected in May 1974 made possible the events of November 1975.

Further, the clear judgement of the people was inadequately reflected in terms of seats. To win the same number of seats in the Senate as the Opposition, the Labor Party had secured 47.29 per cent of the vote, as against the total of 43.88 per cent polled by the official Opposition parties. Labor candidates won some 226000 votes more than the official Opposition candidates. These figures surely have a place in any consideration of the conduct of the Senate in 1975. We suffered badly from a deliberate act of sabotage of the ballot paper in New South Wales. Seventy-three candidates stood; and to register a formal vote electors were required to record a preference for every one of them. The inevitable and intended result was great confusion. There were 332818 informal votes cast in New South Wales— 117000 more than the quota required to elect a New South

Wales senator. A considerable majority of these informal votes was cast in electorates which returned Labor members for the House of Representatives. The conclusion is inescapable; the Labor Government lost a sixth senator in New South Wales because of the deliberate confusion created by the multiplicity of spurious candidates. (Political scientists should research the methods and motives of those who inspired these candidates.)

These are complicated and complex considerations. It is no use repining at what might have been. I state the facts only to emphasise that the Senate as elected on 18 May 1974 was certainly not an anti-Labor Senate.

The most constructive result of the 1974 double dissolution was that we were enabled to pass into law the six Bills which had been twice rejected by the Senate and which, under section 57 of the Constitution, had been the grounds of the double dissolution. The three electoral Acts were challenged in the High Court, which by majority upheld them in October 1975. The Petroleum and Minerals Authority Act was also challenged in the High Court, which by majority invalidated it in June 1975 on the ground that the Senate had not rejected the Bill twice. The outcome of those challenges was to bear indirectly on the events of 1975. That, however, lay in the future; our immediate task was to tidy up the unfinished business of the truncated 28th Parliament and get on with the task for which the people had once more elected us.

Yet on the very measures which had been the basis of the double dissolution and a major factor in the election campaign, the Opposition at once demonstrated that it refused to recognise the legitimacy of our renewed mandate. Section 57 says that, if after a double dissolution the House again passes a disputed Bill and the Senate rejects it, the Governor-General may convene a joint sitting of the members of both Houses. If the Bill is then affirmed by an absolute majority of the total members of both Houses, the Governor-General can sign it into law. Although it was obvious that in such a joint sitting the Government would have a clear majority, the Opposition opposed all six Bills again in the Senate. The three electoral Bills were defeated because the Senate was evenly divided. The Medibank Bills were defeated by thirty votes to twenty-eight and the Petroleum and Minerals Authority Bill by thirty-one votes to twenty-nine. So there had for the first time to be a joint sitting of the members of the Senate and of the House of Representatives.

The joint sitting of 6 August 1974 was the first sitting of Parliament ever to be televised. It was the first sitting convened by a Governor-General for the purpose of resolving disagreements between the two Houses. Its convening was Sir John Kerr's first major official act as Governor-General. I said:

> For, momentous as the sitting is, the reasons for it are not a matter for pride. It has come about because of the repeated refusal of the Senate to pass legislation which has been approved by the House of Representatives—the people's House, the House where alone governments are made and unmade. It has come about because despite two successive election victories by the Australian Labor Party, despite the clear endorsement by the Australian people at the elections only 11 weeks ago of the Party's policies and of the specific measures now before us, the Senate and the Opposition are still resolved to obstruct the Government's program and to frustrate the will of the people . . . Let it be understood that this Joint Sitting is a last resort, a means provided by the Constitution to enable the popular will—the democratic

process—ultimately to prevail over the tactics of blind obstruction . . . Even the sitting itself, an event clearly envisaged and provided for by the Constitution, has been the subject of a desperate last minute, last ditch legal challenge by our opponents. Now, at last—at long last—after sustained stonewalling and filibustering the Parliament can proceed to enact these essential parts of the Government's legislative program.

All six Bills were passed at the joint sitting by majorities of between three and seven votes.

The joint sitting was a further distraction from the real business of the nation and its elected government. This distraction and disruption had lasted since April. The 1974 Budget was delayed until September, a month later than the normal time. It is impossible to exaggerate the damage done by the political preoccupation throughout these critical months. The normal business of government was suspended. The whole Western world was entering the worst economic crisis since the end of the Korean War, the combined result of the oil crisis of October 1973 and the material cost of the war in Viet Nam. Australia's political preoccupation added to the profound economic problems caused by the international crisis.

Soon after the 1973 Budget was brought down, the Treasury and the Reserve Bank stressed that we should take complementary measures to restrict the supply of money. They had not previously advised such steps because they had expected that, with the appreciation of the Australian dollar and the measures to restrict overseas ownership which my Government brought about at the outset, there would be no inflow and probably an outflow of overseas funds. In fact the inflow, largely caused by the McMahon Government's devaluation in 1971, had continued. There was a dangerous amount of money flowing through the economy.

At the outset of the election campaign in April 1974, Russell Prowse, Assistant General Manager of the Bank of New South Wales, claimed that a credit squeeze was already in operation. Neither the Treasurer, Frank Crean, nor I was aware of any such squeeze. I took Mr Prowse's propaganda sufficiently seriously to ask the Secretary to the Treasury, Sir Frederick Wheeler, and the Governor of the Reserve Bank, Sir John Phillips, to discuss the matter with me at Kirribilli House, the Prime Minister's Sydney residence. They assured me that Mr Prowse's statement was indeed election propaganda; they said that the Bank of New South Wales had imprudently overlent and for the first time would be in the embarrassing position of having to borrow from the Reserve Bank. They assured me that our Government's restrictions on credit had been justified and continued to be necessary but denied that our measures amounted to a credit squeeze.

After the elections in May and the election of the Ministry in June, the newly elected Deputy Prime Minister, Jim Cairns, was unwilling to take the responsibility of being Treasurer himself but wanted to take more part in economic matters than he had hitherto taken as Minister for Overseas Trade. In August, during Cabinet's pre-Budget discussions, he asked me if I would agree to his discussing the general economic situation with Sir John Phillips. I agreed. Soon after, he reported to me that Sir John had expressed the opinion that the measures of the previous September had in fact amounted to a credit squeeze, that they had been introduced too late and that they were being continued too long. Soon afterwards the measures were abandoned.

The belated and protracted imposition of the credit squeeze did great damage to Australia's economy. It was a measure which had been introduced and maintained on the advice of the Treasury and the Reserve Bank. One retrospective excuse our advisers gave for having recommended it so late and so long was that statistics available to them were not sufficiently prompt or complete. This was the origin of my decision to have the Commonwealth Statistician given an independent statutory position instead of being merely another official, who, in his case, was subject to the requirements of the Treasury as seen from time to time.

The distraction from economic problems and the destabilisation of the political process which the double dissolution had brought about during the critical months of April, May, June and July 1974 were to have considerable bearing on my handling of the political crisis of October–November 1975. Despite the disruption caused by the Senate's first, but failed, challenge, it is now clear that the double dissolution had really settled nothing. Mr Snedden caused some hilarity at the time by his post-election statement that he had not lost the election but merely failed to get enough seats; with hindsight, the statement can be seen as the first attempt to deny the validity of the verdict of 18 May and to deny the legitimacy of the re-elected government. Senator Withers further refined his post-1972 'aberration theory'; this time he attributed the aberration to the people of Sydney and Melbourne alone.

This new and evenly divided Senate no longer permitted the application of the most original and subtle part of the strategy which Senator Withers had set out in his memorandum to Mr Snedden in October 1973; no motion to defer Supply could succeed in that Senate. It was clear enough that, if they could, the

Opposition would seek to set aside the verdict of the Australian people; but to do so would require other means and other men, for the people had rendered the Withers strategy inoperative. The means and the men were to be found. In mid-1974, however, the most sanguine members of the Opposition could scarcely have realised how powerful an ally they were about to win to their cause when Sir John Kerr took up the high office of Governor-General, to which I had nominated him.

2

WHY SIR JOHN KERR?

'. . . *OMNIUM CONSENSU CAPAX IMPERII NISI IMPERASSET.*'
'(. . . EVERYONE WOULD HAVE AGREED THAT HE WAS
QUALIFIED FOR THE POST OF GOVERNOR-GENERAL IF
HE HAD NOT HELD IT.)'

Tacitus, *Histories* I

How did I come to nominate the Honourable John Kerr, Chief
Justice of New South Wales, as Governor-General of Australia?
The simple and whole answer is that of all those available he
seemed the best qualified and most acceptable to the Australian
people.

Sir Paul Hasluck became Governor-General on 30 April
1969 after eighteen years as a Liberal minister. In May 1973 he
told me that he would not seek or accept an extension beyond
the customary five-year period because his wife had a restricting
and painful rheumatic condition. I expressed my disappointment. I told him that I had intended to ask him to remain as
Governor-General at least till after the House of Representatives
elections due at the end of 1975 because my colleagues and I
found his interest and counsel very valuable and because,

candidly, I wanted to show the Australian people that I had no inhibitions about having a former political opponent in that office.

Sir Paul Hasluck has never expressed any misgivings about the propriety of his relations with my colleagues and me. I am certain he never will because I am certain he had none. He apparently saw no disposition on our part to treat him or any holder of his office as a 'rubber stamp' or a 'robot', to quote Sir John Kerr. Our relations throughout were proper, relaxed, civil and civilised. Throughout, our public and personal relations had been conducted on the basis of a deft, but definitely Australian blend of formality and familiarity, appropriate both to the dignity of his office and to our long association as political adversaries and Australian parliamentary colleagues. He co-operated with goodwill in the process by which my deputy, Lance Barnard, and I, on 5 December 1972, formed the smallest administration having jurisdiction over Australia since the Wellington–Lyndhurst Government in 1834. He facilitated the decisions of our 'duumvirate' during the following fortnight until the full Ministry could be elected and sworn in, notably the release from prison of conscientious objectors to conscription for the war in Viet Nam.

He was not, I believe, unappreciative of our scrupulous endeavours to relieve him of any possible embarrassment, not only as a former Liberal minister but as a highly proficient speaker and writer of the English language, in the delivery of the speech opening the new Parliament and setting out the new Government's program on 27 February 1973. I have always thought that Prime Minister Gorton had shown scant consideration for Sir Paul by the cavalier way he first called upon him to fulfil this duty in November 1969 in a speech of fewer than 200 words, submitted for his perusal a day or two before delivery. Before I left Australia for my first visit as Prime Minister to Papua New Guinea and Indonesia, I instructed the officers preparing the speech that Sir Paul was to have a complete draft not less than a fortnight before the opening of Parliament; his revisions and suggestions—all made very properly within the acknowledged limits of the Governor-General's prerogative—were accepted.

I encouraged Sir Paul in the idea that it was proper for the Australian Governor-General to represent Australia as Head of State abroad. With Sir Paul I gave meaning to the concept of the Governor-General as Australia's resident Head of State. On 30 May 1973 the Queen assigned to the Governor-General all her powers and functions in respect of appointing Australian ambassadors to countries outside the Commonwealth and of high commissioners to Commonwealth countries which were republics or had other monarchs and approving, receiving and withdrawing the credentials of such ambassadors and high commissioners to Australia. We changed the channel for delivering correspondence between the Queen and the Governor-General from the British High Commission in Canberra to the Australian High Commission in London. Sir Paul was utterly sincere in his duty to maintain the interests of the Queen. He trusted me in discussions about her and Prince Philip and Prince Charles. I believe he thought I could keep a confidence; Lance Barnard is the only other man in whom I felt I could confide with such assurance.

Sir Paul's and my relationship was throughout based on openness, frankness, mutual goodwill and mutual respect. At no time right to the end was I aware that my attitude to Sir Paul's successor was in any way different, nor his successor's attitude to me.

Sir Paul agreed to my request to discuss further the matter of his continuing in office with his wife, herself a distinguished Australian author and historian. He later told me that they could not really see their way clear to continue; he was, however, willing to stay on until the end of June 1974 in order to cover the period of the Senate election, which must be held before July. He gave me a handwritten list of eight persons, all of wide experience and high standing, among whom he thought I might choose a successor. The list of persons Sir Paul regarded as worthy included two members of my own Cabinet. I shared his opinion of their worthiness. I doubt if either would have accepted the job gladly. In those days—and throughout our period in government—the most trifling appointment was likely to be attacked as 'jobs for the boys' by those who had had, for twenty-three years, a monopoly on all Federal appointments. The undoubted merits of my colleagues whom Sir Paul had named would have carried small weight with or against the men 'born to rule'.

I approached the youngest man on the list, who was my own first choice for the office. He was a leading Melbourne businessman, a member, by the quaint standards of that city, of one of its well-established families, who had been decorated during the Second World War, had been excluded on the grounds of his race from the Melbourne Club and had undertaken a wide range of tasks on behalf of governments and the community. A week later, he told me that, for family and business reasons, he did not believe that he could accept.

I then thought of Chief Justice Kerr, who was also on Sir Paul Hasluck's list. His wife, Peggy, and my wife had studied together for the Diploma of Social Studies at the University of Sydney in 1942 and 1943. In 1940 he appeared from time to time before the Supreme Court judge whose associate I was. He was looked at somewhat askance by the legal establishment because he belonged to Clive Evatt's 'stable'. I remembered his quick promotion during the war in the outfit headed by Alf Conlon, to whom Bill Taylor, a Labor solicitor and Vice-President of the New South Wales Branch of the Labor Party, had recommended him. After the war we naturally were aware of each other as barristers but my main contacts with him were usually outside the law.

We spent some hours on the beach together in January 1955 at Port Macquarie discussing the impending split in the Labor Party. In January 1956 we both participated in the Australian Institute of Political Science (AIPS) summer school at Canberra on 'Australia's Transport Crisis'. In mid-1957 he and Russell Prowse were ranged against Jim Kenny, the assistant secretary of the Trades and Labor Council of New South Wales, and me on two Sunday afternoons in an early Channel 7 public affairs debate under the chairmanship of the Reverend Dr Malcolm Mackay on the future of the Labor movement. In January 1958 we again participated in an AIPS summer school, this time on 'New Guinea and Australia'.

In mid-1965, when the ALP's Federal Conference in Sydney determined that a statement prepared for it on New Guinea should be redrafted, the Federal President, Jim Keeffe (afterwards a senator), Don Dunstan (afterwards a Premier) and I gathered with John Kerr in his chambers overnight to produce the draft, which the Conference endorsed. My leader at the time, Arthur Calwell, was deeply opposed to any move towards independence for Papua New Guinea, which he wanted Australia to retain as a *cordon sanitaire* against Asia. I was grateful for John Kerr's assistance in promoting the contrary view. At the end of August that year, as President of the Law Council of Australia, he presided over the Commonwealth and Empire Law Conference in Sydney. One of the nights at such conferences is always set aside for private dinner parties. My wife and I said that we would be happy to entertain guests from Commonwealth countries in Asia, Africa and the Caribbean; from this party have stemmed some enduring friendships, for example, those with Eddy Barker, still Minister of Law in Singapore,[1] and 'Sonny' Ramphal, then Attorney-General of Guyana and later, with my Government's support, Commonwealth Secretary-General. John Kerr came to this party at our house; his wife was not well enough to attend.

After John Kerr became a Federal judge I had an especial interest in some of the quasi-judicial tasks he undertook. He was chairman of the Committee on Review of Administrative Decisions and the Committee on Review of Pay and Conditions for the Armed Forces. I was more interested than other parliamentarians of those days in open government; and as Member for Werriwa I always represented more servicemen than anybody else in Parliament.

He was a member of the Court which in February 1969 handed down the judgment in *Moore v. Doyle* which proposed an urgent solution to the demarcation disputes and public exasperation caused by the competing Federal and State arbitration systems. My Government had at once taken steps to carry out the Court's advice as far as Federal power permitted; successive New South Wales, Queensland and Western

---

1   Eddy Barker, Minister for Law, Singapore, 1964–65; Law and National Development, Singapore, 1965–75; Law and Environment, Singapore, 1975–88.

Australian governments have so far done nothing. The most bitter and some of the worst industrial disputes which have occurred in Australia since 1975 are entirely due to the failure of State Governments to legislate to implement Mr Justice Kerr's correct advice in *Moore v. Doyle*. Disputes of this kind will demoralise, if not destroy, Australian unionism and the Australian arbitration system, as we know it.

When the Labor Government was elected, John Kerr was Chief Justice of New South Wales. In informing the House on 17 May 1973 that Mr Justice Hope of the New South Wales Supreme Court had agreed to act as chairman of the Government's proposed task force on the National Estate, I took the opportunity to thank the Premier, his Attorney-General and the Chief Justice for agreeing so readily to make available to the Australian Government the services of yet another distinguished member of the New South Wales Bench. There were no fewer than five New South Wales Supreme Court judges assisting my Government in various important inquiries. Mr Justice Asprey and Mr Justice Toose had been appointed by the McMahon Government to examine the taxation and repatriation systems; my Government extended their terms of reference. Mr Justice Else-Mitchell had been appointed by my Government to examine Systems of Land Tenure and was later to become the first judicial chairman of the Grants Commission; Mr Justice Meares, Chairman of the New South Wales Law Reform Commission, had been appointed with Mr Justice Woodhouse DSC, a judge of the Court of Appeal of New Zealand, to the Committee of Inquiry into a National Rehabilitation and Compensation Scheme. Mr Justice Collins was later appointed as the Royal Commissioner on Petroleum. Chief Justice Kerr made his judges much more readily available for Federal inquiries than did his successor; by that time it did not matter so much, because by then there was an adequate number of Federal judges.

There was a New South Wales Bench and Bar dinner on 25 May. I was the guest of honour; no New South Wales barrister had been Prime Minister for fifty years. They had done well in the early years of Federation: Barton, Reid and Billy Hughes had each become Prime Minister; the last generation of Sydney Bar leaders—Spender, Evatt, Beale, Barwick, Tom Hughes, Bowen and St John—had not. I was amused when, in formally introducing me, the President of the Bar Association, Harold Glass, QC, now a judge of the Supreme Court of New South Wales,[2] explained that despite being the guest of honour I was sitting on his left because Chief Justice Kerr had asked to be present and, since he was Acting Governor, he had to sit on the President's right. I commenced my speech by saying that I had observed the Chief Justice moving further to my right for the last twenty years. Now everyone was amused; one must always start an after-dinner speech on a good note. During the dinner the Chief Justice made it amply evident that he was enjoying his vice-regal role.

The opportunity came for me to raise the position of Governor-General with him and his wife as we were going into a state dinner. It was not in August 1973, as he writes, but on Monday evening 3 September, at the dinner which the New South Wales Government gave in honour of the delegates to the Constitutional Convention meeting in Sydney that week.

The Chief Justice got in touch with me the next day. We exchanged our direct telephone numbers. I said I would call

---

2   See Extended Biographies.

on him at his chambers at 4.30 on Wednesday afternoon 5 September. I walked around from Parliament House in Macquarie Street, where the Convention was meeting, to his private entrance off St James' Road.

It was he, not I, as he asserts, who raised the three questions of salary, pension and tenure. He pointed out that he was fifty-eight years of age and that he could remain as Chief Justice until he was seventy and that thereafter he would receive a pension; if he became Governor-General his income would steadily fall and he would be without a job and without a pension before he was sixty-five; while he had enjoyed a good income at the Bar he had spent freely and for the last seven years had had only his judicial income.

I must emphasise that, in saying that Sir John Kerr first raised these points, I am stating a fact, not casting an aspersion. It was perfectly proper that he should raise these matters. I should have done the same, had I been of his age, situation and position.

I replied that I realised that the tax-free salary of $20 000 prescribed by the Constitution might now be too small, despite the considerable allowances which were made under various guises, and that, since the Constitution says that the salary of the Governor-General cannot be altered during his continuance in office, there would have to be legislation introduced before he took office. I promised to discuss the matter with the relevant departmental heads and to advise him further.

I made a fuller response concerning a pension, because, over many years, I had developed a very definite position of principle on this matter. I told him that I had long been convinced of the propriety of a pension for a retired Governor-General. I recalled that the first Australian to become a State Governor had found the necessity to become a director of a provincial airline on retirement and, pending that, have a relative stand in for him as director; if Australians were to become Governors-General, particularly at an age when they would be regarded as having many years of useful activity ahead of them, it was essential that they have a pension; furthermore the pension must be sufficient for it to be obvious during and after their terms of office that they need not be influenced by government or private pressures during or after their terms. One could not again have a situation where retired judges had accepted the chairmanship of companies applying for television licences.

Over supper at a Queen's birthday reception four years earlier I had said to Lady Hasluck and Prime Minister Gorton that there should be pensions for Governors-General when they retired and, when John Gorton said that my Party would never approve of it, I replied that a Labor Government in New South Wales had introduced judicial-scale pensions for former Governors. Accordingly, I would certainly introduce legislation for a Governor-General, however long or short his term, to receive the same non-contributory retirement pension as the chief justice of Australia.

Sir John Kerr said that he would want a double term—ten years—in the post. The Liberals had let him down on the appointment to the proposed Commonwealth Superior Court which Mr Snedden promised him when he had nominated him to the Supreme Court of the ACT and the Commonwealth Industrial Court in June 1966. Nigel Bowen had replaced Billy Snedden after the 1966 elections and, although he had introduced a Commonwealth Superior Court Bill in 1968, the government had not proceeded with it and Bowen had been replaced by Tom Hughes after the 1969 elections. Hughes had not advanced the proposal before McMahon displaced Gorton as Prime Minister and brought Bowen back as Attorney-General. Whatever Bowen's attitude might now have been to the Bill he had been transferred after four months in favour of Greenwood, who was hostile to the concept and finally announced its abandonment. So, Sir John said, he would need some undertaking from the Leader of the Liberal Party in the light of his experience at the hands of the Liberals. In his six years as a Federal judge the Liberals had had five changes of attorney-general. In the same years, their record for stability of party leadership had not been much better; he had been appointed under Holt and there had been three since—Gorton, McMahon and now Snedden.

I said that I appreciated his frustration because two other judges who had accepted appointments from the Liberals shortly after him had also been left in the lurch. I was the first member of Parliament to propose the Federal Superior Court, at the Legal Convention in Perth in 1957 and in the debate on the estimates for the Attorney-General's Department in 1958. I could scarcely, however, mention his tenure to Mr Snedden before I had recommended his appointment to the Queen. I undertook, however, that I would take the very first opportunity to mention it to Mr Snedden after the Queen had agreed to appoint him.

In the ensuing months we had several further conversations. He called in at Kirribilli House a couple of times on his way home to Wahroonga. I had lunch with him in his chambers; again I walked there so that no official or police cars would attract attention, because he was most anxious that no word of my approach should escape even to the Premier, perhaps especially to the Premier. We spoke occasionally on the telephone; once my wife came upon me speaking to 'John' about the governor-generalship and thought I was offering it to Mr Justice John Moore, the President of the Australian Conciliation and Arbitration Commission. Sir John Kerr, to whom she told this afterwards, would for long playfully ask me, in her presence, 'Have you told Margaret any secrets today?'

Reflecting on this, when reading Sir John's memoirs, I was reminded of the remark made to King William III by the first Earl of Marlborough about some highly secret military operation: 'Sire, I have told only my wife.' To which the King replied: 'I have not told even my wife' (who, of course, happened to be the Queen of England in her own right). Because of the necessity to keep the situation confidential, I discussed it with only one other person, Mr Barnard.

In his book, Sir John says that in October 1973 I told him that I would like to be in a position to put a name before the Queen while she was in Australia for the opening of the Opera House; that if he would indicate only that he would seriously consider accepting I would be able to say to her that I wished to ask him to undertake the task. No such conversation took place; no such suggestion was made by me. No one in my position could be crass enough to inform the Queen that anyone would hesitate to accept the honour of representing her. What would I have said to the Queen? 'Ma'am, the person I have in mind is the Chief Justice of New South Wales, but he's not quite sure yet whether he wants to be your representative.' The idea is preposterous.

On 13 October, the Saturday before the Queen arrived, the Kerrs and we were guests of Sir Howard and Lady Beale at dinner at their Sydney residence. Sir Howard had been a Liberal minister in the Menzies Government and a former ambassador to Washington. Neither the Kerrs nor I mentioned the appointment. Next Monday, he wrote to me about an article he had been reading in *Encounter* and again he made no reference. The Queen arrived on Wednesday 17 October, opened the Opera House the following Saturday and departed on the Monday. I told her that Sir Paul Hasluck would not be able to accept an extension of his term beyond June and that I would hope to put a nomination before her when she came to open Parliament in the following February. Chief Justice Kerr's name was not mentioned; I was in no position to mention his name to the Queen.

It was only in November and December that I pressed the Chief Justice to make up his mind in time for me to nominate him or someone else to the Queen. He was particularly attracted to my suggestion that the Governor-General should from time to time represent Australia overseas. In these days of rapid transport, one of the functions of the Head of State is to make visits to other countries. Australia's Head of State cannot do so because when she makes a visit outside Britain she is perceived as Queen of Britain. When President Suharto had visited Australia in February 1972 one of his suite had taken umbrage that our Head of State was not in Australia but on her way to Thailand.

Sir Paul Hasluck and the Governor-General of Canada had, in the absence of the Queen, been accorded a status similar to that of a Head of State at the Persepolis celebrations in 1971 to commemorate the 2500th anniversary of the founding of the Iranian monarchy by Cyrus. (After all, the Persians invented the system of satraps.) The Governor-General of Canada had also been received as Head of State on a visit to France, Belgium and the Netherlands. There were some, I pointed out, and there would soon be more Commonwealth countries in the South Pacific which were likely to retain the Queen for some years as their Head of State: Fiji, Papua New Guinea, the Solomons and, perhaps, the New Hebrides. I thus envisaged a role for the Governor-General of Australia in preserving ties with such countries of our origins and countries of our neighbourhood as were familiar with our institutions. This whole aspect proved immensely fascinating to Sir John.

I have also to record that he noted the domestic amenities and advantages for him in the position. Just as his wife's health had made it impossible for him to pursue a political career in the mid-1960s, so now there would be staff available to assist him as Governor-General in a way that there would not be as Chief Justice. And I have to say, however offensive to him it might be to recall it, he did indeed put this very point to me.

On 10 December he was received by Sir Paul Hasluck at Admiralty House. He also saw Sir John Bunting, the head of the Department of the Prime Minister and Cabinet and, like Sir Paul, a man of great experience and utmost discretion. Sir John's mind was now fully made up. I recommended his appointment to the Queen at Yarralumla late in the afternoon of 27 February and she agreed. By this protracted process, Sir John Kerr became the first Governor-General in Australia's history whose name had been placed before the monarch, by the Australian Prime Minister, in person, in Australia.

Earlier that day I had ascertained where I could telephone Sir Robert Askin and Mr Snedden. On returning to Parliament House from Yarralumla, I immediately telephoned them. I told Mr Snedden that I had promised Sir John that if I were in government in five years' time I would recommend another five-year appointment for him. I told him that I had also told Sir

John that I would commend the same course to Mr Snedden. Mr Snedden was delighted with the appointment, recalled that he had nominated Sir John as a Federal judge and asked if he could give the news to the press conference he was holding in his office as I was speaking to him. I agreed that he should. So it happened that Sir John Kerr's appointment started on a magnificently bipartisan note. Neither Mr Snedden nor I were to benefit from it. We joined Evatt and Alf Conlon in the company of those who had helped John Kerr and were discarded by him.

In the second chapter of his book, Sir John Kerr gives his version of his appointment. He poses these questions: 'Is the Governor-General, under the Constitution, a robot, a rubber stamp, a cipher? . . . Did Mr Whitlam have such a concept of the office in mind when he nominated me for it? Did he aspire to reduce the office to such a level?' Sir John leaves his questions hanging, although the mere posing of them in that form is clearly meant to suggest an affirmative answer. Yet in another context, he partly answers his questions. Acknowledging that I did not ask him anything about his political views or his attitude to the political parties or their Federal policies, he writes:

> I had no reason to think, nor do I now believe, that Mr
> Whitlam in approaching me about appointment had any
> expectation of political partisanship or subservience from
> me in the office of Governor-General.

Precisely. The real answer to Sir John's rhetorical questions lies in the record of my conduct towards him and his predecessor, Sir Paul Hasluck. Nothing in that record suggests that my colleagues or I regarded the Governor-General as a rubber stamp or a robot. Nor, of course, does Sir John directly claim so. At the time I nominated Sir John, I held exactly the same concept of the governor-generalship as all my predecessors as Prime Minister would have held, including Sir Robert Menzies whom he quotes approvingly at the beginning of his second chapter. None of us regarded the Governor-General as a robot. All of us, however, would have upheld the basic principle of our system of responsible government—that the Governor-General in his official actions must act on the advice of his elected ministers. And none insisted on this more staunchly than Sir Robert Menzies.

Sir John seems to chide me for failing to get a clear understanding with him about his views of the role of the Governor-General and his interpretation of the so-called reserve powers. I do not believe any Prime Minister in 1973 would have thought it necessary to do so or to make that a bargaining point about the appointment to so great an office. I do not believe any of my predecessors as Prime Minister have ever thought it necessary to do so or to demean the prime ministership or the governor-generalship by doing so. My successors will naturally be more circumspect. That is just one measure of the damage Sir John Kerr has done to the office he held and the Constitution under which he held it.

My references to the governor-generalship were a matter of public record. I had startled some conservatives by referring to the Governor-General's position as that of viceroy. As early as 1 June 1973, the late Senator Greenwood, the last Attorney-General in the McMahon Government and the first Attorney-General in the Fraser Government, asked Senator Murphy in the Senate:

Is it a fact that the Government is intending that the role
and functions of the Governor-General should become those

of a Viceroy so that State Governors would become responsible to the Viceroy and act upon the advice of Commonwealth Government Ministers and not, as at present, on the advice of State Government Ministers? Has the Government made any approach to the United Kingdom Government along those lines? If there is no such intention and if no such approach has been made, will the Government make a clear and unequivocal assertion repudiating any such intention?

The answer I provided stated (in full):

The Governor-General is the viceroy of the Queen of Australia (Constitution sections 2, 6 and 68). Consequently, his prerogatives are not the concern of the British Government.

My view was, and is, that, when the Queen of Australia is not resident in Australia her representative in Australia has all the power which she has while resident in Australia, no more, no less. That means that the Governor-General will act on the advice of his Australian ministers, not on the advice of the Queen's British ministers; he will act on the advice of his ministers as the Queen does on the advice of hers. I might have added, had it occurred to me, that I should expect the Queen's representative to behave as honourably to his Prime Minister as the Queen does, and that the monarch's representative should be as honest, open and honourable in his conduct towards the Prime Minister as all monarchs and their representatives have been since William IV.

The sections of the Constitution which I cited in my reply to Senator Greenwood vest in him 'such powers and functions of the Queen as Her Majesty may be pleased to assign to him' and 'the executive power of the Commonwealth ... exercisable by the Governor-General as the Queen's representative'. It is indeed a curious assertion (made, at least by implication, by Sir John) that to regard the Governor-General as viceroy is to downgrade the office to that of a rubber stamp or its holder as a robot. Is it a derogation of the Queen to assert the unchallenged constitutional fact that she will exercise her powers only upon the advice of her British ministers in Britain and her Australian ministers in Australia?

I would, if asked, have agreed with the view put by Professor L. F. Crisp in *Australian National Government* (Longman, 1978) that the governor-generalship 'provides a dignified ceremonial leadership to the government and the nation; it offers an adequate symbol of national unity and continuity above the day-to-day warfare of parties'. So would all my predecessors. So would the overwhelming majority of Australians, at least until 11 November 1975. This was the common view of all Australians—Labor or Liberal—about the governor-generalship until that day. It was never a question at issue.

The public reaction to the appointment confirmed my assessment of its acceptability. The *Age* editorialised on 28 February 1974:

> The Governor-General is the Queen's representative in
> Australia and is formally appointed by Her Majesty. By
> constitutional convention, he is chosen by the Australian
> Government and recommended by the Prime Minister. In
> nominating Sir John Robert Kerr, Chief Justice of New
> South Wales since May 1972, the Whitlam Government has

made, by any standards, an excellent choice . . . We admire
the Queen's, and the Prime Minister's, good judgement.

The *Sydney Morning Herald* was equally complimentary to
both Sir John and me:

Mr Whitlam deserves credit for the appointment of an
eminent, and eminently suitable, Australian to be the next
Governor-General. It was also most appropriate, and will
undoubtedly please many Australians who value our ties
with Great Britain and with the monarchy, that Mr Whitlam
was able to consult the Queen personally about her new
representative while she is in Canberra . . . The appointment
of the Chief Justice of New South Wales, Sir John Kerr, will
be welcomed, not least because it plainly owes nothing to
partisan considerations.

Sir John came to Parliament House to be sworn in as
Governor-General on 11 July 1974. As I met Lady Kerr at the
foot of the steps she greeted me 'Many happy returns, Prime
Minister'. Parliament gave a reception for Sir John and Lady
Kerr that night. They had my wife and me to Yarralumla for
lunch next day. Lady Kerr entered hospital soon after and died
on 9 September. She and my wife had been loyal friends for over
thirty-two years.

When Sir John Kerr arrived in Canberra on 10 July 1974 to
take up his position as Governor-General he made a favourable
impression by asking that women should not curtsy to him or
his wife. His official secretary was quoted as saying that night
that Sir John 'favours the shaking of hands—both for men and
women—as a reciprocal gesture of greeting and respect. A slight

bow to the Governor-General and his wife by both men and women at the time of shaking hands would not be inappropriate.'

The following day Sir John arrived for his installation, to my surprise shared by many others, in morning dress of ample proportions and a top hat a size too small. This uniform was to be a cartoonists' delight until he went into exile.

In a prepared 'address' at a dinner given in his honour by members of the Union Club, Sydney on 3 April 1975 he spoke about 'the office of the Governor-General in this day and age and why I find the office so pleasant and interesting'. His first comments were:

> There is of course a lot of ceremonial and social activity which would not necessarily appeal to everyone. I shall deal with this simply by saying that I enjoy it all. I do not mind the ceremonial side at all. I believe that ceremony is an important part of life.
>
> At the bar, on the bench, and in other ways, I have always been associated with the dressing up and ceremonies of a particular way of life. We know that in academic life, in other professions, in the church, in the services and so on, ceremonies are important.

Sir John's book amply confirms his interest, amounting to obsession, in honours, awards and decorations. Soon after taking up office he asked me if I would recommend to Harold Wilson, then Prime Minister of Britain, that he should be appointed to the Privy Council; he was the first Governor-General not to be a member. Also as a former judge he would enjoy the title which had been reserved for justices of the High Court. (I knew the lure of the Privy Council for them. Forty years earlier Sir Frank Gavan Duffy had refused for well over a year to stand aside as Chief Justice for Sir John Latham, who had in anticipation stood aside for Menzies as MP for Kooyong and Attorney-General, until he was appointed to the Privy Council.) I pointed out that I was the first Prime Minister who had not been a Privy Counsellor since Alfred Deakin. I had resisted the temptation for the same reason as Deakin; we did not think it appropriate that the Australian Head of Government should be beholden to the British Head of Government for such favours. I accepted the view of Pierre Trudeau that there could conceivably be conflicts between oaths of allegiance to the Queen of Australia and the Queen of Britain; in Australia's case these could have occurred during Australia's intervention and Britain's abstention in Viet Nam, and indeed ships flying the British flag regularly sailed to Haiphong while the Australian flag was flying over Nui Dat.

Early in 1975, when we were discussing the establishment of the Order of Australia, he speculated that the Liberals would retain the Order but could introduce a class of knights and dames. I told him I thought he correctly judged their likely attitude. After his honeymoon in Fiji and New Zealand, he suggested that, since he already had a title, I would not be contravening Labor Party policy if I were to recommend his promotion from KCMG to GCMG,[3] as the Governors-General of Fiji and New Zealand were and all Governors-General of Australia had been. I gently disabused him but he revived the suggestion after his visit for the Independence ceremonies in

---

3   KCMG: Knight Commander of the Order of St Michael and St George; GCMG: Knight/Dame Grand Cross of the Order of St Michael and St George.

Papua New Guinea, whose first Governor-General was created a GCMG. Unconsciously he could not accept that the greatest Governor of New South Wales had not been knighted; I playfully chided him when, looking across Sydney Harbour from Admiralty House, he referred to 'Lady' Macquarie's Chair.

Alfred Deakin once dismissed the governor-generalship as a 'gaudy glittering toy'. Sir John Kerr certainly had a hankering for the baubles of the office. As I have described, I was unable to meet his wishes. His conduct was to show that his interest far transcended the mere trappings. He was developing a concept of his role far beyond anything envisaged by any of his predecessors. His book confirms it. I was unaware of it. He gave every sign of satisfaction with his role and his relations with my Government and me personally.

Early in 1975 Sir John Kerr delivered two speeches which indicated his preoccupations and growing pretensions. Neither of them was shown to me. The first was an address to the Indian Law Institute in New Delhi on 28 February. He had six copies of this address made in the High Commissioner's office. He carried them all off, leaving no copy with our High Commissioner, Bruce Grant. The second speech was made at the Union Club in Sydney on 3 April. In his Indian Law Institute address Sir John drew heavily on the Queale Memorial Lecture delivered by Sir Paul Hasluck in Adelaide on 24 October 1972. The three speeches taken together are notable not only for the contrasting emphasis which their authors give to their own personal significance but also the emphasis they give to the opportunities they have to see documents and cables and to have discussions with the Prime Minister and other ministers. In his Queale Lecture Sir Paul only once referred to the negative interpretation of the role of the office as a 'cipher'. By contrast

Sir John Kerr was elaborate in denying that the Governor-General could be so regarded. At the Indian Law Institute he said: 'People are always interested in the question whether the Governor-General is a mere figurehead or whether he has any significant role to play.'

He did, however, expand on his ceremonial role and status:

> Abroad I am accorded the Head of State status on all occasions when I am present but Her Majesty, the Queen, is not . . .
>
> I am still accorded a vice-regal salute which consists of six bars of the Royal Anthem 'God Save the Queen'. This was used at the aerodrome on my arrival here but it should not be thought that because of this Australia is in any sense dependent upon the United Kingdom or that the vice-regal salute has anything to do with the Queen's position and status in her other realms. My salute relates solely to my position as her representative in her capacity as Queen of Australia.

At the Union Club he told that egalitarian assembly that in Nepal, India, Pakistan, Afghanistan and Iran 'I was treated, not as a cipher or figurehead or rubber stamp, but as a person who at home occupies the position which I have been describing'.

It is particularly interesting to compare the views of Sir Paul Hasluck and Sir John Kerr on the relationship between the Governor-General and the Prime Minister and his other ministers. Sir Paul had said:

> The Executive Council provides regular and close association between the Governor-General and his Ministerial advisers. In addition, opportunities arise and can be made from time

to time for direct and personal conversation in private.
The Governor-General may ask a Minister to call to discuss
matters of current interest.

Sir Paul continued:

With the Prime Minister the Governor-General can be
expected to talk with frankness and friendliness, to question,
discuss, suggest and counsel.

In his address to the Indian Law Institute Sir John Kerr said:

There is ample opportunity both during and after meetings
of the Executive Council and in other ways for the
Governor-General to be fully informed about national affairs
and policies. There is full and frank discussion with the
Prime Minister. The Governor-General can ask questions,
discuss broad or detailed matters, make suggestions, provide
counsel—he can advise and warn.

In the Union Club address Sir John said:

He is entitled to be told why things are being done. He is
entitled to think about them. He is entitled on occasions to
make a suggestion, to give advice, even to utter a warning.

Again:

I have found it most rewarding to be fully informed about
the nation's affairs; to read the Cabinet papers, the Cabinet
decisions, the cables.

And yet again:

> I find the work of the Executive Council particularly
> interesting and of course it affords considerable
> opportunities for me after the formal business is over to talk
> to the ministers present. Over a period of time these talks
> can be most informative and rewarding in their frankness
> and background information.

It is important to note the dates of these speeches. Sir Paul's
lecture was delivered two days before the Parliament rose for
the elections of 1972 which returned my Government to office.
Both as a senior minister and Governor-General during three
prime ministerships—Gorton's, McMahon's and mine—he was
able to draw on long and close experience. Sir John Kerr's
experience related solely to the period of my prime ministership.
Accordingly, his comments in February and April 1975 must be
presumed to be his assessment of his relations with me and my
ministers after an association of nine months. There was not the
slightest hint of the doubts and reservations which he now
claims in his book to have held *at that time*. He told his fellow
members of the Union Club that he proposed to explain to them
'why I find the office so pleasant and interesting'. He told them
how rewarding he found it to be 'fully informed' about the
nation's affairs. And the quotations I have recorded show that he
was completely satisfied with his opportunities for 'full and
frank discussion with the Prime Minister' and 'to make a
suggestion, to give advice, even to utter a warning'.

In Chapter 4, I shall examine in detail the use Sir John Kerr
made of these opportunities with which he professed himself to
be completely satisfied in April 1975. At this point I merely

stress again the dates on which these speeches were made and I set them in the context of the claims Sir John makes in his book about matters which were causing him concern and from which he claims he had already drawn a lesson about his future conduct and his relations with the Government and in particular with his Prime Minister. He never conveyed the slightest concern to me at the time or thereafter. He made no suggestions, provided no counsel, uttered no warning. Nor did I know that as early as November 1974 he was privately expressing anxiety about the possible course of events in 1975 and the role he might be called upon to play in them.

3

DOWN CAME THE SQUATTER

'. . . I'D WANT TO FIND A SITUATION IN WHICH WE MADE
THAT DECISION AND MR WHITLAM WOKE UP ONE
MORNING FINDING THE DECISION HAD BEEN MADE AND
FINDING THAT HE HAD BEEN CAUGHT WITH HIS PANTS
WELL AND TRULY DOWN.'
Malcolm Fraser, 21 March 1975

November 1974 proved to be a much more troublesome month
for the Liberal Opposition than for the Labor Government. I
have since learnt, however, that it was in that month that Sir
John Kerr expressed his concern about the likely course of
political events in 1975. He expressed them, not to me, the Prime
Minister, but to the press proprietor, Rupert Murdoch, in the
presence of other newspapermen. For the following account
from an unpublished manuscript I am indebted to Ian Fitchett,
doyen of the Canberra Press Gallery at a time when the Gallery
was at its professional peak. Mr Fitchett—journalist, wit, and
above all Australian gentleman and Australian patriot, writes:

> Just when Murdoch became friendly with Kerr is not known
> but they were close enough for the Governor-General to

make the 50-mile journey to Cavan on the banks of the
Murrumbidgee late in the afternoon of Sunday 17
November 1974, almost a year to the day before Kerr
dismissed Whitlam.

Murdoch had been back in Australia for some weeks
and was entertaining a party of his senior men at Cavan that
weekend. His mother, Dame Elisabeth, had come from
Melbourne to play the hostess in place of Rupert's wife.

Included in the guests were cartoonist Paul Rigby and
his wife and James Hall, editor of the *Australian*, unaware
that he was due to lose his job early the following year.
Adelaide was represented by Ron Boland, Murdoch's senior
man on the *News*. Owen Thomson, editor-in-chief of the
Daily and *Sunday Telegraph* was also a weekend guest.
Invited out for a barbecue lunch was Ian Fitchett, who had
just commenced writing the Cassandra column in the
Sunday Telegraph.

It was a hot November day and there was some air of
mystery during lunch beside the swimming pool, Rupert
going to the phone on at least two occasions. This led to very
little speculation as Murdoch rivals Billy McMahon as a
telephone compulsive. However, in mid-afternoon Rupert
told those present that the Governor-General, John Kerr
would be coming out later in the day. John Kerr did not
arrive until well after 5 p.m. accompanied by his late wife's
private secretary, Jean Lester. Miss Lester was an old
Government House hand, her secretarial appointments
there, on and off, going back to Lady Slim, almost twenty
years before.

Rupert brought John Kerr and Miss Lester round to the
side verandah of Cavan, with its beautiful long sweeping

outlook down to the river, where they were welcomed by
Dame Elisabeth and introduced to the guests. After a few
pleasantries Dame Elisabeth, ever charming, took Mrs Rigby
and Jean Lester into the homestead and left the men to
themselves. Kerr at once said that he had to be on the road
by 6.30 at the latest.

Rupert, a gracious host, offered late-afternoon drinks,
Kerr asking for Scotch. The Governor-General at once
opened the conversation by expressing his concern over the
prospect of Gough Whitlam having to run the country with
a hostile Senate throughout 1975. Kerr spoke not only of the
certain rejection of much of Whitlam's legislation by the
Senate but also of the ever present possibility of refusal of
Supply in the autumn session of the Parliament or of the
outright rejection of the Budget later in the year.

The conversation that followed included talk about the
double dissolution granted Menzies by Sir William McKell
on 19 March 1951.

It was at this point that John Kerr looked at his watch,
said that it was 6.30 p.m. and that he must go.

Kerr, widowed only nine weeks before, struck me at the
time as a rather sad and lonely man. However, it was quite
obvious that he had quite a close relationship with Rupert
Murdoch.

But as Supply until the following 30 June had gone
through the Senate, only three days before, on 14 November,
Kerr's fears seemed rather far-fetched on that particular
Sunday.

There are many significant aspects about Mr Fitchett's
account of the Cavan meeting. It shows a degree of intimacy

between Sir John Kerr and Mr Murdoch which had great importance in the events of 1975. There was a contemporaneous and parallel intimacy between Mr Murdoch and Mr Fraser, equally important in the events of 1975. Most of all, it shows that Sir John was willing to open his mind, his concerns and his worries to people who had no real entitlement to know of them—in a way in which he never was willing to do so—and certainly never did—to those most entitled to such information, his constitutional advisers, and above all, the Prime Minister of Australia.

Further, as Mr Fitchett points out, this meeting took place only three days after the Senate had actually passed the Budget and provided Supply. There had been no crisis that year, nor any atmosphere of crisis. Nor did the Senate, as elected by the people only six months before, have it in its power to force a crisis in the way it was able to do a year later.

Mr Murdoch dined with me at the Lodge on the following Wednesday 20 November. He was very forthcoming about Mr Snedden's problems with his Party. He did not mention Sir John's concern at the course events might take in 1975.

The events of October–November 1975 could never have taken place if the Senate elected by the people on 18 May 1974 had remained intact and retained its integrity. That the Senate of the 29th Parliament became, in the words of my 'dear enemy' and friend, Jim Killen, as of writing Australian Minister for Defence, a 'tainted Senate' had nothing to do with the decision made by the people. Two State anti-Labor Premiers procured the corruption of the Senate and a gross distortion of its composition as determined by the people. Sir John seems to take my plagiarism of Mr Killen's epithet as hard evidence of my implacable hostility towards the Senate as an institution. In fact,

I used the phrase only in reference to that particular Senate, on the authority of the most honest and honourable of all Liberals, one who knows how to call a spade a spade; although given his delight in the richness and variety of the English language, he might exhaust the thesaurus before actually doing so. Nevertheless it was indeed a deeply tainted Senate by 1975.

The elections of 1949 were the first in which the Senate, its numbers increased from thirty-six to sixty, was elected under the proportional representation system of voting. Despite his landslide win in the House of Representatives, Menzies was in a minority in the Senate. It was this situation which led to the double dissolution of 1951 and which later led Menzies to describe the use of numbers in the Senate to reject government legislation as 'a falsification of democracy'. In 1951 a Labor senator from Western Australia, Dick Nash, died. Under the Constitution, if the place of a senator becomes vacant it is filled until the next Federal election by the person chosen by the State Parliament or if that Parliament is not in session, by a person appointed by the State Government until the State Parliament can make its choice. The Liberal Country League, which had a majority of members in both the Legislative Assembly and Legislative Council, resolved that the new senator should belong to that party. Premier McLarty stalled the appointment until he could consult Prime Minister Menzies. He wrote to Menzies on 20 December 1951 and to the other Premiers, of whom three were Labor, on 10 January 1952. They all agreed that, whenever a casual vacancy occurred in the Senate, the replacement should come from the same party as the former senator. The communications establishing this convention were not recorded in any Federal files; this was a main reason for my pressing on with archives legislation. Don Dunstan, the Premier of South

Australia, had no records because Premier Playford had responded to McLarty by telegram from the Gold Coast. Sir Charles Court, the Premier of Western Australia, lent me his State's file.

The convention thus established was unfailingly adhered to until 1975. In each case, irrespective of the political complexion of the State Government responsible for filling the vacancy, a nominee of the party to which the former senator had belonged filled the vacant place. Eight of the vacancies were caused by the death or resignation of a Labor senator; the other eighteen were caused by the death or resignation of non-Labor senators. In ten of the twenty-five cases, the new senator for the State was a political opponent of the existing State Government. No convention could have been better established by practice and precedent.

The Australian people's endorsement of the realities of the Australian party system was given at the referendum of May 1977 when they wrote the convention into the Constitution. That endorsement was given most resoundingly in New South Wales, the State where the Premier first broke it in 1975. The people of Queensland served a similiar rebuke on their Premier. By then, the breach of the convention in 1975 had served its only and intended purpose, the destruction of the Labor Government.

On 29 November 1974 Mr Justice Menzies of the High Court died suddenly. Early in December Senator Murphy indicated to me through Dr Cairns that he would be willing to go to the High Court. I recalled to Dr Cairns that, when our Government had been formed in December 1972, I had told Cabinet that there would be no appointments from its ranks during our first term. (The term I then envisaged was the normal three years.) I said, however, that I was prepared to vary that ruling in the case of Senator Murphy, who had been a great reform Attorney-General; in particular, he had persuaded the Senate, which we did not control, to pass two outstanding pieces of legislation, the Family Law and the Trade Practices Bills. Cabinet agreed to his appointment on 9 February 1975, just before the High Court commenced its sittings for that year.

Sir Garfield Barwick and Senator Murphy were the fifth and sixth Federal Attorneys-General to be appointed to the judiciary; Isaacs, Higgins and Latham to the High Court and Senator Spicer as founding Chief Judge of the Australian Industrial Court. The Menzies Government also appointed Percy Joske, QC, MP, to the Industrial Court and several Territorial Supreme Courts. In 1973 Nigel Bowen, MP, a former Liberal Attorney-General, had been appointed to the New South Wales Supreme Court by the Askin Liberal Government; in 1976 he was to be nominated as founding Chief Judge of the Federal Court of Australia by Mr Fraser's second Attorney-General, Bob Ellicott.

Senator Murphy's achievements in office, his experience and standing at the Bar, his appearance before the International Court of Justice, his familiarity with the decisions of the Supreme Court of the United States, all made him eminently suitable for appointment to the High Court of Australia. Why, then, the outrage which followed the announcement? I conclude that, to the degree it was not synthetic, it resulted from the double standard which conservatives, deeply convinced of their natural right to rule, apply to all appointments involving power or prestige. The double standard is expressed in the simple equation: Liberal = good; Labor = bad. None of the significant appointments my Government ever made has ever been shown to be unsuitable on the grounds of professional qualifications or personal character; all of them which involved a person with any association, however remote, with the Labor Party were criticised as 'jobs for the boys'—with the notable exception of that of Sir John Kerr himself.

The Premier of New South Wales, Tom Lewis, announced that he would not follow the convention established by Menzies and adopted by every State Premier since 1951. On 27 February 1975 a joint sitting of the New South Wales Parliament nominated a former mayor of Albury, Cleaver Bunton, to replace Senator Murphy, amid scenes of tumult and disorder remarkable even for that legislature. The new senator declared that he would sit as an Independent. During the crisis of October–November, Senator Bunton staunchly supported the Government. Thus, the loss of the vote of a Labor senator chosen by the people of New South Wales in 1974 was not itself decisive in that crisis. The real damage done by Mr Lewis and the New South Wales Liberals lay in the overturning of established convention. It showed how easy it was to break the rules.

Yet the first victim was to be the Leader of the Opposition, Mr Snedden. He opposed what his New South Wales colleagues were doing; he did nothing to stop them. He declared, with resounding ambiguity:

> I, Billy Mackie Snedden, have no power to determine who that successor [to Senator Murphy] will be. I have no power under the Liberal Party constitution. I have no power under the Australian Constitution. I have stated my view clearly, frankly, without fear and without seeking favour. That is my view and I maintain it.

This ringing declaration of principle was made to a Liberal Party rally at Randwick Racecourse, Sydney. Both the declaration and the occasion itself were evidence of Mr Snedden's gravely weakening hold on the leadership of his Party. The Randwick rally was part of an effort by the Liberal Party organisation to bolster Mr Snedden's position against the challenge being directed against him on behalf of Mr Fraser.

An abortive move against Mr Snedden had been made at the Liberal Party meeting on 27 November 1974. After this failed move on his behalf, Mr Fraser stoutly denied the slightest knowledge of or involvement in it. There may be some who believe him; and, indeed, Mr Fraser has a remarkable and enviable record of being the beneficiary of the actions of others who kept him in utter ignorance of their mighty efforts on his behalf. It soon became clear, however, that another push would be made on Mr Fraser's behalf as soon as a decent interval elapsed after the failed coup of 27 November 1974. Only a fortnight later, a meeting of Mr Fraser's supporters was arranged at the Poolaijelo Hall some thirty minutes from Mr Fraser's Western District property of Nareen. It was arranged by Reynolds Rippon, a leading grazier whose family had held large interests in the *Hamilton Spectator*. Mr Snedden might have had a much better idea of the forces being shaped against him had he been a close reader of that newspaper in the following weeks. In particular, he might have gained an insight into the likely role of his deputy, Mr Lynch.

The *Hamilton Spectator* of Tuesday 17 December 1974 reported:

Six Liberal Party branches have unanimously affirmed their 'complete confidence' in Mr Malcolm Fraser (Lib. Wannon).

About 90 members at the Poolaijelo Hall supported a
confidence vote in Mr Fraser—just over a fortnight since a
controversial Federal Liberal Party leadership challenge.

Senator Sir Magnus Cormack told the meeting Mr
Fraser had been much maligned in city media concerning
Liberal Party leadership. He said he knew Mr Fraser had
no part in proceedings that took place concerning the
leadership.

At this 13 December meeting at Poolaijelo, it was resolved to
hold a rally in support of Mr Fraser at the Mechanics Institute
Hall in Coleraine on 14 February 1975. On 1 February the
Hamilton Spectator announced that the rally would be addressed
by the Deputy Leader of the Liberal Party. It was a clear sign
that Mr Lynch had abandoned his leader. The mandate of
heaven was moving to Mr Fraser.

On 18 February the *Spectator* reported that both Fraser and
Lynch had joined forces on the Coleraine platform in 'declaring
themselves in favour of an early election'.

Mr Snedden was deposed as Party leader and replaced by
Mr Fraser on 21 March 1975. His handling of the Lewis breach
of convention and his poor performance in Parliament in its
wake undoubtedly contributed to his downfall. In November
1974 Mr Fraser's first challenge to Mr Snedden was lost by
eleven votes. In the House of Representatives a majority of the
Liberals voted for Mr Fraser but the Senate Liberals solidly
backed Mr Snedden. In Mr Fraser's second challenge in March
1975 Senator Withers had swapped sides, bringing enough
senators with him to topple Mr Snedden by eight votes, thirty-
six to twenty-eight. In particular Senators Cotton and Carrick,
former president and secretary of the State branch of the Party,

had persuaded all New South Wales Liberals in both Houses to support Mr Fraser. It has been suggested that in the parliamentary confrontation with Mr Snedden I resorted to 'over-kill' and that accordingly I myself created the condition by which Mr Fraser could supplant him. This, I believe, takes insufficient account of the character of the Liberal Party and the character of Mr Fraser. The events of February and March may have hastened Mr Snedden's end and determined the timing by Mr Fraser and his friends. The *Hamilton Spectator* reports made it clear that Mr Snedden was doomed, certainly from the time that Mr Lynch cast his lot with Mr Fraser. But then I was no more an avid reader of the *Hamilton Spectator* than Mr Snedden.

I realised, of course, that Mr Fraser was a more formidable opponent than Mr Snedden. I was disposed, however, to take at face value his statement of the principle that would govern his attitude to the Supply question. At his first press conference as leader, he said:

> The question of Supply—let me deal with it in this way. I generally believe if a Government is elected to power in the lower House and has the numbers and can maintain the numbers in the lower House, it is entitled to expect that it will govern for the three-year term unless quite extraordinary events intervene.
>
> I want to get talk about elections out of the air so that the Government can get on with the job of governing and make quite certain that it is not unduly distracted by these particular matters.
>
> Having said that, let me also say that if there are any questions about when an election might be held or when someone might want to do something about it, I would not

be wanting to answer that particular question or trailing my coat about what our tactics or approach would be, because if we do make up our minds at some stage that the Government is so reprehensible that an opposition must use whatever power is available to it, then I'd want to find a situation in which we made that decision and Mr Whitlam woke up one morning finding the decision had been made and finding that he had been caught with his pants well and truly down.

The advent of Mr Fraser as Liberal leader was, of course, to transform the future prospects of my Government. It escaped me altogether, however, that his advent had transformed Sir John Kerr's view of his own future prospects even more sharply. In Chapter 2, I described Sir John's request to me to secure certain undertakings about his tenure from Mr Snedden. The new Leader of the Liberal Party had given no such commitment. In the circumstances of his accession, he was not likely to take over automatically the commitments made by the man he had deposed. Obviously, I was not in a position to seek from Mr Fraser a renewal of the undertaking I had secured from Mr Snedden. Sir John Kerr did not ask me to try to do so. But with Mr Snedden's deposition, Sir John Kerr's bipartisan guarantee of security of tenure disappeared. The rest of this story is not least an account of how Sir John Kerr came to terms with the new situation in which all of us found ourselves.

4

RESOURCE DEVELOPMENTS

'I FIND THE WORK OF THE EXECUTIVE COUNCIL
PARTICULARLY INTERESTING AND OF COURSE IT AFFORDS
CONSIDERABLE OPPORTUNITIES FOR ME AFTER THE
FORMAL BUSINESS IS OVER TO TALK TO THE MINISTERS
PRESENT. OVER A PERIOD OF TIME THESE TALKS CAN BE
MOST INFORMATIVE AND REWARDING IN THEIR
FRANKNESS AND BACKGROUND INFORMATION.'

Sir John Kerr, 3 April 1975

Sir John Kerr's book has a chapter entitled 'The Loan Affair and Justiciable Issues'. His treatment of the 'loan affair' is plainly intended to serve as justification of and set the stage for his conduct in November 1975. It is all an exercise in hindsight. He writes of his 'great shock' and his 'deep worry'. If such was his state of mind, he never indicated it to me or any of my colleagues, at any time from 14 December 1974, when he first became involved, to 11 November 1975. Sir John shared the responsibility for authorising Rex Connor, the Minister for Minerals and Energy, to borrow large amounts overseas to secure energy resources for Australia and to develop them in Australia; he was fascinated with the potential of such projects; he became embarrassed when the Liberals and the newspapers misrepresented the proposition; and finally his actions operated with theirs to harass Rex Connor.

From its first Cabinet meeting my Government had been intent on developing Australia's immense mineral and energy resources without letting them pass into foreign hands. This was the motivation for the Pipeline Authority, the Petroleum and Minerals Authority and the enhanced Australian Industry Development Corporation. When oil supplies became unexpectedly precarious and expensive following the Middle East War in September 1973, the Cabinet received many submissions and made many decisions to safeguard energy supplies to Australia and to promote energy projects in Australia. The successive Governors-General saw the Cabinet papers including Cabinet decisions. Sir John confirmed this in his address to the Union Club on 3 April 1975.

On 14 December 1974 Mr Connor received Executive Council authority to borrow up to US$4000 million and to determine on behalf of the Australian Government the terms and conditions of the borrowing. The authority was revoked on 7 January 1975 since it had not been used and it conflicted with a Deutsche Mark loan then pending. On 28 January the Executive Council authorised the minister to raise a loan not exceeding US$2000 million. The authority was revoked on 20 May 1975 since negotiations were in train for a loan through Morgan Stanley and Company Incorporated of New York.

The purpose of both borrowings, as set out in the explanatory memorandum for the Executive Council, was to meet the needs of the Australian Government for:

> ... substantial sums of non-equity capital from abroad for
> temporary purposes, amongst other things to deal with

exigencies arising out of the current world situation and the international energy crisis, to strengthen Australia's external financial position, to provide immediate protection for Australia's supplies of minerals and energy and to deal with current and immediately foreseeable unemployment in Australia.

What were the international circumstances the Australian Government had to confront? In 1973 and 1974 eruptions of unprecedented magnitude shook the financial world. Balance-of-payments surpluses from the sale of oil began to accumulate in enormous quantities in the Organisation of Petroleum Exporting Countries world, principally the Middle East. Surpluses amounting to no less than US$55 000 million to US$60 000 million are believed to have accumulated in this way in 1974 alone.

As Bill Hayden later pointed out:

It is acknowledged that the actions of the Minister for Minerals and Energy and of other Ministers in these matters were not orthodox in the sense that they did not turn to the old established finance houses of the rich industrial countries. But those very institutions are prepared to search out the new sources of funds, so why is it wrong for Australia to do so? . . . It is my belief that a great deal of the surprise which is apparent in the community on these matters springs from the unorthodox, the unconventional. I remind the House that France, England, Japan, Italy and Denmark have already trodden that so-called unorthodox, unconventional path.

The proposals were neither grandiose nor sinister. In September 1974 the Shah of Iran visited Australia and discussed closer links between the two countries in developing and sharing their respective energy and agricultural resources. In March 1975 Dr Cairns, as Deputy Prime Minister and Treasurer, and Ken Wriedt, as Leader of the Government in the Senate and Minister for Agriculture, visited Iran, Saudi Arabia, Kuwait and Bahrain to discuss similar arrangements. In 1977–78 the Australian Government borrowed over US$2000 million overseas. In November 1978 the Australian Loan Council unanimously and eagerly approved overseas borrowings by all the States for projects which, with the sole exception of the Melbourne Trade Centre, had been among those which my Government was proposing to finance with any loans which Mr Connor raised. (In the same month Mr Anthony made his ministerial statement endorsing Mr Connor's guidelines on export contracts for Australian minerals.) The 1975 proposals, however, foundered because of the animosity between the Treasury and the Department of Minerals and Energy right from the top. Public controversy was fomented by disaffected and disloyal officers of the Treasury peddling snippets of information to the Liberal Opposition, particularly its deputy leader, Mr Lynch.

In his account, Sir John relies heavily on the misrepresentation and misunderstanding which were deliberately created among the public and which persist in the public memory. In giving this brief history, I must emphasise two cardinal points: at every stage of the negotiations, the most senior officials of the Australian Government were actively involved, not least the law officers; and at no stage did Sir John Kerr express to me the slightest doubts about any aspect of the matter, neither about what we were trying to do nor how we were going about it.

There was nothing hugger-mugger about these operations. Before the proposal became public, there had never been such close scrutiny of a loan proposal in Australia's history as was given by officials to this one; after it became public, there has never been such close scrutiny of every detail connected with a loan as this one.

It is nothing to the point that Treasury officials opposed our proposal. Treasury is the sole repository of neither the wisdom nor the integrity of Australian Government. I was vastly diverted even if more than somewhat surprised to read that Sir Frederick Wheeler declared at his last Treasury Christmas party in December 1978 that 'all politicians are bastards'. I might say, though never about Sir Fred himself, *vos quoque*. Sir John Kerr states that, had he known of the departmental disputes about our loan proposal, this would have confirmed him in his decision to accept the advice of his ministers. This is a first-class example of how later political developments and revelations have distorted Sir John Kerr's judgement of both his proper role and his actual behaviour.

Late in September 1974 Jerry Karidis, an Adelaide businessman, told my colleague Clyde Cameron that he believed it would be possible for the Australian Government to raise a large overseas loan at about 8 per cent interest. Mr Cameron informed Mr Connor, who said he would like to discuss the matter with Mr Karidis. Early in October Mr Cameron arranged for Mr Karidis and his solicitor, Tim Anderson, to meet Dr Cairns, who was Acting Prime Minister while I was at the United Nations General Assembly, Mr Connor and Sir Lenox Hewitt, Secretary of the Department of Mines and

Energy. In November Mr Karidis told Mr Cameron that he was in touch with Tirath Khemlani, who claimed to be in a position to make direct contact with Middle East oil interests which had large sums of money to lend. Mr Cameron and Mr Karidis took Mr Khemlani to meet Mr Connor. Mr Connor, Sir Lenox and Dennis Rose of the Attorney-General's Department also had talks with John Broinowski of Darling and Company, the merchant bankers.

On Monday 9 December I arranged a meeting at my office in Parliament House with Dr Cairns, Mr Connor, Senator Murphy, Sir John Phillips, Sir Roland Wilson, Chairman of the Commonwealth Banking Corporation, Sir Frederick Wheeler, Sir Lenox Hewitt, Maurice Byers, QC, the Solicitor-General, Clarrie Harders, Secretary of the Attorney-General's Department, and Mr Rose. Further discussions took place during the week between some of us and John Menadue, Secretary of the Department of the Prime Minister and Cabinet, and other officers of the Treasury and Attorney-General's Department.

It was finally decided that Mr Connor should be authorised to raise an overseas loan of US$4000 million. At about 7 o'clock on Friday evening 13 December I sought an Executive Council meeting. My staff told me that the Governor-General had left Canberra for Sydney that afternoon. I then spoke to a member of his staff at Admiralty House and was told that he had gone to the ballet and it was not known when he would be back. I asked that his staff telephone me on my direct number as soon as he was known to be awake on Saturday morning.

At this stage I can write no more about the documents and discussions involving Sir John Kerr on 13 and 14 December because they are *sub judice*. On 20 November 1975 a private

citizen, Danny Sankey, issued summonses against me, Dr
Cairns, Mr Connor and Mr Justice Murphy, as he now was, in
which he alleged, first, that we had conspired with each other to
contravene the Financial Agreement, which regulates loan
raisings, and, secondly, that we had conspired with each other to
deceive the Governor-General by recommending that he
approve the authority for Mr Connor to raise a loan in
contravention of the Financial Agreement. In November 1978
the High Court held that the first charge was bad in law. The
second charge, however, is still before the courts.[1]

Sir John's book makes it abundantly clear that none of us
deceived him in any respect whatsoever. It is irrational to
suppose that any illegal project would have got past four
ministers including two QCs, the heads and senior officers
of four departments including the Attorney-General's
Department, the heads of the Reserve and Commonwealth
Banks and the Solicitor-General. If any State Government
thought that my Government's action was improper or illegal it
could have challenged that action in the Loan Council or before
the High Court; none of them did. If the Liberal Attorney-
General of New South Wales or any of Mr Fraser's three
attorneys-general thought that any minister had broken the
criminal law he should have prosecuted him; none of them did.

On Saturday afternoon 14 December Lionel Bowen, the
Special Minister of State, and I left on a mission to Europe; Sir
Lenox Hewitt and Mr Harders came with us. (The Liberals
were most caustic at our chartering a Boeing 707 from Qantas.
Four years later to the very day, the Fraser Government went
one better: they announced that they were getting two 707s from

1   This matter was concluded. See Extended Biographies.

Qantas for such voyages, and not just chartering them but buying them!) Except in a telephone call to Mr Byers, Sir John Kerr never raised the matter of the loan minutes with any minister, departmental head or legal adviser before a public controversy arose in June and July. In July and August he told me that he was being embarrassed in the clubs by snide questions whether he had been approving any billion-dollar loans recently. He was apprehensive that people might regard him as slack in not having presided over a meeting of the Executive Council instead of merely signing the documents when they were sent to him.

It is as simple as that; and all Sir John's thousands of words cannot change it. He became concerned about his complicity in the events of 13–14 December 1974 only when they became a matter of political controversy, and when the people with whom he wished to ingratiate himself started ribbing him about it. Legality or propriety had nothing to do with it.

Sir John would have us believe that the Executive Council is at the very centre of government in Australia. It is not. Before the 'loan affair' not 1 per cent of our people would have been aware of its existence. I daresay even now less than 1 per cent are aware of its functions.

Like any body which meets in private the Executive Council is thought to move in a mysterious way its wonders to perform. Let me dispel the mystery. The Constitution mentions the Federal Executive Council; it does not mention the Cabinet or Ministry or Government. The appointments which governments make, the treaties they conclude, the acquisitions they ordain, the authorities they give, derive their legal effect from being given formal approval at meetings of the Executive Council. Business comes before the Executive Council in the form of a minute accompanied by an explanatory memorandum from the minister or ministers primarily responsible for the subject.

At a meeting of the Executive Council on 12 January 1901 it was decided that a quorum should be three. The Governor-General is the president of the Executive Council. The Constitution often refers to the Governor-General in Council; even where the Constitution states that the Governor-General may do this or that, it has always been thought that he does so when authorised by the Executive Council. There is a vice-president of the Executive Council, who is a minister appointed by the Governor-General on the Prime Minister's recommendation to preside when the Governor-General cannot himself preside at a meeting. If neither the Governor-General nor the vice-president attends, the senior minister in attendance presides. Meetings are convened quite informally and quickly by telephone calls between the Prime Minister's and the Governor-General's staff.

'If', to quote an affidavit sworn on 12 November 1976 by Mr Carmody, Secretary of the Department of the Prime Minister and Cabinet, 'the Governor-General is not present at the meeting of the Executive Council the minute and the schedule are subsequently submitted to him for signature'.

There were ninety-seven meetings of the Executive Council while Sir John was Governor-General and I Prime Minister. At thirteen of these meetings the senior minister presided—Mr Hayden and I twice each and Mr Crean, Mr Connor, Senators Wriedt and Willesee and Messrs Daly, Barnard, Beazley, Uren and Bryant once each. The Vice-President presided at seven of the meetings and the Administrator, Sir Roden Cutler, at six of them. Fourteen of the meetings were held to suit the convenience of the Governor-General at Admiralty House.

Before a person becomes a minister he is sworn as a member of the Executive Council. He swears that he 'will not directly or indirectly reveal such matters as shall be debated in Council'. When a person ceases to be a minister, he remains a member of the Executive Council but can no longer be called to its meetings. A person who is or has been a member of the Executive Council is entitled to the prefix 'Honourable'. It is most exceptional for a person to be removed from the Executive Council; Senator Glenister Sheil is the only instance I know.

In his book Sir John runs on for more than fourteen pages about his doubts and difficulties over the Executive Council minute he signed on 14 December 1974. They all seem to have been resolved before 28 January 1975, because on that date he signed a similar Executive Council minute to which he devotes much less than a single page.

Let me point up the significance of this. Sir John had more than six weeks to reflect on the minute of 14 December 1974. That minute was cancelled on 7 January 1975. All his retrospective concerns are about that one. Yet it had become inoperative in less than a month. Even if the concerns he now claims to have felt had any foundation, they were presently laid to rest by the revocation of the borrowing authority granted to Mr Connor by that minute. Yet we are asked to believe that a matter which had caused him 'great shock' in December 1974 deserved his approval and acquiescence on 28 January 1975. And indeed, Sir John himself admits these very points, for, discussing the question of whether the minute of 14 December was valid, he writes:

It was never tested and *the point became an academic one*. It was however one to be left to the courts. *For this reason I expressed no view to Mr Whitlam as to the validity of the meeting.* [My italics]

This is a preposterous assertion. The question of validity, if there was ever any doubt about it, certainly became academic on 7 January, when the first authority was rescinded. But to suggest that the very fact that its validity might become a matter for the courts—'justiciable', Sir John's word—was itself the excuse and the reason for not raising it with me is monstrous. Elsewhere, he asserts that the central role of the Governor-General is to prevent illegal conduct by ministers; that assertion forms part of his defence for his conduct on 11 November 1975. Yet, in this case, he says that he could not raise the matter with me precisely because he thought it might be invalid!

What is the truth about Sir John's state of mind during those days and weeks of December–January? Let the witnesses of the conduct of the Governor-General of Australia in the summer of 1974–75 balance the reflections of the author of *Auvergne* in 1978.

Sir John asserts that his absence from Canberra on Friday night 13 December was due to his attending 'an official engagement' at the Sydney Opera House. It was in fact a performance of the ballet *Romeo and Juliet*. There was nothing wrong or unusual in the Governor-General's absence from Canberra; nor is there the slightest reason why he should not go to see the ballet. But why dress it up, years later, as 'an official engagement'. Even the vice-regal notice in the *Sydney Morning Herald* did not try to sustain such a pretence, such pretensions or such pretentiousness. Simply, the Prime Minister could not contact the Governor-General, because he was at the ballet. That is all there is to say about it.

On the following Thursday 19 December, Sir John presided over an Executive Council meeting in Canberra attended by Mr Connor and Mr Enderby. Mr Connor noticed how eager Sir John was to discuss the progress of the talks about overseas loans and the immense potential of the projects which they would finance. Mr Enderby, who as a resident of Canberra frequently attended the Executive Council and who did not become involved in the subject till he became Attorney-General in February, had never seen Sir John so enthusiastic.

I had to leave London on Boxing Day to return to Australia in the wake of the devastation caused to Darwin by Cyclone Tracy. I was due in Sydney from Darwin on Saturday evening 28 December. Elizabeth Reid, my adviser on women's affairs—Sir John had asked her to Yarralumla on 20 December—and Patti Warn, my media secretary, came in the early evening to Kirribilli House, intending to help me with any preparations for the Cabinet meeting which I was calling on the Darwin tragedy. They were sitting in the drawing room about 8.30 p.m. when to their astonishment the Governor-General tapped on the french windowpanes demanding admittance. They asked him in and got him a bottle of scotch. Sir John explained that he had been walking in the gardens of Admiralty House when he saw the lights on at Kirribilli House. Knowing that I was to return from Darwin that evening he felt he should come over in case he could do anything.

The three went out onto the verandah. Sir John reminisced about his courting days when as a penniless barrister he had taken his late wife on ferry trips to while away many an afternoon. She had always liked the look of Kirribilli House; it had been in those days her dream home, he said. When he had been appointed Governor-General, Sir John said, he had apologised to her that his job took him to the wrong house. He may once have dreamt of being Prime Minister but not of being Governor-General.

The women told him that they were worried about a telephone call earlier in the day to the effect that one of my ministers was proposing to make a controversial appointment to his personal staff as soon as I had gone back to Europe. Sir John recalled that the proposed appointee had previously received an exemption from some provisions of the Public Service Act in order to take up an earlier ministerial appointment. He said he would see if anything could be done to block the appointment. He got in touch with his aide-de-camp, Captain Chris Stephens, RAAC, and told him to telephone Mr Cooley, the Chairman of the Public Service Board, for information on the terms of appointment as formally approved and the extent to which they departed from the norm. After some time the aide told Sir John that he had been unable to contact Mr Cooley at home but had ascertained that he was at a party in Canberra where he was trying to reach him with His Excellency's request. Mr Cooley was later extracted from the party and agreed to have the papers ready in the morning.

When the women received a call that my aircraft might not reach Sydney until nearly 11 p.m., they decided that I would probably not want to see anybody by the time I reached Kirribilli House and that they should go to a party which was being held at Miss Warn's flat not far away.

They issued a light-hearted invitation to Sir John to join the party. He noted the address but said it was unlikely he would come, lamenting how restrictive the life of the Governor-General was, particularly as far as a personal life was concerned. He could not just drive off into the night without explaining his comings and goings. It was very lonely upstairs at Government House and Admiralty House when the day's work was done.

Sir John was seen to the postern between the two mansions. The housekeeper, Jo Holloway, told the women that Sir John might very well turn up and gave them another bottle of whisky for him. They walked around to the flat. The remaining guests did not believe that they had been entertaining the Governor-General. They started speculating on which of them would be the new Lady Kerr and whether the next party would be at Admiralty House or Yarralumla. When there was a buzz from the security intercom on the ground floor it was cheerfully suggested that it would be the Governor-General. On answering, my secretary found that it was his aide and himself. They were asked up.

It was now midnight. Conversation wandered over the Darwin disaster, protocol, women's needs, the plight of Aboriginals and the Queen. They talked about the remarkable progress that had been made in Papua New Guinea since self-government, largely due to the accelerated localisation program which Labor had encouraged.

One of the men at the party then had the poor taste to inquire how he should go about getting in touch with the Queen. Sir John made it quite clear that he was the only person in Australia who could get in touch with Her Majesty. This was absolutely vital to the concept of the role of the Governor-General in Australia. He and he alone was entitled to engage in direct communication with Her Majesty. Others, however eminent, had to go through her private secretary. The more the guests queried this isolation of the Queen from her loyal Australian subjects, political or otherwise, the more persistent he became on what he saw as his role and his unique relationship to the Queen.

So, on a rather sour note, the Governor-General of Australia eventually withdrew.

My account is not exaggerated but bowdlerised. It gives an extraordinary insight into Sir John's state of mind, his conduct and his view of his role at that time. It extended apparently to intervention in the business of ministerial staff appointments. Further, it illustrates much about the relationship which existed between Admiralty House and Kirribilli House. Sir John felt no inhibition about turning up at Kirribilli House because 'the lights were on' and, knocking off a bottle or two of my dutiable scotch. Yet I now learn that he had a total inhibition against talking to me about his 'great shock', his 'deep worry' on an important matter of state! (He continued to seek out Ms Reid— dinner at Admiralty House, calls at Kirribilli House, lunch, dinner and other visits at Government House. He had her private number. His theme was why should she work for the second man in the country when she could be married to the man above him. At last, just before she left with me in April for the Commonwealth Heads of Government meeting in Jamaica, she told him she was still married and, although she could take steps to end her marriage under the existing law, she was not proposing to take them.)

On Monday 30 December I had all the appropriate ministers at Kirribilli House to make arrangements for the rehabilitation of Darwin. That afternoon when the meeting had concluded but some of the ministers and I were still putting the finishing touches to various documents and announcements, Sir John appeared on the verandah. We asked him in. For well over an hour he joined in all our discussions very fully and interestedly. That night I went back to Europe, to resume the itinerary on which much time and money had been spent by many governments.

(During my absence Mr Bowen had made the scheduled visit to Malta; no Australian Prime Minister had yet visited that Commonwealth country. I rejoined the party in Greece and became the first Head of Government to visit Constantine Karamanlis, head of the restored Hellenic democracy. Our political opponents made something of my dash from the ruins of Darwin to the ruins of Greece. Greek migrants in Australia were not particularly amused by such criticism and are still not. They appreciate the fact that I was and am the only Australian Prime Minister to have taken an interest in their homeland.)

Although all four ministers who had signed the minute on 13 December were together at Kirribilli House throughout his call, Sir John never raised the matter with any of us. He had plenty of other opportunities, none of which he took.[2]

He presided at an Executive Council meeting at Admiralty House on Tuesday 7 January 1975 at which the minute of 13 December was rescinded; it was attended by Frank Stewart, the Vice-President of the Council. He presided at another Executive Council meeting there a week later attended by Dr Cairns, the Acting Prime Minister, and again by Mr Stewart. He did not refer before, during or after these meetings to the minute of 13 December. Two nights later he had Jim Cairns and his wife to dinner at Admiralty House; again he made no reference to the minute of 13 December.

---

2   Sir John did not raise the matter with Senator Murphy, who had just returned from Darwin, during the broad discussion followed by the long lunch which he had with Murphy at Admiralty House before Kerr himself went to Darwin on Thursday, 2 January 1975. Nor did he do so with Dr Cairns, who sat beside him at the Darwin Relief Fund Concert at the Opera House on 4 January.

On 22 January, two days after we returned from Europe, my wife and I were his guests at luncheon at Government House; he did not raise with me the minute of 13 December. On 28 January he presided at a meeting of the Executive Council at Government House attended by Mr Connor and Senator Murphy at which he signed a minute in the same terms as the minute of 13 December except that the amount was changed from US$4000 million to US$2000 million. He did not express any qualms about the minute of 13 December or the new minute before, during or after this meeting with the ministers.

On Sunday 2 February, on the eve of the ALP National Conference to be held at Terrigal through the following week, he received me at Admiralty House and did not mention either minute. On Monday 10 February there was a series of meetings at Government House. He received Mr Justice Murphy and then me. He commented on the resounding endorsement of Mr Connor's policies at Terrigal; I said he would have been given an even bigger reception if it had been known that there was a prospect of a petrodollar loan to consummate them. He presided over an Executive Council meeting attended by me, Dr Cairns and Mr Cameron. Later again he commissioned Kep Enderby, QC, as Attorney-General and his closest professional friend, Senator Jim McClelland, as Minister for Manufacturing Industry. At no time in this series of meetings on that day did he express any misgivings about either minute. On 14 February he received Sir John Phillips, who had been involved in the discussions in December; again he expressed no qualms whatever.

There was still not the wispiest cloud over Sir John's relations with my ministers when on 20 February 1975 I farewelled him and his daughter, Gabrielle Kibble, and their entourage when he left on his first overseas tour by RAAF aircraft. He first visited Nepal where he had been invited to the coronation of King Birendra. In February 1970 Lord Casey had represented Sir Paul Hasluck at the wedding of the King when he was Crown Prince; he had been punctilious in sending me a copy of his report on his visit. Later in April 1971 King Mahendra of Nepal and his Queen had made a state visit to Australia and had been tendered a dinner by the Parliament. It was appropriate, therefore, that Sir John himself should attend this further royal occasion to which Australia's Governor-General had been invited. He also wished to take up the invitation which the Shah had given him the previous September. I also arranged for him to visit India, Pakistan and Afghanistan on his way from Nepal to Iran.

On Saturday 15 March, immediately on his return he received me at breakfast at Admiralty House. He was still elated over his reception in Katmandu and New Delhi. In the former he as the Queen's viceroy had been greeted at the airport by the King himself and thereafter had been ranked and seated in precedence above her son and heir and the Duke of Gloucester and Earl Mountbatten of Burma. 'I was treated,' he was to tell the Union Club in Sydney on 3 April, 'not as a cipher or figurehead or rubber stamp but as a person who occupies the position of Head of State'. (Moreover, Australia was alphabetically ahead of all the other countries represented.) In New Delhi Mrs Gandhi had been most forthcoming in response to my request that she should meet him. He did not mention to me or give me the address which he had given to the Indian Law Institute on 28 February but which contained this passage:

It is the duty of the Executive Council to ensure that what is done is in conformity with the Constitution, the laws of the

Commonwealth and the established and recognised practices
of the Australian Government. The Governor-General, as
President of the Council, has real and important duties in
this connection and can obtain legal advice especially from
the law officers of the Crown if he feels that he needs it.

Clearly he had no misgivings about the two Executive Council
authorities to Mr Connor at the time he spoke in New Delhi.
Nobody in Australia saw the text of this speech before the
Journal of the Indian Law Institute was received by the National
Library on 23 December 1975. Sir John gave the Department of
Foreign Affairs and me a report on the countries he visited. He
did not attach a copy of the speech to the Law Institute to the
reports he gave the Department and me.

Sir John stayed at Admiralty House and my wife and I next
door at Kirribilli House until we all returned to Canberra the
following Tuesday, 18 March.

My wife and I were his guests on 23 March at his dinner for
the Prime Minister of New Zealand and Mrs Rowling. He
received me on Thursday 27 March. On Saturday 5 April my
wife was among his guests when, to quote the vice-regal notices,
he held an 'at home' at Miegunyah, Toorak, to inaugurate his
use of the establishment as an official residence in Melbourne.
That night my wife and I were his guests at dinner at the Hotel
Windsor in Melbourne.

Sir John visited Papua New Guinea from 11 to 17 April and
presided over a meeting of the Executive Council in Sydney
on Friday 18 April. Then on Monday 21 April, prior to my
departure with Mr Bowen for the Commonwealth Heads of
Government Meeting (CHOGM), he confided in me that on 29
April, during my absence, he would be marrying Mrs Nancy

Robson. He had known her since their days together at the Australian School of Pacific Administration thirty years before. She had intended to go to Paris as an interpreter with UNESCO. She had accepted his offer to stay in Australia as his wife. (He did not tell me that Mrs Robson had become free to marry him only three days before and that on that very day they would have to give the statutory seven days' notice of their intention to marry.)

I congratulated him on marrying such an accomplished lady, whom I had come to know as a French interpreter at conferences arranged by the Department of External Affairs in the 1950s and 1960s. He told me why she had divorced her husband, Hugh Robson. I reminisced that Hugh and I had been judges' associates together in the Supreme Court. He had arranged the bachelor dinner for me before my own marriage and I had known him at the bar; our political views had diverged, because in 1950, when I gained Labor selection for the new State seat of Sutherland, he had sought Liberal selection for the new State seat of Collaroy against Bob Askin, who twenty years later appointed him to the District Court.

It surprises me to discover nearly four years later that Sir John Kerr was a deeply troubled man at that time and that, as he writes, 'he had learned some lessons from the loan affair'. I can only repeat he never mentioned his 'lessons' to me. And the truth is, of course, that all his 'lessons' were learnt retrospectively.

Sir John's doubts about the loan minutes were triggered by newspaper stories about Mr Khemlani and questions in Parliament. Mr Connor had made it plain to Mr Khemlani from the outset that he would only make the loan arrangements with the lenders themselves. Mr Khemlani would have to look to the lenders for any recompense for his services. Mr Khemlani was already irritated and alienated by February. The cancellation of the second authority in May would have been the last straw for him, for he must have incurred heavy expenses. He set out to recoup his losses by selling his story and his documents to the newspapers and the Liberals.

On 9 July 1975 the Government called a special session of the Parliament 'to consider the matter of overseas loan negotiations'.

Mr Fraser said that the 'infamous Executive Council decision on 13 December 1974 . . . raises the most serious possibility of a deliberate conspiracy to deceive and to defraud'. Mr Lynch said that my conduct amounted to a conspiracy. They were outdone by Mr Ellicott, who had been Solicitor-General before entering Parliament and who was now the shadow Attorney-General. He declared that the Government should get rid of Mr Connor and Sir Lenox Hewitt and he attacked the honesty of Mr Justice Murphy. He proceeded then to ask:

> By the way, where was the advice of the Solicitor-General?
> If this Government wanted the impartial advice of a lawyer,
> where was the advice of the Solicitor-General? That has not
> been produced . . . We know that Messrs Byers and Harders
> were at a meeting in the Attorney-General's Department.
> They were good enough to prepare this document 'J', this
> farrago of fact and falsity. Why was the Solicitor-General not
> good enough to be asked for advice on this particular matter
> and where is his advice? If it were tabled here it might
> satisfy a lot of us.

Mr Ellicott concluded that we must have deceived the Governor-General into approving the Executive Council minute. He read a notice of motion to call Mr Byers and public servants who had been concerned with the Executive Council meeting of 13 December before the bar of the Senate. Half an hour later Senator Withers so moved.

The time of the Senate was taken up with this exercise on 15, 16 and 17 July and with evidence from Mr Karidis on 22 July. The mountain went into labour and not even a mouse was produced.

I am convinced it was these events which gave rise to Sir John Kerr's concern over the 'loan affair'. His real concern had nothing to do with the validity or otherwise of the Executive Council minute of 13 December 1974; it arose only when that cancelled minute became a matter of political controversy. If this is not so, if Sir John Kerr's professed concern antedated the events of June and July 1975, then he is all the more blameworthy for his gross breach of the duty he owed me not only as Governor-General but as a man of honour. If he had doubts, it was his duty as Governor-General to 'advise and warn' his Prime Minister of them. If he had doubts, it was the obligation of any man of honour to speak man to man about them.

5

STACKING THE SENATE

'LET IT BE REMEMBERED THAT THE OPPOSITION
SUCCEEDED ONLY BECAUSE A LABOR SENATOR DIED.
THEY DID IT OVER A DEAD MAN'S CORPSE.'
Senator Steele Hall, 15 October 1975

On 30 June Senator Bert Milliner, one of our Queensland senators, died. The Premier of Queensland, Joh Bjelke-Petersen, announced that he would refuse to accept Labor's nominee as Senator Milliner's replacement. This was Dr Malcolm Colston, who had narrowly failed to win the tenth Queensland place in the 1974 double dissolution. (He was elected to the Senate in December 1975.) On 9 September Mr Bjelke-Petersen procured the nomination of Pat Field, an individual of the utmost obscurity, from which he rose and to which he sank with equal speed. He was said to have been a former member of the Labor Party; he promptly announced that he would vote against the Labor Government on all occasions. As police reports say, nothing more is known of this person. (When he faced the people as a candidate in December,

he secured 2909 out of the 1 053 209 votes cast in Queensland.)
Yet this appointment was the crucial event leading to the
political crisis of October–November 1975.

The Senate elected in May 1974 was now thoroughly
debauched. The people had elected twenty-nine Labor senators,
twenty-nine Liberal and Country Party senators and two
Independents. As a result of the actions of Premiers Lewis and
Bjelke-Petersen and the return of Senator Townley to the
official Liberal fold, the Senate now consisted of twenty-seven
Government senators, thirty-one anti-Government senators and
two Independents (Senators Hall and Bunton). The conditions
for the operation of the Withers strategy of 1973 again existed. If
Senator Milliner had not died, or if the Queensland Premier had
not followed Mr Lewis in sweeping convention aside, the Senate
could not have deferred Supply. Senator Hall put it with lurid
precision when he said in October that the Liberals 'were
marching on the sleazy road to power over a dead man's corpse'.
On the Opposition's first motion to defer consideration of the
Budget on 15 October, he continued: 'Let it be remembered that
the Opposition succeeded only because a Labor Senator died.
They did it over a dead man's corpse.'

Nevertheless, there was still no inevitability about the crisis.
We were emerging from the winter of our discontent. I had felt
obliged to agree to the resignation of Lance Barnard and his
appointment to an ambassadorial position. There was no man to
whom I owed so much. He was my first and always my firmest
Caucus supporter. No Labor leader ever had a better deputy or
a better friend. As Minister for Defence, he presided over the
most complete reorganisation of the armed services ever
achieved in peacetime.

He was depressed by his defeat for the deputy leadership

after the 1974 elections. A hearing defect, a legacy of El Alamein, appeared to worsen, reducing his effectiveness in Cabinet and Parliament. His general health suffered from the Canberra climate and his prolonged absences from home and family. His resignation necessitated a by-election for his electorate of Bass, centred upon Launceston. The outcome was a disaster. The Bass result undoubtedly increased the pressure on Mr Fraser to try to force a general election.

Incidentally, it was during the Bass campaign that I first heard the canard that I had ordered the replacement of the Queen's photograph with my own in government offices and public buildings. Nothing of the sort ever happened and no such instruction was ever given. This myth was revived in one piece of recent correspondence to newspapers about Sir John Kerr's book as evidence of my dictatorial leanings. When I was in London in mid-1976, I was asked on television by Peregrine Worsthorne, who is described as a Tory intellectual, why I had replaced the Queen's head with mine on Australian stamps!

In July in deeply distressing circumstances I was obliged to secure the dismissal of the Deputy Prime Minister, Dr Cairns. There was a clear principle at stake: through inadvertence and inattention Dr Cairns had been responsible for a wrong and misleading answer being given to the Parliament. I made it clear in Parliament on 9 July that that was the sole reason for Dr Cairns' dismissal and that the principle would apply to any minister as long as I was Prime Minister.

The new team settled down quickly and well, with Mr Crean as Deputy Prime Minister, Mr Hayden as Treasurer and Senator James McClelland as Minister for Labour and Immigration.

The reception given to the Hayden Budget was highly satisfactory. The *Australian Financial Review* commented on 20 August:

There is a lot more courage and creativity in Mr Hayden's budget last night than his deliberately unemotional speech suggested. If it works—and there is an undeniable plausibility about the economic aggregates produced by Mr Hayden and his bureaucratic advisers—then Mr Hayden will be a Treasurer of considerable significance in Australian history.

The *Sydney Morning Herald* said:

In framing its budget strategy for 1975–76 the government has aimed to fit in with the prevailing conventional wisdom about what constitutes sound budget policy. Much of the pre-budget discussion has been conducted in terms of the desirable size of the budget deficit, with a rather surprising amount of agreement on a figure of $2500 million. In aiming for an overall deficit of $2798 million and a domestic deficit of $2068 million in 1975–76 Mr Hayden has been successful in holding himself close to this consensus figure. Although the way the deficit is arrived at and the stance of other policies, notably monetary policies, are much more important than the size of the deficit in economic policy terms, there were important psychological reasons for keeping the deficit within these bounds. A larger deficit would have fed inflationary expectations and a further decline in business confidence while a much smaller deficit would have set off early demands for a reversal of a too severe budget strategy.

The *Sydney Morning Herald* concluded:

All in all, it is a clever budget strategy, combining deficit restraint with a major tax restructuring. If it works, growth will be about 5 per cent over the year and 7 or 8 per cent on a June to June basis. While unemployment cannot be expected to improve much, against that is the prospect of at least a stabilisation of inflation. While the government has extended some specific concessions to the ailing corporate sector in the form of a 2½ per cent cut in company tax and a continuation of the accelerated depreciation allowance, it is obviously relying much more on a recovery in consumer demand and a stabilisation of inflation to stimulate the corporate sector.

Under the heading 'Realism, Restraint, Reform', the *Age* wrote:

The strategy adopted by the Treasurer was not, of course, the only option open to him. He could have offset a joyless deficit by a tough monetary policy, but this would mean higher interest rates, financial disruption, further depression of business confidence and serious company failures. Or he could have chosen the short, sharp, shock approach suggested by the Treasury last year. This would certainly have brought down inflation—but with what a thump. Such shock treatment would have meant a massive rise in unemployment and widespread business failures—a policy as unacceptable today as it was when the government rejected it last year. Instead, Mr Hayden opted for a middle way that would seek to achieve real growth of 5 per cent in

1975–76 while bringing down inflation gently over two to
three years—provided the private sector and especially the
trade union movement play their parts.

Throughout the entire Budget crisis, our opponents never
claimed that the Budget itself was the reason for blocking it.
Indeed it was not until May 1976 that they announced any
economic measures of their own to modify the strategy of the
Hayden Budget. The events of October–November had nothing
to do with the Hayden economic strategy of 1975; they had
everything to do with the Withers political strategy of 1973.
Only the death of Senator Milliner and the machinations of Mr
Bjelke-Petersen had made it applicable. Mr Fraser said after the
Budget had been brought down: 'We'll be following normal
procedure in the Senate and with the knowledge we have at the
moment, at this stage, it would be our intention to allow it a
passage through the Senate.'

Sir John Kerr deals at exhaustive length with press articles
during the second half of September, speculating on the
possibility of a Senate refusal of Supply and the course the
ensuing crisis might take. These articles included speculation on
the role of the Governor-General and the possible dismissal of
the Government. Sir John uses this accumulation of quotations
to suggest that as early as September the question of his
dismissal of my Government was already a live issue and his
power and right to do so taken for granted. Moreover, he
implies that the very existence of these articles must prove that
such considerations were, or should have been, to the forefront
of my mind. The fact is of course that in September such
considerations were speculative in the extreme. It seemed
increasingly likely that the Budget would pass. A reading of

Hansard in those weeks attests this. The Opposition cast around for its 'extraordinary and reprehensible circumstance'; its efforts were as fruitless as its motives were transparent. The articles to which Sir John refers, including one he quotes with becoming modesty ('Sir John is a big man. A formidable intellect. A generous personality . . . he, more than anyone else, may become the man of the moment', the *Australian* 18 September), were all written by able journalists, admirable fellows all, but they were not my advisers, and more to the point, they were not the Governor-General's advisers.

The week beginning Sunday 12 October may be taken as the onset of the real crisis. The events of that week encompassed all the essential elements of the crisis as it was to develop over the next month, especially as they were to influence the conduct and action of Sir John Kerr. The crucial events are these:

On Sunday 12 October a meeting of the Federal Council of the Australian Liberal Party recommended that State Liberal Governments should not issue writs for a half-Senate election if I were to advise one.

On Tuesday 14 October, I asked for, and received, the resignation of the Minister for Minerals and Energy, Mr Connor.

On Wednesday 15 October, Mr Fraser announced, after the joint party meeting, that the Opposition would use its numbers in the Senate to defer Supply. That afternoon, the Senate decided not to proceed further with consideration of the 1975 Loan Bill.

Also on 15 October, the Governor of Queensland, Sir Colin Hannah, delivered a blatantly political attack on the policies and performance of the Australian Labor Government.

On Thursday 16 October the first of the great parliamentary debates of the crisis took place and the Senate deferred consideration of the Appropriation Bill.

That afternoon, Mr Ellicott issued a press release which in fact contained the scenario for 11 November.

And that evening, I attended a dinner at Government House in honour of the Prime Minister of Malaysia, Tun Abdul Razak, before which I made a passing remark which, judging by his book, had a traumatic effect upon Sir John Kerr and entered profoundly into his calculations throughout the crisis.

On 10 October the majority of the High Court (with Barwick CJ in the minority) ruled valid my Government's legislation to provide representation in the Senate for the people of the Australian Capital Territory and the Northern Territory. It had been one of the Bills which formed the grounds for the double dissolution of 1974 and had been passed at the joint sitting in August 1974. It had been then challenged before the High Court by the anti-Labor Governments of Queensland and Western Australia.

The High Court decision had great relevance to subsequent events. It transformed the Opposition's attitude. It became a matter of urgency to them to force an election for the House of Representatives before a half-Senate election, and before the new Territorial senators could take their places.

The normal election for half the Senate had to take place before 30 June 1976, when the term of half those elected in 1974 would expire. It had been the regular practice (Menzies in 1964, Holt in 1967, Gorton in 1970) to hold half-Senate elections towards the end of the previous year, six months or more before expiry. Should I choose that option, the thirty new senators from the States would not begin their term until 1 July 1976. The four new Territorial senators, however, would be seated immediately in the existing Senate.

It was within the bounds of political possibility that Labor could win both ACT seats, with the certainty of one of the two Northern Territory seats. Further, the two States of New South Wales and Queensland, for which the bogus replacements had been installed, would each elect six senators instead of five; proportional representation would almost certainly have ensured Labor three senators in each. Most important of all, the elected senators filling the casual vacancies currently usurped by Messrs Field and Bunton would, like the Territorials, have taken their places immediately; they would not have had to wait until 1 July 1976.

It can be seen how this would have transformed the Senate, for at least six months. The best result for the Government would be: thirty-two Government senators, thirty-one Opposition senators and one Independent. The worst result would be: thirty-one Government senators, thirty-two Opposition senators and one Independent (Steele Hall, supporting the Government on the vital question of Supply). In short, to borrow from Canning, I could call a new Senate into existence to redress the balance of the old.

The Liberal Party determined to prevent this result and circumvent the Constitution. The newly installed President of the Liberal Party was John Atwill, a close friend of Sir John Kerr. He had been active on Sir John's behalf in persuading Sir Robert Askin to make him Chief Justice of New South Wales.

Under section 12 the writs for elections of senators for a State are issued by the Governor of the State. On twenty-four occasions since Federation, the Governor-General had suggested to the State Governors the date which they should set for elections of senators for their States. On four of these occasions, 9 May 1953, 5 December 1964, 25 November 1967 and 21 November 1970, an election of the House of Representatives was not held jointly with the elections for the Senate. On all twenty-four occasions, the State Governors had routinely met the Governor-General's request.

Yet, on 12 October 1975, the Liberal Party Council recommended that State Liberal Governments should break the convention of seventy-five years and refuse to allow their Governors to issue the writs for a Senate election. On 21 October Sir Robert Menzies was induced to publish a letter urging the 'impertinence' of a 'premature' Senate election, six months before its necessary date, although he himself had advised exactly such a course four times on even earlier dates and his two successors on 26 September 1967 and 1 October 1970 had given such advice in respect of the election of senators due to begin their terms on 1 July 1968 and 1971 respectively. The Liberal Party establishment was well and truly engaged.

It is a supreme irony in the history of Australia and a remarkable example in the history of hypocrisy, that on the very day the Liberal Council urged one breach of convention they urged the restoration of another; while urging State Governments and Governors to break the tradition of seventy-five years, they recommended that in future State Governments should abide by the convention that deceased or resigned senators should be replaced by a senator of the same political party. Once their breach of one convention had served its purpose, they were determined to break another to secure the same purpose.

This threatened breach of yet another constitutional convention—one that had not been varied in the history of Federation—was an important factor in my hesitation about exercising this key option in the ensuing political struggle. And my hesitation largely involved the position of Sir John Kerr. I did not wish him to be the first Governor-General to be humiliated by the refusal of State Governors to accept his request.

On Monday 13 October, I received from Corr and Corr, Solicitors, of Melbourne, acting for the Herald and Weekly Times Ltd, a number of documents in confirmation of some articles the Melbourne *Herald* had been running the previous week. These documents indicated that Mr Connor had been responsible for my having given a misleading reply to Parliament on 9 October in these terms: 'I am assured by the Minister for Minerals and Energy that all communications of substance between him and Mr Khemlani were tabled by him on 9 July 1975.' One telex message in the documents sent to me by Corr and Corr—and one message only—cast doubts on this answer I had given. It was a telex to Mr Khemlani dated 23 May, three days after Mr Connor's loan-raising authority had been revoked. It said: 'I await further specific communication from your principals for consideration.'

I was faced with this choice: to stick to the first principle of ministerial answerability to Parliament, dismissing a senior and respected colleague and provoking, obviously, a first-class crisis; or run away from the principle and try to gloss over its breach. As I told Parliament on 15 October, in this exchange:

MR SINCLAIR: What is the Prime Minister's current attitude to the Westminster doctrine of ministerial responsibility? Does the Prime Minister accept any responsibility for any of the actions of his Ministers? If not, what responsibility does he accept as leader of his Government?
MR WHITLAM: It is because I do accept the principle of the Westminster doctrine, that Ministers are answerable to

the Parliament for what they say and do in it, that I have in the last three months had to take two of the most painful decisions of my life.

In a statement on 14 October I said:

In Mr Connor's judgement, these are not communications of substance. I have already said that in my judgement, they are. But further, it was for me both as head of Government and as the minister accepting responsibility for the answer I gave to the Deputy Leader of the Opposition, to be in a position to make that judgement. I regret I was not in that position.

In these circumstances therefore I today advised the Governor-General to terminate the commission of the Minister for Minerals and Energy.

I wish to make it absolutely clear that the reason for my decision rests solely and wholly on the matter of the answer I was led to give last Thursday. It is a precise, clearly defined issue. I have made it clear throughout the life of this Government that there is the one standard which, once departed from, must carry the heaviest penalty. It is a principle on which the integrity of Parliament itself depends.

There was I believe a departure caused from that principle. The principle and my insistence upon it was made amply clear, tragically clear, only three months ago in the case of the Honourable Member for Lalor. In that case and in this there was and is no reflection whatsoever on the personal integrity of the Minister involved. The error of judgement in both cases was the same; the consequences of that error of judgement, the same. But let me emphasise, those consequences spring not from misconduct, but from standards in relation to a narrow, precise but fundamentally important principle which this Government and I as head of this Government must insist upon.

I want to make the clearest possible distinction between the conduct of the Member for Cunningham in his capacity as Minister, the manner in which he fulfilled his duties, including all his involvement in overseas loan raisings and this one precise principle. In particular, his communications with Mr Khemlani after 20 May were not of themselves improper or irregular. It is not the contents of those telex messages which constitutes any breach of propriety. It is the discrepancy between those communications and the assurances the Member gave me last Thursday.

Up to 20 May, the Minister for Minerals and Energy had Executive Council authority to conclude a special loan-borrowing overseas. That authority was revoked.

On 20 May, that authority was revoked. The revocation of that authority did not mean that the Minister for Minerals and Energy or indeed any other Minister should not even discuss possibilities of loan borrowings with any intermediaries nor did it mean that the Australian Government would not receive information about the possibility of loan raisings. When this whole matter was debated on 9 July, I said specifically (page 3595) 'Executive Council authorities are usually sought only when a loan matter approaches finality. This does not mean that negotiations or discussions about possibilities are precluded without Executive Council authority.' Nothing in the communications after 20 May between the Minister for Minerals and Energy and Mr Khemlani or any of his associates indicates that the Member for Cunningham went beyond these guidelines. There was no impropriety involved in his receiving messages and there was no impropriety in his response to one of them. The error was in his failure to inform either the Treasurer or myself about these activities. This was an error of procedure, not an error of propriety. It is because that error of procedure led to a breach of Parliamentary standards last week that I asked for the resignation of the Minister.

The basic facts remain as they have always been and have always been revealed in this Parliament. They are as I stated them on 9 July and nothing has changed them. Since 14 December 1974, the Minister for Minerals and Energy (Mr Connor) had Executive Council authority to borrow up to US$4000 million and to determine on behalf of the Australian Government the terms and conditions of the borrowing. The Minister was also authorised to sign and deliver promissory notes for the purposes of the borrowing, or to authorise any other person in writing to sign and deliver the promissory notes. That authority was revoked on 7 January 1975 since it had not been used and it conflicted with a Deutsche Mark loan then pending. On 28 January 1975, the Executive Council authorised the Minister to raise a loan not exceeding US$2000 million. The authority was revoked on 20 May 1975 since negotiations were in train for a borrowing of US$100 million through Morgan, Stanley and Company Incorporated, of New York.

In all the scrutiny to which this matter has been subjected, for all the money offered to informers, for all the travels of the Deputy Leader of the Opposition there is still not one allegation of impropriety, illegality, malpractice or

malfeasance charged against this Government or any
Minister. There has been no specific charge of impropriety in
negotiations of an illegal or corrupt conduct on any member
of the Government involved in these transactions at any time
from 14 December to the present day. A specific charge, a
specific allegation can be investigated; no such charges, no
such allegations have been made. In two cases breaches of
the Parliamentary principle have been alleged, investigated
and punished. But in no case has there been an allegation of
improper conduct, of dishonest conduct, of reprehensible
conduct of an illegal or corrupt nature. No such allegation or
charges were made at the special sittings to discuss this
matter on 9 July. No such charges were made in the Senate
for all their abuse of Parliamentary privilege. No such
charges have been made by the Deputy Leader of the
Opposition even after his foray into the highways of New
York and the byways of Europe. No such charges have been
made by any of the newspapers who have investigated this
matter. Never has so much been paid by so few for so little.

The wisdom of the Government's effort to raise overseas
loans on behalf of Australia and for the good of Australia
is a perfectly legitimate subject for political debate. We
defended and continue to defend it. That particular effort
failed and so, while Australia has received nothing, Australia
has paid nothing and is under no obligation to pay anything.

It was the week of broken conventions. Not the least
egregious was the intervention of the Governor of Queensland,
Sir Colin Hannah. At a luncheon of the Brisbane Chamber of
Commerce he not only attacked the record of the Australian
Government but expressed support for the Opposition. He

justified his grossly partisan remarks by saying that he would be 'guilty of sheltering behind convention' if he remained silent.

State Governors are still appointed by the Queen of Britain on the recommendation of the British Government (the Secretary of State for Foreign and Commonwealth Affairs).[1] The senior State Governors hold a dormant commission to act as Administrators of Australia in the absence or incapacity of the Governor-General. I believed Sir Colin Hannah had by his deliberate display of gross partisanship disqualified himself from holding such a commission or fulfilling such a responsibility. I advised Sir John Kerr to request the Queen to revoke Sir Colin's dormant commission. He unhesitatingly agreed. A day or two later, he suggested to me that it might be more appropriate if I tendered the advice directly to the Queen. I did so. On 26 October, the Queen, on my advice, revoked the dormant commission. In 1976 the British Government refused to accept Mr Bjelke-Petersen's request that Sir Colin's term be renewed. Mr Fraser refused to reinstate Sir Colin's dormant commission as Administrator.

Many books have already been published dealing with aspects of the dismissal of my Government. Only one author had the benefit of speaking to Sir John Kerr. Alan Reid, in his book *The Whitlam Venture* (Hill of Content, 1976), suggests that my advice to the Queen on the Hannah affair was one of two matters which were decisive in conditioning Sir John Kerr's attitude. The other was the remark I made to the Prime Minister of Malaysia, Tun Abdul Razak. Reid writes (p. 371):

---

1 Since the *Australia Acts 1986* the Governor of each State is appointed by the Queen on the advice of the Premier of the State.

'Additionally Kerr had what he believed to be "or else" warnings in the shape of the Whitlam observation in Tun Abdul Razak's presence and in the promptitude with which Whitlam had moved on Hannah.'

All I can say is that after the events Sir John Kerr vouchsafed to Mr Reid concerns which he never did to his Prime Minister during them.

6

THE SENATE ON STRIKE

'IF A PARLIAMENT BECOMES UNWORKABLE BY
DESTRUCTION OF CONVENTION, DEMOCRACY ITSELF
BECOMES UNWORKABLE, BECAUSE DEMOCRACY RESTS
MUCH MORE ON ADHERENCE TO CONVENTION THAN TO
THE RIGID APPLICATION OF RULES AND LAWS.'
Malcolm Fraser, 2 March 1975

From 15 October to 11 November the Government pursued a single purpose—to put an end to the Opposition's tactic of deferring consideration of the Budget and to force the Senate to a direct vote, either to grant or reject Supply. We had Supply until 30 November. We had thus a full six weeks in which to bring pressure to bear on the Senate, to force it to a clear-cut vote. From the outset of the crisis it was known that there were at least two, and probably five, Liberal senators who, while they were prepared to go along with the tactic of deferral, would not vote for the outright refusal of Supply or the outright rejection of the Budget. Our hopes for success lay with the consciences of these senators. It is now known that our hopes were justified; the week my Government was dismissed was the week the Senate would have cracked. Only the intervention of Sir John

Kerr saved the Senate from what would have been an historic climb-down and saved Mr Fraser from a devastating humiliation.

The crisis of October–November 1975 was in truth a political crisis, fully capable of resolution by political means. It was a true constitutional crisis only in the sense that the Constitution was manipulated and constitutional conventions flouted by politicians for political purposes. The very first resolution by the Senate deferring consideration of the Budget acknowledged this: that resolution did not pretend that the Opposition's motives rested on any constitutional issues; it was simply a demand that an election be held for the House of Representatives at the behest of the Senate, at a time and in circumstances overwhelmingly favourable to the Opposition.

More than forty years previously the first Australian Governor-General, Sir Isaac Isaacs, forcefully and accurately described the action of a Governor-General who would uphold the view of the Senate against the advice of his constitutional advisers having the confidence of the House of Representatives; such an act, said Sir Isaac Isaacs, would be 'the act of a partisan'. Sir John Kerr acted as a partisan to dismiss his constitutional advisers in the very week, perhaps on the very day that their efforts to maintain the Constitution, the unbroken convention of seventy-five years, and the rights of the House of Representatives were about to be crowned with success.

Sir John Kerr had no need to try to read my mind or interpret chance remarks; he had only to read Hansard. During that month I made six major speeches on formal motions in the House. On every sitting day Question Time was dominated by the issue. Every aspect of the issue—every constitutional, legal, financial and political aspect—was exhaustively canvassed. In the formal speeches I drew heavily on the advice of Mr Byers and Mr Harders. Throughout the crisis I put my views and declared my intentions as forcefully, fully, frankly and openly as I could. I dealt fully with my beliefs about the proper role and responsibilities of the Governor-General and his relationship to the elected government, his constitutional advisers. Yet at no time throughout the crisis did Sir John Kerr query any of my statements, demur at any of my interpretations or contest any of my claims. On the contrary, as I shall show, he gave every indication to my colleagues and me that he supported our case, applauded our course, and approved our cause.

The principle at stake was clear; our path towards enforcing the principle was straightforward; our strategy was simple—to apply pressure at all points to bring the Senate to a direct vote. On 139 occasions since 1913 Appropriations Bills had been passed by a Senate with an Opposition majority.

I never volunteered the expression 'smash the Senate' attributed to me by Sir John Kerr; nor was that my aim, even supposing that such an objective could ever be remotely feasible. Nor did I use the expression 'toughing it out'; and if the expression is a fair description of our strategy, it was much more relevant to the conduct of Mr Fraser. It was he, not I, who had precipitated the crisis; it was he, not I, who had to hold his supporters in line and bring reluctant and troubled members of his own Party to the barrier; it was he, not I, who knew that, at all costs, he must prevent the Senate from voting directly to reject the Budget and refuse Supply, for he knew, as I did, that such a motion would fail; it was his nerve, not mine, which was being tested. I was not trying to 'smash the Senate'.

I was determined to uphold the ancient and fundamental principle that it is the Lower House which must control the supply of money to the elected government, to the ministers who are the constitutional advisers of the Crown precisely and solely because they have the confidence of the Lower House. I was determined to assert the equally fundamental principle that a government having the confidence of the House of Representatives cannot be forced to dissolve at the whim or behest of senators, who themselves need not face the electors. Our determination was strengthened by the fact that the majority in this particular Senate was fortuitous in its creation and fictitious as an expression of the decision of the electors eighteen months previously, though that fact was not central to the principles involved.

These principles were first set out fully in the first motion I moved in the first of the momentous debates on the crisis on 16 October 1975:

> *Considering* that this House is the House of the
> Australian Parliament from which the Government of
> Australia is chosen;
> *Considering* moreover that on 2 December 1972 the
> Australian Labor Party was elected by judgment of the
> people to be the Government of Australia; that on 18 May
> 1974 the Australian Labor Party was re-elected by judgment
> of the people to be the Government of Australia; and that
> the Australian Labor Party continues to have a governing
> majority in this House;
> *Recognising* that the Constitution and the conventions of
> the Constitution vest in this House the control of the supply
> of money to the elected Government;
> *Noting* that this House on 27 August 1975 passed the
> Loan Bill 1975 and on 8 October 1975 passed the

Appropriation Bill (No. 1) 1975–76 and the Appropriation Bill (No. 2) 1975–76 which, amongst other things, appropriate moneys for the ordinary annual services of the Government;

Noting also that on 15 October 1975, in total disregard of the practices and conventions observed in the Australian Parliament since Federation, the Leader of the Opposition announced the intention of the Opposition to delay those Bills, with the object of forcing an election of this House; that on 15 October 1975 the Leader of the Opposition in the Senate announced that the Opposition parties in the Senate would delay the Bills; and that on 15 October 1975 the Senate, against the wishes of the Government, decided not to proceed further with consideration of the Loan Bill 1975;

Considering that the actions of the Senate and of the Leader of the Opposition will, if pursued, have the most serious consequences for Parliamentary democracy in Australia, will seriously damage the Government's efforts to counter the effect of world-wide inflation and unemployment, and will thereby cause great hardship for the Australian people;

1. This House *declares* that it has full confidence in the Australian Labor Party Government.

2. This House *affirms* that the Constitution and the conventions of the Constitution vest in this House the control of the supply of moneys to the elected Government and that the threatened action of the Senate constitutes a gross violation of the roles of the respective Houses of the Parliament in relation to the appropriation of moneys.

3. This House *asserts* the basic principle that a Government that continues to have a majority in the House of

Representatives has a right to expect that it will be able to govern.

4. This House *condemns* the threatened action of the Leader of the Opposition and of the non-government parties in the Senate as being reprehensible and as constituting a grave threat to the principles of responsible government and of Parliamentary democracy in Australia.

5. This House *calls upon* the Senate to pass without delay the Loan Bill 1975, the Appropriation Bill (No. 1) 1975-76 and the Appropriation Bill (No. 2) 1975–76.

All subsequent motions in all subsequent debates merely amplified these basic principles. In my speech I quoted the constitutional authority of Quick and Garran, a book written at the time of the foundation of the Australian Parliament:

'The House of Representatives is not the only national chamber: it is the democratic chamber; it is the grand depository and embodiment of the liberal principles of government which pervade the entire constitutional fabric. It is the chamber in which the progressive instincts and popular aspirations of people will be most likely to make themselves first felt . . . by the Constitution, it is expressly intended to be such a House and by its organisation and functions it is best fitted to be the area in which national progress will find room for development.'

I commented:

And this, with a prescience, prophetic insight, that Quick and Garran would not have claimed for themselves, gets

to the heart and the root of this present grave crisis. It is
because this Government has attempted to make this
Parliament the instrument of reform, for long overdue
change, for progress, for the redistribution of wealth, for the
uplifting of the underprivileged, for the reduction of the
privileges of great wealth and deeply entrenched vested
interests, an instrument towards equality of opportunity for
all Australians, that our opponents and those vested interests
have from the very beginning, as Senator Withers revealed,
embarked on a course to destroy this Government at the
earliest opportunity. But what they are really doing is
destroying the very basis of parliamentary democracy in
our country.

Concluding my speech I reminded the House indirectly that
the Government had available indirectly the option of an
election for half the Senate, which would immediately fill the
new Territorial seats and the two casual vacancies in New South
Wales and Queensland and provide an outcome almost certainly
to our advantage. Mr Fraser was later to reveal in a speech on 30
October that the fear of such an election was at the heart of his
anxieties. He had done his sums very well. I concluded on 16
October:

The Senate resolution talks about 'submitting to the
judgement of the people'. Precisely! This matter should be
submitted to the judgement of the people. It will be
submitted to the judgement of the people. The issue is the
unconstitutional and undemocratic conduct of a chance
majority in the Senate. The issue is the rejection by the
Senate of a Budget designed to bring great benefits to this

nation. It is the Senate which is on trial. It is the Senate
which will have to submit to the judgement of the people.
It is the Senate which has rejected the Budget. It is the Senate
which must face the people. Again, in the indelible words of
Senator Steele Hall, it is the Senate, the Liberal Party and the
Liberal leader which, by the course they are now attempting,
have sown the seeds of their own destruction.

In that first debate neither I nor Mr Fraser canvassed the
role or the responsibility of the Governor-General. I had, however, the previous day—Day One of the crisis, immediately after
Mr Fraser announced his intention to block Supply—made my
position clear enough. On that day I answered two questions
bearing on the Governor-General's role. In answer to a question
from Mr Fraser I said:

> If a money Bill were rejected in this House I would go to the
> Governor-General. If the Government were defeated on any
> vote of confidence in this House I would go to the
> Governor-General. There is no doubt about that. What is
> important is to preserve the principle, which I am certain
> everybody who has sat or stood in my place in this House
> would also have asserted in the three-quarters of a century
> that we have had a national Parliament, that it is the
> government formed in this House and answerable to this
> House that determines financial matters. This has been the
> situation not only in every English speaking democracy but
> also in every other country. No other country would have a
> situation where an upper House could reject a Budget.
> Nowhere in the world would there be the idea that State
> governments could decide the date of an election for one of

the Federal Houses. These are utter distortions of the parliamentary system in Australia. However much the honourable gentleman may squirm on this matter he will be the guilty man if this practice which has endured for three-quarters of a century, and this practice which is observed throughout the world today, is broken. I will not let him off the horns of his dilemma. He could not carry a motion of no confidence in the Australian Government in this House.

I maintained that position throughout. As inspired speculation about possible intervention by Sir John Kerr grew, I repeated and expanded upon it. Sir John Kerr could have had no doubt as to my position. Not once did he seek amplification, explanation or modification.

The second answer I gave to Parliament on 15 October is particularly interesting in the light of Sir John Kerr's claims in reference to the dismissal of the Lang Labor Government of New South Wales by the Governor, Sir Philip Game, in 1932. In his book Sir John asserts that I must have been utterly aware of the possibility of his using the reserve power to dismiss my Government because I allegedly remarked to him at Government House, Melbourne, that he would have 'to do a Philip Game'. My full opinion on that matter was given at length in an answer to my colleague Barry Cohen on 15 October. In his book Sir John Kerr quotes my answer. In it I drew on a letter which Mr Menzies (as he then was) had written when he was Attorney-General and Deputy Premier of Victoria to Sir Philip Game. I said that Mr Menzies' 1932 letter was relevant to the present circumstances 'because there have been suggestions that in this day and age the viceroy of Australia, the Governor-General of Australia, should withdraw the commission of the

Prime Minister who has the confidence of the House of Representatives'. I continued:

> It is suggested that the Governor-General of Australia, the viceroy, should take this action because, for the first time in history, the Senate, which cannot initiate and cannot amend money Bills might make so bold as to reject a money Bill. The last time in Australia that a vice regal representative— it was a State Governor, a Crown Agent, in other words a British official—cancelled the commission of a head of government was in 1932. But what Mr Menzies, as he then was, wrote to Sir Philip Game is very relevant to present circumstances.

I then quoted Mr Menzies' letter. It should be noted that he wrote his letter after Mr Lang's dismissal and in support of the action taken by Sir Philip Game. It sets forth with perfect Menzian clarity the situation which both the Governor-General and I faced in 1975 and the principles on which I acted and Sir John Kerr should have acted in 1975. Mr Menzies' letter of 1932 is as follows:

> . . . the newspaper demand that you should dismiss a Premier on the ground that there was some reason for believing that he no longer enjoyed the confidence of the electors always seemed to me to be based upon an absolute misconception of the constitutional position of a modern Governor. *Under the Australian system of universal suffrage and triennial Parliaments, with a legally recognised and responsible Cabinet, it must, in my opinion, follow that so long as a Premier commands a majority in the Lower House, and so long as he is*

guilty of no illegal conduct which would evoke the exercise of the Royal Prerogative, he must be regarded as the competent and continuing adviser of the representative of the Crown. For a newspaper to urge a dissolution because in its opinion the Government has lost the confidence of the electorate is a mere impertinence. The constitutional authority of a Premier rests almost entirely upon his success at a general election, and upon his continued authority in the popularly elected House, and not upon irresponsible speculations as to whether he would have lost his majority if the Constitution had provided for annual and not triennial elections. Moreover, these are days (and now I speak as a politician) in which any Government may, in the stern discharge of its duty, be compelled to take steps which render it unpopular with the electorate. This, however, so far from being a good cause for its recall, may constitute its greatest claim to reputation, and one of the factors which strengthens the hand of a Government fresh from victory at the polls is that it may look forward to a period of office in which its policy may be dictated by convictions and not by the mere necessity for vote catching. It would, in my respectful opinion (and in this I am expressing the majority view among reputable lawyers in this State), have been nothing short of a calamity if during the very great constitutional crisis, New South Wales had possessed a Governor who had subordinated the constitutional authority of a Governor to the purely opportunist demands of those who found the constitutional restrictions irksome. This represents my considered view, in spite of the fact that politically I am a vigorous opponent of Mr Lang and his policy, and at all material times considered that policy to be actually disastrous to Australia. [My italics.]

The campaign against the Senate's action extended far beyond Parliament. As I had promised on 16 October we took our cause to the people. In Melbourne on 20 October and in Sydney on 24 October my parliamentary colleagues and I and Bob Hawke, the President of the ACTU and the ALP, addressed large rallies. Even so apolitical an event as the Gymea Lily Festival spontaneously became a demonstration of support for the Government. The turnaround in public opinion was swift and spectacular. The change in the political climate was perceptible, almost tangible, well before it was confirmed by the opinion polls towards the end of the month. Those polls showed that 70 per cent were opposed to actions of the Senate and in favour of passing the Budget. As our campaign strengthened and public outrage deepened, the standing of the Government itself as recorded in the opinion polls improved markedly. Even as early as 20 October, less than a week after the onset of the crisis, leading newspapers were having second thoughts, despite Mr Fraser's efforts by telephone on Tuesday night 14 October to win prior support from the press proprietors for the action he intended to announce the following day. On 20 October the Melbourne *Herald* said:

> We believe the Opposition should not continue to refuse Supply. If they gained office by radical strategy Mr Fraser and Mr Anthony would quite possibly find a permanently ungovernable Australia on their hands.

The Adelaide *Advertiser* said:

It was Mr Fraser who first threw away the rule book and made this a boots and all fight. He and his supine followers cannot now complain if they get hurt.

The strategy of Mr Fraser and his colleagues may be seen as the mirror-image of ours. Our object was to secure a direct vote of the Senate; Mr Fraser's object was to prevent it. It can now be seen that Sir John Kerr's attitude was crucial to Mr Fraser's ability to hold the line.

In his 1977 autobiography Senator Don Chipp, who was one of Mr Fraser's shadow ministers and first ministers, has written:

> During the weeks up to our decision to block Supply Fraser saw Kerr on several occasions . . . at each Shadow Cabinet meeting he showed an unbending confidence that Kerr was 'on side'.

The earliest and fullest description of the Opposition tactics comes from Andrew Peacock, now Minister for Foreign Affairs.[1] He and his wife stayed over in Bali from 24 to 28 September 1975 on their way home from Iran. They were met at the airport by Mr Lim Bian Kie, private secretary to General Ali Murtopo, Chairman of the Centre for Strategic and International Studies, and Mr Harry Tjan, a member of the staff of the Centre.

A record of the conversation was made in Jakarta three days later. I learnt of the existence of the record in May 1976 and asked Mr Peacock a question about it upon notice. My colleague Ken Fry learnt about it in March 1977 and asked him a question

---

1 Andrew Peacock, Minister for Foreign Affairs, 1975–80. He resigned from Federal Parliament in 1994.

without notice. The text was published by the *National Times* at the beginning of May 1977. The paper stated, 'there seems little doubt that the document originated from Indonesian intelligence sources'. It was not, however, released publicly or privately by Indonesia; it was purloined by an Australian. Indonesian specialists at the Australian National University are convinced that the record is authentic. Most attention has been given to the portions of the document which deal with Portuguese Timor and Australian foreign policy generally. Half of it, however, deals with Australian domestic politics as follows:

1. According to Mr Peacock at the present moment the Opposition parties were leading 20 per cent in the opinion polls over the Labor Party Government. In order to win a general election, it was sufficient to have only three per cent. The Opposition parties wanted to force an early general election this year (November 1975) or next year (May 1976). He personally, along with John Malcolm Fraser (candidate for PM), really wanted to see the three-year term fulfilled, not to force a general election by rejecting the Supply Bill in the Senate. But he felt his Party would be forced to agree to bringing on a general election because pressure was already strong enough (nine out of eleven members of the Shadow Cabinet agreed with the bringing on of an election). A problem that might arise was two Liberal senators who would not follow the command of the Party. So we will just have to wait and see what happens in the next few weeks.

2. If the Supply Bill can really be rejected by the Senate the following scenario will develop:

   a. PM Whitlam is not prepared to dissolve the Parliament and Senate (a 'double dissolution'). He will continue to govern without a budget. As a result he will not be able to pay salaries and so on. The situation would become chaotic.

b. PM Whitlam appeals against the Senate to the High Court. A constitutional court battle would result.

c. PM Whitlam will not agree to a double dissolution or to hold a general election, but also does not want to work. In this case the Governor-General Sir John Robert Kerr would be forced to ask John Malcolm Fraser (Opposition) to form a cabinet. But this cabinet would not be able to get a mandate to govern, because Parliament is controlled by the Labor Party. What can happen is: John Malcolm Fraser is appointed PM, a minute later he asks the Governor-General to dissolve Parliament and the Senate, following which a general election is to be held.

A more subtle and more accurate scenario for a dismissal was published by Mr Ellicott on 16 October. Mr Ellicott had been Solicitor-General during the first year of my Government. I knew that he had unsuccessfully sought the Liberal selection for Berowra in 1972. Under my Government he completed the negotiations for a seabed boundary with Indonesia which were much more advantageous to Australia than the Fraser Government will now be able to negotiate past the Timor gap.[2] He had accompanied Senator Murphy to the International Court of Justice to present Australia's case against French nuclear tests in the South Pacific. I ensured he was closely involved in drafting and reviewing any of our legislation which could possibly be challenged in the High Court. In 1973 he told me of his intention to seek the Liberal selection for the

_____

2   The term of the Fraser Government was 1975–83.

blue-ribbon seat of Wentworth, based on Sydney's wealthier eastern suburbs. I wished him good luck and told him that, if he did not win the selection, he could be assured that his position in the service of my Government would remain unimpaired. In a review of Sir John Kerr's book for the *Age* he seemed to suggest that he found our relations difficult. I was never aware of it.

Mr Ellicott's press release of 16 October took the form of public advice to the Governor-General. It began with the assertion that the Governor-General performed his role 'with the advice of Ministers whom he chooses and who hold office during his pleasure'. Mr Ellicott went on: 'The Prime Minister is treating the Governor-General as a mere automaton with no public will of his own, sitting at Yarralumla waiting to do his bidding.'

This, be it noted, was issued on 16 October (and presumably written on 15 October). The crisis precipitated by Mr Fraser's announcement was not twenty-four hours old. Nothing had been tested, and nobody, including the Governor-General, had been treated in any way whatsoever, automaton-like or otherwise. The ground was already being laid for shifting the blame for the crisis and the deadlock between the Houses away from Mr Fraser and his use of chance numbers in the Senate onto me and my alleged misuse of the office of the Governor-General. Mr Ellicott then went on to invite Sir John Kerr to make a range of purely political judgements and highly speculative assessments, relating to the prospects of my Government being able to secure Supply. The Governor-General, Mr Ellicott argued, should not merely respond to political events as they unfolded, but predict, pre-empt and even prevent them (for example, in the case of his not being satisfied that the election for half the Senate would have a favourable result for the Government). Mr Ellicott did not specify who should be responsible for advising the Governor-General on these critical political matters. Mr Ellicott concluded:

> If the Governor-General was not satisfied that the Government would have supply until the election result in the Territories was known he would only have one option open to him in the interests of good government. He is entitled to and should ask the Prime Minister if the government is prepared to advise him to dissolve the House of Representatives and the Senate or the House of Representatives alone as a means of ensuring that the disagreement between the two Houses is resolved.
>
> If the Prime Minister refuses to do either it is then open to the Governor-General to dismiss his present Ministers and seek others who are prepared to give him the only proper advice open. This he should proceed to do. The proper advice in the circumstances is to dissolve both Houses of the Parliament or the House of Representatives alone with or without a half Senate election.

This gratuitous advice, given on the very first day of the crisis, was, of course, the same as the improper advice sought, received and acted upon by Sir John Kerr from Mr Ellicott's double cousin, the Chief Justice, Sir Garfield Barwick, on the last day of the crisis.

On 21 October Sir John Kerr telephoned me at Parliament House during a meeting of the Federal Parliamentary Labor Party. I left the Caucus to take the call. He said: 'This Ellicott thing ... it's all bullshit isn't it?' He added that in any case it would be best if I provided him with an opinion on the legal propositions contained in it. I immediately returned to the Party room, told Mr Enderby of our conversation, and asked that he and Mr Byers provide the opinion Sir John requested. This they did in a document dated 4 November containing some 6000 words, comprising thirty-nine closely argued numbered paragraphs. At the end of pages of detailed argument involving the Constitution itself, High Court rulings on the Constitution, the opinions of British and Australian and Canadian constitutional authorities, the precedents established in the English and other Dominion parliaments since 1783 and past practice and established conventions of the Australian Senate, the law officers concluded:

> 38. It seems to us, if we may respectfully say so, that assumptions underlie Mr Ellicott's press statement which present dangers to the orderly workings of Government. Those dangers are significant ones. That the possibility of their existence is a disquieting one cannot, we venture to think, be seriously doubted. For they may be indefinitely repeated and may involve deleterious consequences to the working of the constitutional provisions. That that working requires restraint on the part of both Houses is hardly open to doubt. A view which looking only to the existence of the legal power disregards or ignores constitutional practices hitherto apparently governing the exercise of those powers, requires, we venture to think, the gravest consideration before its adoption could even be contemplated.
> 39. We have found ourselves for the reasons we have stated firmly of the opinion that Mr Ellicott's expressed views are wrong.

Sir John Kerr received their opinion from Mr Enderby on 6 November. He made no comment.

The law officers, of course, had treated only constitutional aspects of the crisis. Throughout October and the first week of November it remained essentially a political crisis. Each day which passed brought its solution appreciably nearer. It is important to recall this. While the financial aspects naturally became more serious as the margin of time available to the Government narrowed with Supply usually running out at the end of November, the atmosphere of political crisis did not deepen; it perceptibly lightened; at least on our side. Tension in the House eased; proceedings became more relaxed, at times hilarious, particularly under the brilliant leadership of Fred Daly. It was largely due to a parliamentary tour de force by him that an attempt to resurrect Mr Khemlani and revive the loan affair flopped (see Chapter 10). We foreshadowed financial arrangements through the banks to carry essential payments to public servants, servicemen and government contractors beyond 30 November, should it prove necessary. This was not a sign that we had despaired of reaching a political settlement of the crisis before then; it was part of the pressure we were applying at all points to achieve it. The essence of that political settlement would be to force a direct vote on Supply.

On 28 October, Mr Fraser gave Parliament a reason for the Senate choosing to vote to defer rather than vote to reject Supply. 'While the measures are deferred', he said, 'it is within our power to resurrect these measures once it is known there is to be a House of Representatives election. That is the reason for deferral. It is the reason we stay with deferral.'

It was, as events were to show, only part of the reason. This was, of course, a key part of the Withers strategy set out in

October 1973, two years before. It was not, however, the sole or principal reason Mr Fraser stuck to the tactic of deferral because he was stuck with it. He knew that the Senate would not vote to reject Supply; the numbers were not there to do so.

While Liberal senators had been prepared to go along with the tactic of deferring a vote on the Budget, it was common talk that many of them would never vote against this or any other Budget because they would regard that as a usurpation by the Senate. There were some Liberal senators whose terms of office were due to expire at the end of June and who were not proposing to seek re-election or had been given an unwinnable position on their Party's Senate ticket. They served with Labor senators on all party committees, where a high degree of friendship is fostered and confidence shared. Quite apart from the question of the principle involved, they would see no point in losing over seven months' membership of the Senate through having the Senate as well as the House of Representatives dissolved. The same consideration arose in the case of those senators whose terms of office did not run out till June 1979; they could not be sure whether they would be given winnable positions on their Party's ticket if the Senate were dissolved.

It was left to Senator Withers on this issue, as on so many others, to confirm and augment the facts. He told the press last August that over the traditional glass of champagne following the swearing-in ceremony of the Fraser caretaker ministry at Government House on 12 November, Sir John Kerr remarked that in weighing up the various factors in the difficult decision he took he was at least confident that the Senate would hold firm. Senator Guilfoyle interjected *sotto voce* 'We've got news for you'. The news was that several Liberal senators were regarded by Senator Withers as likely to cave in within two days and let the Budget pass. They included Senators Carrick and Cotton.

Further, two senators—Bessell (Tasmania) and Jessop (South Australia)—had gone on public record to state that they would not vote to reject Supply. As early as 25 October Senator Bessell had appeared on the ABC program *Four Corners*. This exchange took place:

> INTERVIEWER: And if it came to a vote of pure rejection of Supply you wouldn't vote?
> BESSELL: I would not vote for a rejection.
> INTERVIEWER: Well, in point of fact, you could be a very important senator if it came to that crunch situation?
> BESSELL: I would think that there would be a good many others who would feel the same as I do on that particular item, on that particular matter, on the question of rejection.

This was on 25 October. As each day passed, the pressure on these senators increased. It came from unexpected sources. In the first week in November, South Australia's Sir Thomas Playford, who had been the longest serving Premier in Australia's history, whose name among Liberals was one to conjure with second only to Menzies himself, circulated his views by telegram to the South Australian Liberal senators. He said that the Budget should be passed on economic grounds and warned of a public backlash if the Liberal and Country Party senators continued to block it on political grounds.

At the outset of the crisis Sir John Kerr asked me if it was appropriate for him to consult with Mr Fraser. I said it was.

On Tuesday afternoon 21 October 1975 Sir John Kerr received me and later swore in Rex Patterson as Minister for Agriculture and Paul Keating as Minister for Northern Australia. He received Mr Fraser at Government House that night.

On Thursday 30 October Sir John Kerr had Senator McClelland and me to lunch and an Executive Council meeting, and in the afternoon received Mr Hayden and Mr Fraser.

On Monday afternoon 3 November, before going to the Governor's Cup Eve party and becoming his guest at Government House, Sir John Kerr received Mr Fraser at the Governor-General's office, Treasury Place, Melbourne.

On Thursday morning 6 November Sir John Kerr received Mr Fraser at Government House and in the afternoon received me, held a meeting of the Executive Council and received Mr Enderby and Mr Hayden.

After that meeting on 3 November Mr Fraser announced a proposal which purported to be a compromise but in fact was a diversionary tactic. On 4 November I responded to his proposal in these terms:

> I would like to warn honourable gentlemen that the proposals derive no greater sanctity from the fact that they were divulged to the Governor-General at the request of the author before they were made public. l have no doubt that His Excellency was amused. One of the proposals is, l gather, that I should seek an audience of His Excellency and advise him that in six months I intend to advise him to issue writs for an election of the House of Representatives. This is a most diverting proposal. When I advise the Govenor-General to issue writs for an election for the House of Representatives I shall do it at a time of my own choosing.
>
> It is in this House that such decisions are made, and the decisions as to when there will be elections for it are made by

persons responsible to this House. Those elections can be held up to the third anniversary of its first meeting after an election. I gather that there is some proposition that the Leader of the Opposition, who on the most favourable issues at most can depend on the votes of half the senators, should himself give advice to the Governor-General as to when there should be elections for the House of Representatives—a very novel proposition.

Beyond the basic principles involved there was an overriding reason for rejecting this proposal. It was in fact a proposal—for indeed Mr Fraser was serious about it—for a six-month long election campaign. The four months' disruption in 1974 would have paled into insignificance compared to what would have happened in 1976, had I agreed. In the same answer on 4 November I said:

> My ordinary view is that elections should take place closer to the expiry time of the shorter term senators. Nevertheless, I am influenced by the advice of the editorials in the *Age* and the *Australian Financial Review* to consider an earlier Senate election—on a date such as Sir Robert Menzies and most of my predecessors would have advised. But I want to assure honourable gentlemen and right honourable gentlemen that I am still thinking over the matter. I am not over-euphoric because of the overwhelming results of the opinion polls. I am not unduly swayed by the editorials in the *Age* and the *Australian Financial Review*. I still want to look at the matter. I am not distraught as those opposite are by the High Court having held what would obviously have been the case in the

minds of most honourable gentlemen, that senators may be elected from Territories and may vote.

On 6 November I indicated to Sir John Kerr that my mind was working along these lines. In his book Sir John writes that Mr Fraser had told him that morning that any proposal for a separate Senate election was unacceptable to his Party. These two discussions, Sir John Kerr asserts, were decisive in making up his mind. He writes:

> I had no doubt, after these two conversations that the leaders were on the point of collision. I knew on 6 November that I would have a weekend of very serious private deliberations which I intended to undertake alone.

That night Sir John flew to Melbourne. He was accompanied by Lady Kerr and their artistic adviser, Richard Cobden. The vice-regal notices do not record his activities for Friday. On Saturday, Sir John Kerr reviewed a parade to mark the 50th Anniversary of the foundation of the Royal Australian Corps of Signals at Watsonia Barracks and opened the Corps Museum. In the evening, he opened the 29th Congress of International Organisations for Motor Trades and Repairs at the Melbourne Hilton Hotel. On Sunday, he arrived at Admiralty House, Sydney. His weekend of 'private deliberations' had not been altogether an ascent to Mount Sinai.

7

THE GOVERNOR-GENERAL
CONSULTS

'WE ALL LAUGHED.'
Sir John Kerr, 1978

Sir John Kerr's deception was two-fold. At all stages, he failed to 'counsel and warn'; he never disclosed to his constitutional advisers his concerns or the course he had in mind. It follows by necessary inference that he deliberately misled us: at the very time he had determined to dismiss us, he consciously and deliberately left us to believe that he understood and supported what we were doing. His was a double deceit—by omission and by commission.

It has been said that the differences in any account of conversations between Sir John Kerr and me would, in the final analysis, boil down to his word against mine. Sir John Kerr's apologists were extremely anxious to sound this cautionary note before the publication of his memoirs, which have so disappointed them in their lack of incriminatory matter against me. The fact is, of course, there is no evidentiary equality whatsoever between us. As Prime Minister I was head of a Cabinet of twenty-seven very independent, even wilful individuals, meeting regularly, some of whom are writing their own memoirs; answerable to Caucus; responsible to Parliament; chief of a great department of state; working hourly with a large staff; in constant contact with a host of persons, official and non-official; under the closest scrutiny of the press and other media, to many of whom I spoke daily. Simply, I have too many witnesses. It is just not worth my while to concoct, even after the lapse of three years.

The real evidence about what I said to Sir John Kerr is to be found in my public statements. I do not assert that everything I said in private is to be found in public speeches. I do not assert that everything I said in public was said in private. I do assert that nothing I said in private was inconsistent with what I said in public. That applies not only to my relations with Sir John Kerr. It has been a cardinal rule of mine throughout my public career.

In his book Sir John makes no bones about never having raised directly with me the possibility of using the Governor-General's reserve powers to dismiss my Government. To justify himself he goes to great pains to describe conversations with me during which I made my attitudes clear but during which he remained silent about his 'thought processes'. He sums up by saying there were four occasions on which 'Mr Whitlam gave clear evidence of his awareness of the reserve powers':

1 in Port Moresby on 15 September 1975;
2 in his study at Government House on 16 October 1975;
3 on 18 October 1975, but he does not say where; and
4 at Government House, Melbourne, on 3 November 1975.

The first, second and fourth of these occasions were purely social and the third is imaginary. I shall deal with it first.

Sir John says flatly 'on Saturday 18 October I had another talk with the Prime Minister'. He says we talked about the Supply crisis between the House of Commons and the House of Lords when Asquith was Prime Minister. He says that I also raised the possibility of bank credit for the 'public servants, troops, police, contractors and so on', whom the Government could not pay until the Budget was passed. He says he was being *told* by me and he never again felt he could *talk* to me.

Sir John, however, does not say where this discussion took place, and for good reason; it did not take place. He was in Canberra on the day and I was in Sydney (I opened the Gymea Lily Festival, which was given extensive cover on television). I had gone to Sydney on the Friday and I returned to Canberra on the Monday. He had gone from Sydney to Canberra the previous Monday and stayed there till he went to Sydney on the following Monday. There was, however, a significant conversation between me and Sir John Kerr that weekend, the first weekend of the Supply crisis. It gains its significance from Sir John Kerr's subsequent conduct.

On Sunday 19 October 1975 Sir John telephoned me at Kirribilli House. He raised two matters. First, he was embarrassed by the articles in the newspapers which were intimidating him, as he said, about how he should act on the deferral of Supply by the Senate. He expressed particular concern over the cover story carried by the *Australian* the previous day under the headline 'Will Sir John Kerr act?' I did not then know of the close relationship which had developed between Sir John Kerr and the proprietor of the *Australian*, Mr Murdoch. Secondly, Sir John asked me whether he should consult with Sir Garfield Barwick, the Chief Justice, on the crisis.

I at once gave him my view that he should not consult with the Chief Justice. Only one Governor-General, Sir Ronald Munro Ferguson, had consulted with a chief justice; he had done so, with his Prime Minister's approval, in 1914 at a much earlier stage of Australia's constitutional development, and the Chief Justice had been Sir Samuel Griffith, one of the founding fathers. In 1921 the High Court had said that it would not give advisory opinions; if the Court as a whole could not give such opinions, still less could a single justice of the Court do so. Although the Chief Justice might be *primus inter pares,* in cases where the Court had been divided under my Government, Sir Garfield had been in the minority. In any case the matter upon which the Chief Justice or any other justice gave advice could come before another justice and almost certainly before the Full Court for argument and decision.

Sir John did not demur in any way at my response. Immediately I went upstairs and told Graham Freudenberg, who was working with Joy O'Brien on my speech for the following Tuesday, to make appropriate references to the press intimidation of the Governor-General. I told Mr Freudenberg: 'He says it's intimidation.'

Accordingly the following passage was included in my speech:

> The proprietors are having second thoughts [about the denial of Supply]. So should the Leader of the Opposition. So should his supine followers. The conditioning which the Leader of the Opposition and the proprietors sought to impose upon the public last week, and indeed for weeks

before that, they now seek to impose upon the Governor-General himself. There have been those long months of conditioning by the political, the business and media interests who have never been prepared to accept the legitimacy of an Australian Labor government. Now we are seeing a fresh phase in this exercise. Now we have the headlines: 'Will Sir John Kerr act?' and 'Fraser says Kerr must sack PM'. Where will this intimidation stop? I find it thoroughly depressing that the honourable member for Wentworth [Mr Ellicott], a former Solicitor-General, one who discharged his office with distinction and impartiality, lends himself to this disgraceful episode.

Sir John Kerr himself quotes this passage of my speech of 21 October and adds this comment: 'Statements like this made publicly and to me confirmed my belief in an irreversible attitude by Mr Whitlam against an election.' Thus, a statement made because of his own expressed concern and out of regard for his office becomes evidence of my intransigence and a justification for his secrecy!

To strengthen his assessment of attitudes, Sir John Kerr purports to record conversations he is supposed to have had with me even before the eruption of the real political crisis in October.

The first of these is supposed to have taken place at an Independence Day reception in Port Moresby on 15 September. (It is fascinating that so many of the conversations which Sir John found, or now claims to have found, of deepest significance in this period took place at receptions or dinners—the Independence reception in Port Moresby, before a dinner for the Malaysian Prime Minister and a Melbourne Cup reception, for example; nothing of significance seemed to have passed on the more serious and substantive occasions.) Sir John Kerr writes:

> In Port Moresby on 15 September the Prime Minister told
> me that he was thinking he might, if the Senate rejected the
> Appropriation Bills, present them to me nevertheless for
> assent, with advice that the Senate had no legal power to
> reject them. This discussion took place at an Independence
> Day reception. I parried this by saying that if he did that
> there would be an uproar but doubtless the High Court,
> assuming that I did assent, would hear immediately a case to
> declare the resulting 'Acts' invalid. He agreed.

This discussion did not take place. Over a year before at Admiralty House Sir John raised this proposition with me; his reasoning was that if, as the Constitution ordained, the Senate could not amend money Bills, still less could it reject them. I told him that I was not attracted by the proposition, which would invite a challenge in the High Court with a probable rebuff and certain delay. I was particularly careful and invariably successful in seeing that our legislative acts and administrative actions would survive challenge in the Court. Sir John and his old friend and new minister, Joe Riordan, had recently discussed the idea. It would have been odd for me to revive it with him in Port Moresby.

The three functions we attended together that day were a lunch at our High Commissioner's residence, a flag-lowering ceremony at the Hubert Murray Stadium and refreshments at Mr Somare's residence for the midnight fireworks display. Sir John and I were never seated or standing together and there was always a great number of others speaking to each of us and the guests of honour and their spouses. The only actors in the cast on 10 and 11 November 1975 who had a private conversation in Port Moresby were Mr Fraser and Sir Garfield Barwick.

Sir John places great significance on a remark I made at his dinner for the Prime Minister of Malaysia, Tun Abdul Razak, on 16 October, the day after Supply was first deferred in the Senate. What were the circumstances of this terrifically significant remark?

When the Governor-General gives a state dinner at Yarralumla it is the custom for the Prime Minister and his wife to be invited to have a drink and some light conversation in his study with him and the guest of honour and their wives before joining the other guests who are waiting in the main reception room for the arrival of the vice-regal couple and the guests of honour.

Malaysia is a federation; it has a Federal Parliament of two Houses; it has a constitutional monarch elected for a five-year term. Razak had been Premier of the State of Pahang before Independence and then became deputy to Tunku Abdul Rahman, the first Prime Minister. He was a cadet member of the royal family of Pahang. The Sultan of Pahang was the most charismatic of the Malay rulers and could have been expected to serve a term as King. The Tunku was wary of having a popular King and prevented the Sultan's election.

I knew Razak was interested in the role of the Crown in a constitutional monarchy. Razak knew me better than he knew any Australian and I knew him better than I knew any Malaysian. He was a lawyer. I had known him since my visit to Malaysia in June 1962. I had visited his country three times as Deputy Leader of the Opposition and four times as Leader of the Opposition. Each time I had been received by him not only in his office but in his home with his wife and five sons. We became so close that he discussed Australia's clandestine intelligence operations in Malaysia with me many years before I was officially briefed about them. As Prime Minister I had met him not only in his country but also in Indonesia and at Commonwealth Heads of Government meetings.

In the light of our friendship, the current circumstances and our immediate surroundings, it is not surprising that Razak raised the role of the Governor-General in the event of the Senate rejecting the Budget. Nor is it surprising that, to break up this subject and pass to another, I should make the flippant remark 'it all depends who gets to the phone first, he to dismiss me or I to have him recalled'. As Sir John writes, we all laughed. Precisely! If Sir John had regarded the remark as so sinister why did he not take it up with me afterwards?

He also writes about me three pages before his description of the Razak incident: 'He told me on 16 October he would not be out to Yarralumla on the crisis for some time.' Presumably this is supposed to be a declaration that I would not be advising an election. The only occasion when Sir John and I were together on 16 October was at the dinner for Tun Razak; I do not know at what stage I am alleged to have made this remark.

The fourth occasion on which Sir John says I gave 'clear evidence of my awareness of the reserve powers' was at Government House, Melbourne, on 3 November. The Governor of Victoria and Lady Winneke were giving their Melbourne Cup Eve party in the state ballroom. Sir John and Lady Kerr and the Governor of New South Wales and Lady Cutler had become their house guests that day. The Premier of Victoria and Mrs Hamer and my wife and I assembled, according to custom, with the three vice-regal couples in the anteroom for a few minutes before entering the ballroom. It was not the time nor the place for political pronouncements or confidences. I knew Sir John had just come from receiving Mr Fraser in his office in Treasury Place. I was alert for the slightest indication from him of what had transpired; none came. I had to wait for his book to learn what passed between them at their four meetings. Not even readers of the book are told what passed between them in their many telephone conversations.

There are seven other occasions which Sir John specifies for talks on Supply.

The first was on 25 August at Admiralty House. We met with Stuart Devlin to discuss the insignia he was designing for the Order of Australia. The three wives were present.

The next was on 29 September when he received me at Government House.

The third was, he says, shortly before Mr Connor resigned on 14 October. The last time I spoke to him before that date was at a meeting of the Executive Council which Fred Daly and I attended on 7 October. He says he told me that, if I held an election and lost, I was still young enough to have a second term as Prime Minister, 'as Wilson did in England'. I would certainly have remembered such a remark; I would certainly have responded to it. It was never made, as Mr Daly confirms. Sir John is imagining that he put to me the argument he was to put to Mr Hayden on 6 November and to the Speaker, Gordon Scholes, on 11 November.

The fourth occasion which he alleges was on 14 October at Government House, when Senator Wriedt was sworn in as Minister for Minerals and Energy. It was a very short meeting because Senator Wriedt and I had come from our Party meeting in the morning and had to return for Question Time in our respective Houses. Supply was not discussed.

The fifth time was on 21 October at Government House. It was the first occasion in his account which took place after the Senate had deferred the vote on Supply. His account is accurate.

The sixth time was on 30 October at Government House. Sir John gives a correct description of his suggestion that the Opposition senators should 'grant supply on the condition of a half-Senate election delayed until the following May, with an undertaking that the Senate would not meet before 1 July 1976'. This was a condition he could enforce, because the State Governors had always held the Senate elections on dates proposed by the Governor-General. It was also an undertaking he could enforce, because the Governor-General appoints the times for holding the sessions of the Parliament. He had made the suggestion to me at Admiralty House the last time we were both in Sydney, three weekends previously, as a contingency if the Senate were to defer Supply. He said that Mr Fraser had to have an escape or he would be ousted like Mr Snedden and that it would be bad for the parliamentary system to have three Leaders of the Opposition in one year.

After the Senate deferred Supply he twice put the suggestion by telephone to Jim McClelland, with whom he had long exchanged direct home and office numbers. On 30 October the Senate and House sat in the morning and afternoon. He asked us both to lunch before an Executive Council meeting. We knew that he had invited Mr Hayden and Mr Fraser to call that afternoon. All reviewers of Sir John's book have noted that it contains not a single reference to Jim McClelland, who had been his most enduring and intimate friend. The senator gave an account of this meeting on 18 February 1976 in the Senate. Mr Hayden has written a review of Sir John's book. I shall be quoting both.

The seventh and last occasion Sir John cites was Thursday afternoon 6 November at Government House. At a meeting of the Executive Council which Mr Keating also attended I made a passing reference to the advice which I did in fact give him by telephone five days later. I knew he had seen Mr Fraser that morning. I arranged for him to see Mr Enderby and Mr Hayden after me. I did not know he had arranged for officials of the Department of Housing and Construction to follow us; no one knows with whom he made these arrangements, because the Department has mislaid the files.

On only three of the eleven occasions Sir John mentions in his book were there actual or meaningful discussions between us—on 29 September, before the Senate deferred a vote on Supply, 21 October and 30 October. He had, however, in prepared addresses in February and April, let it be publicly known how easy and valuable it was for him to ascertain facts and discuss issues with me and my ministers during and after meetings of the Executive Council.

Sir John had told the Indian Law Institute on 28 February:

There is ample opportunity both during and after meetings of the Executive Council and in other ways for the Governor-General to be fully informed about national affairs and policies. There is full and frank discussion with the Prime Minister. The Governor-General can ask questions, discuss broad or detailed matters, make suggestions, provide counsel—he can advise and warn . . .

He can obtain the reasons for what he is being asked to do and make suggestions about it but he must not get into political controversy, be partisan or try to act politically himself. He must not try to manipulate the political process.

In his prepared 'address'—not a mere 'speech'—at the Union Club dinner on 3 April 1975 Sir John said:

> He [the Governor-General] is entitled to be told why things are being done. He is entitled to think about them. He is entitled on occasions to make a suggestion, to give advice, even to utter a warning. He would, of course, be rather silly to do this unnecessarily or frequently or except on important occasions; but the right is there, as is the opportunity.
>
> I find the work of the Executive Council particularly interesting and of course it affords considerable opportunities for me after the formal business is over to talk to the ministers present. Over a period of time these talks can be most informative and rewarding in their frankness and background information.

If Sir John had wished to have further or fuller discussions on Supply or other matters with me he could have done so at or after the Executive Council meetings I attended over this period on 26 September with Mr Enderby in Melbourne or 7 October with Mr Daly in Canberra or 3 November with Bill Morrison, the Minister for Defence, in Sydney or 6 November with Mr Keating in Canberra. There was another official occasion when he could have done so: on 21 October I was present when he swore in Dr Patterson as Minister for Agriculture and Mr Keating as Minister for Northern Australia. The truth of the matter is, however, that in Parliament I had frankly and fully explained my attitudes and principles. He was not able or willing to face me. I did not and I do not say different things in private from what I say in public.

Sir John has been at pains to detail what he says have been

his conversations with me on selected occasions. When it suits him, as in his account of the Winnekes' Cup Eve party, he makes a point of elaborating on what could only have been the merest casual conversation. He does not, however, claim even a casual conversation took place on the multitude of other occasions when we met informally during a period when he claims he was wracked with misgivings. He did not even discuss the multitude of newspaper articles which he has stored in his scrapbook, even those which particularly impressed a man of his messianic and feudal proclivities, such as the articles by the *Australian*'s writer on religious affairs and the broadcast by an expert on Polynesian monarchies and mediaeval justiciars.

If, as he seems in his book to imply, he thinks it appropriate to discuss such matters with me on social or ceremonial occasions, he had manifold opportunities to do so during Princess Margaret's visit. We and our wives were together when the Princess arrived at Canberra airport on Wednesday morning 22 October and at dinner at Government House that night and at Canberra airport when the Princess left on Friday morning and when she left from Sydney airport on Monday morning 3 November. My wife and I went over to Admiralty House to meet the Princess in the late afternoon of Sunday 2 November. She said she would like to see Kirribilli House as her sister had told her about it. So Sir John and Lady Kerr and my wife and I waited until she left Admiralty House to drive around next door to Kirribilli House and then we walked quickly across through the postern to be in time for her arrival. After the Princess left, the Kerrs stayed talking with us for quite some time. It would have been very easy for Sir John and me to have a talk together on this occasion or more briefly on the earlier occasions during Princess Margaret's visit. He never raised the subject of Supply.

PRIME MINISTER

CANBERRA

that This House declares
that it has confidence
in the Whitlam govt
and that this House
informs HM the Queen
that, if the HE the G·G
proports to commission
the hon member for Wannon
as PM, the House does
not have confidence in him.
or in any govt he forms.

The resolution written by Mr Whitlam
at the Lodge, 11 November 1975

With Sir John Kerr and Margaret Whitlam at the
Governor-General's swearing-in in 1974 (Newspix/News Limited)

With supporters at a Labor Party rally at Hyde Park, Sydney, in
October 1975 (Anton Cermak/Fairfaxphotos)

Sharing a platform with Opposition leader Malcolm Fraser at an
ethnic affairs meeting in July 1975 (Newspix/News Limited)

While Sir John has purported to give his conversations with me he has given no information about his conversations with Mr Murdoch, Sir Garfield Barwick or Mr Scholes. Last August Senator Withers told the press that there were several un-publicised telephone conversations between Sir John and Mr Fraser during the twenty-five-day period between the blocking of the Budget and the dismissal of my Government. The final call was initiated from Yarralumla and took place shortly before Sir John sacked me. These calls were separate from the ones arranging the well-publicised meetings between the two. Sir John makes no reference to any of these telephone conversations he had with Mr Fraser.

Nor does Sir John mention the opportunities he had to discuss the Supply problem with my colleagues and how on occasions he used those opportunities. Bill Hayden has written:

Sir John Kerr as Governor-General was a totally different personality from his predecessor, Sir Paul Hasluck.

The termination of an Executive Council meeting with Sir Paul was usually followed by coffee and intellectually stimulating discussion on a surprisingly wide range of subjects.

Sir John adopted a much more convivial style, inevitably anecdotal about industrial skirmishes in which he had been involved in earlier years. He reflected, it seemed to me, many of the values and outlooks of old-style Labor men I have known—men who had been used to exercising tough and effective control over the now defunct Labor machine of the inner-Sydney region.

Hospitality was generous, although coffee was notably less popular.

Sir John asked Senator Jim McClelland to call on him at Admiralty House on 28 July. He had the senator and Mr Enderby to lunch at Admiralty House on 25 August. In reviewing Sir John's book Mr Bowen says 'there are at least four Ministers to my knowledge—Keating, Patterson, Senator McClelland and Enderby—who claim to have been misled. For example, Mr Enderby is adamant that Sir John clearly led him to believe that Mr Ellicott's publicly expressed views were nonsense.'

Sir John says that he knew that one minister was worried about the policy of 'toughing it out'. This was John Wheeldon, whom Sir John and Lady Kerr had to lunch at Government House. Senator Wheeldon made it plain that Caucus was standing fast. He was reassured about Sir John's attitude. On his return from Government House he hastened to tell me this and also told several of his colleagues in the Senate.

Joe Riordan, the Minister for Housing and Construction, who had had a longer and closer association with Sir John than anyone except Jim McClelland, has a very clear recollection of their conversation about the role of the Senate. Mr Riordan gave Sir John two reasons for his view that the Senate would never reject Supply. First, he had very reliable information from an impeccable source that there were several Tasmanian senators who would not vote for an actual rejection of the Budget. Secondly, he recalled an opinion his union had received twenty years before concerning the invalidity of an attempt by a body to use a general power in order to overcome a deficiency in a specific power. The opinion relied on a judgment of Sir Owen Dixon. Sir John smiled and asked if the advice was given by a good lawyer. Mr Riordan replied that he had thought it the best advice available at the time and that his counsel had progressed to the highest levels of the judiciary and now occupied the principal vice-regal post in Australia. They both laughed.

Mr Riordan's point was that since the Senate was denied the power to amend money Bills it could not have its way by rejecting them. Sir John gave Mr Riordan to understand that he accepted Mr Riordan's assessment on senators' intentions and Senate pretensions.

Jim McClelland gave a full public account of Sir John's deceptive conduct in the Senate on 18 February 1976:

> ... From the outset of the Supply crisis I did my best to avoid any contact at all with the Governor-General. I believed that it was improper as an old friend for me to try to influence him in any way. I thought that it might be embarrassing to him if it were known that he had had conversations with me. So I did my best to avoid Executive Council meetings. I was on terms with the Governor-General where I could phone him and have immediate access to him, and where he could phone me and come to visit my home incognito, if you like—even after he became Governor-General. But I believed in pursuance of the niceties of the situation that I should try to keep out of his way and not embarrass him during the crisis.
>
> But there came a time in an ordinary routine meeting of the Executive Council where I found myself with the then Prime Minister at Yarralumla. I was invited to lunch by my old friend, the Governor-General. At that lunch he freely discussed the constitutional crisis. I can assure all honourable senators that the only deduction which could not be drawn from what he said to us was that he contemplated in any way exercising the option which he ultimately exercised. In fact,

he led us to believe that that was not on his mind and would never be on his mind. On another occasion, he said to me privately: 'I do not concede that there is any crisis requiring my intervention until the money runs out.'

. . . a little more than a week before 11 November, the Governor-General phoned me at my home. We know what has been said about what he did, about the option which he ultimately exercised being the only option available to him. But that was not what was on the Governor-General's mind that day. The Governor-General spoke to me about Mr Fraser having painted himself into a corner and how we could get him off the hook, how he and I and the Labor Government could collaborate to solve the problem by finding a solution for Mr Fraser which would not involve a total loss of face. What the Governor-General suggested was that the Whitlam Government should undertake to him that he should convey to Mr Fraser a proposition that we have a half Senate election but that it would not call the Senate together until 1 July of this year and therefore would not attempt to gain any adventitious advantage about all of the things that were speculated upon at that time when it was said that we might have an accidental majority until 1 July.

The Governor-General said to me: 'I believe that what is primarily on their mind is a worry that if you get a majority for a short period you will introduce electoral reform that will put the Country Party out of business'. He said: 'I believe that the best contribution that I could make in this crisis would be to call up Mr Fraser and suggest to him that he could save face by agreeing to a suggestion such as that'. That may not strike honourable senators as such a dishonourable or extraordinary suggestion. I am not criticising the Governor-General for having that idea. As a matter of fact, I think it was a perspicacious idea and quite a shrewd way out of the crisis. But the questions that do really arise are these: Certainly I was an old friend, but why should he go out of his way to ring me? I was also a partisan. I had an interest in the outcome as a member of a government which was likely to be dismissed if he took a certain course of action. One wonders how many others he talked to. We know that he talked to Sir Garfield Barwick. One wonders whether he had private chats with Mr Ellicott or with his old, good friend Mr Atwill, the President of the Liberal Party of Australia. Why did he talk to me? Why did he single me out?

. . . The reason the Governor-General rang me was to lull me and my Party into a false sense of security. I believe now that he had made up his mind before Supply was deferred and that at all times the leading figures of the Liberal Party knew that they had this ace up their sleeve.

On 2 December 1978 Mr Hayden described how Sir John had pursued his course of deception till the very day on which he made up his mind to dismiss my Government:

. . . On November 6, I called on him at his Yarralumla residence at his request.

The invitation came through the Prime Minister's office and through the then Attorney-General. Both sources requested that I outline fully and candidly to him proposals the Government had in mind to meet the public and defence services' salaries in the event of Supply and Treasurer's advance running out.

I advised Sir John that although somewhat messy, the scheme was workable and furthermore it was legal on the advice of the Attorney-General's Department.

It has been claimed by some sources that this was an improper device to get around the authority of Parliament.

The assumption implicit in many such statements appears to be that all spending authority for Government must be approved annually by Parliament.

In fact, some 60 per cent of each year's annual expenditure by the national Government is covered by automatic appropriations which do not come before the Parliament.

The more significant comment I made to Sir John, however, was that in my view the Prime Minister, Mr Gough Whitlam, was manoeuvring to outface the Senate in tactics of bluff, that he could probably win and, I suspected, within a week, or at most not much more. There were several Liberal Senators, as was well known at the time, who had made quite plain their discontent with the tactics of Senate obstructionism.

They were ready to break. It was explained to Sir John that Supply would last to about December 11 but that the Treasurer's advance would sustain the Government's liability to fund the public and defence forces' payrolls for a few weeks after that.

. . . I was taken by surprise to find Sir John apparently little, if at all, interested in much of what I said.

He unexpectedly embarked on a discursive commentary about how highly he regarded Gough Whitlam's magnificent fighting ability, especially with his back against the wall. He said that Gough Whitlam fought like a lion, but even if he were defeated next time he would certainly fight his way back the time after that.

I recall observing rather wryly that it was easier to get out than to get back in. Sir John dismissed, graciously, but quickly, discussion about diffident senators retreating from the brink as too uncertain.

. . . It is clear that Sir John had embarked on an exercise designed to thoroughly mask his real intentions in this matter from the Prime Minister.

That is inexcusable and inconsistent with the role of either a monarch or the representative of a monarch in our system of parliamentary government.

It lacks the frankness and character toward the Prime Minister which was displayed respectively by Kings Edward VII and George V towards their Prime Minister, Asquith, in the great British constitutional conflict between 1909 and 1911.

There, the kings were able to play constructive and influential roles. Sir John Kerr could never make that claim.

Mr Hayden recalls Sir John's opinion that I could 'do a Wilson'. He claims in his book that he made these remarks to me. As I have said, he did not. He presumably prints this as evidence of sympathy, frankness, even personal goodwill. That he should now regard them as meaningful advice, as some sort of substitute for his real duties and obligations to be open and honourable with his ministers, seems to me to go to the very heart of his character and to demonstrate his fundamental lack of true understanding of the nature and purpose of politics in Australia. Ours is not a game of 'ins' and 'outs'; it is not a matter of 'Buggins' turn'. My Party had been out for twenty-three years; one generation of Australian Labor supporters had passed away with their deepest hopes of a Labor restoration in their lifetime unfulfilled; another generation had witnessed years of frustration and bitterness; a new generation had at last seen their hopes realised, had shared the tantalising disappointment of 1969, the victory of 1972 and the vindication of 1974; many of my principal colleagues had wasted the prime and most productive years of their lives in the wilderness and bitterness of two lost decades; millions of Australians still reposed their deepest hopes and aspirations in us, on the basis of the hard-won verdicts of 1972 and 1974; those verdicts, those victories, had raised new expectations among groups of Australians— migrants, Aboriginals, the handicapped, the poor and under- privileged—which can never again be set aside.

All this, according to Sir John Kerr, was to be thrown away without a fight, without demur—because I could 'do a Wilson'! And I was to do it because a corruptly created Senate, a Senate quite different from that elected only eighteen months before by the Australian people, was being manipulated by Mr Fraser, at the behest of his outside backers! At no time was it merely a question of one man's fortunes or ambitions; it was throughout greatly a question of the fate of a whole government, a party, a generation of Australians, and a whole set of basic principles. If I had any right at all to be Prime Minister and Leader of the Labor Party, it was because I was the custodian of all those people's hopes and the custodian of all they had fought for. It was that and that alone which motivated me in the great crisis. Throughout I was sustained by the staunch support of my colleagues and the determination of millions of my fellow Australians.

8

AMBUSH

'BY GOD, MR CHAIRMAN, AT THIS MOMENT I STAND
ASTONISHED AT MY OWN MODERATION.'
Clive of India, 1773

Even at the height of the most severe political crisis in our history, Australia's public life was not without the civilities. I had spent Monday 10 November in Melbourne. My evening engagement was to be present and speak at the traditional Lord Mayor's banquet. The Leader of the Opposition also attended. I had invited the parliamentarians who had been guests at the dinner—Mr Fraser, Mr McMahon, Mr Lynch, Mr Peacock and my own parliamentary colleague Ted Innes, MP for Melbourne—to accompany me on the RAAF aircraft back to Canberra. During the flight Mr Fraser, relaxed and even jocular in his fashion, said to Mr Innes, 'I thought this flight was for VIPs only'. Mr Innes' response must fall in the 'expletives deleted' category. By contrast Mr Peacock was in a sombre mood. Discussing events with a journalist on board, the ABC's

George Negus, he said, 'Malcolm's got us into this terrible mess'. It was well after midnight when we landed in Canberra.

Mr Fraser and Mr Lynch were driven off together by Eric Kennedy. They spoke very quietly but at the end were relaxed enough to say, 'He doesn't seem to know anything about it. All we have to do now is hope the press doesn't get hold of it, because then it could all blow up in our faces.'

At 9 a.m. as agreed the previous day, Mr Fraser, Mr Lynch and Mr Anthony came to my office in Parliament House to meet Mr Crean, Mr Daly and me. I put to them the proposition that, if they would allow their senators to pass the Budget, I would defer the elections for half the Senate until it would be too late for the four initial Territorial senators to take office before the new State senators were due to take office on 1 July. (This was the proposition put to me by Sir John Kerr himself, as a face-saving device for Mr Fraser, and also twice put by him to Senator Jim McClelland.) Mr Anthony seemed not averse to the idea; Mr Fraser and Mr Lynch would not accept it.

Mr Fraser asked that I should not give my proposition or their response to the press. I agreed, because, as I told him, I had always taken the attitude that advice should be given to the Governor-General directly before the nature of it was announced publicly in advance. One now knows that Mr Fraser did not want his Party and colleagues to know what my offer was. After Mr Fraser and his two colleagues left, Mr Crean commented reflectively, 'They seem very cocky'.

I immediately tried to speak to the Governor-General on the telephone. My secretary was told that Sir John could not come to the telephone. I then telephoned him myself on his direct number. I told him that I wished for an early meeting with him; I had put the proposition which he had suggested to defer the half-Senate elections; since the Opposition had now rejected it, I wanted to ask him to set the process for those elections in train straight away. I also told him I would advise him to submit the Constitution Alteration (Simultaneous Elections) Bill to the electors on the day of the Senate elections. Sir John said he was sorry he had not been able to take my call at first as he had been worried about a grandchild's illness—his daughter Gabrielle's son; he had now to get ready for the Remembrance Day service at the National War Memorial. After an appropriate interchange about his grandson, I said, 'Then I won't be able to see you till after one o'clock because there is, as you probably know, a notice of motion to censure the Government. Obviously, I have to be in the House while that is being debated, and I can't call on you until the luncheon adjournment. I shall have to tell my Party meeting what my advice will be to you. I know that my predecessors have told the House what their advice to the Governor-General is going to be.' (Holt in 1967 and Gorton in 1970 had first told the House they intended to advise the Governor-General to have a half-Senate election; in March 1974 I had advised Sir Paul Hasluck before informing the House.) I told Sir John, 'I have not thought that was courteous and I think I should give you the advice first. Nevertheless, since I must tell the Party, it is quite likely it will become public knowledge before I see you. Do you agree?' He said, 'Yes, certainly.'

So it was arranged that I would call on him immediately the House adjourned for lunch. I telephoned the Independents in the Senate, Cleaver Bunton and Steele Hall, about the advice I was to give the Governor-General and then told my own Party meeting. Thus, the only members of Parliament who were kept in the dark about my intended advice to the Governor-General were the members of the Opposition—at Mr Fraser's insistence.

At a press briefing after the Liberal Party meeting, Mr Lynch told journalists: 'We believe events will work themselves out. We believe the present course is sound for reasons which will become apparent to you later.'

Before the House met I received a call from Mr Frank Ley, the Chief Electoral Officer. He told me that Mr Fraser had telephoned him to inquire the last date upon which a Federal election could be held. He had told him that the last date upon which the school premises would be available for an election would be 13 December. To meet this deadline, in particular to compile and print the electoral rolls, the writs should issue within the next couple of days. It would be possible to issue them a week later but it would impose a great strain on the system and would leave very little margin for delays in deliveries of ballot papers. Mr Ley's response to Mr Fraser concurred with what he had told me over the previous week and was the basis of my telling Sir John that he should send requests to the State Governors to issue writs for a half-Senate election that week.

The House sat at 11.45 a.m. so that members could attend the War Memorial Service at 11 a.m. I was represented at the ceremony by Mr Enderby, who had been in frequent contact with Sir John Kerr during the crisis. Sir John did not speak to him except on departure from the War Memorial, to say, 'Goodbye, Mr Attorney.' It was indeed. When the House assembled Mr Fraser moved his censure motion—the first and only motion of censure or no confidence he had moved against my Government during his eight months as Leader of the Opposition. At 12.34 p.m. I moved an amendment to substitute a censure of him for his censure of my Government. Mr Anthony followed me and the House adjourned at 12.55 p.m. when he finished speaking.

In moving his motion of censure, Mr Fraser made two references to the role of the Governor-General which made it clear that he had foreknowledge of Sir John Kerr's action that day. His opening words were:

> The evasion and contempt of Parliament and of the
> Constitution have become a critical issue in the attempt of
> the Prime Minister [Mr Whitlam] to hang onto power. He
> believes that he alone is the Constitution; that he alone is the
> Parliament. The Parliament is very clearly the Queen—in
> our case the Governor-General—the Senate and the House
> of Representatives. All have a proper part and proper powers
> under the Constitution. The Prime Minister cannot pre-
> empt their powers and their prerogatives.

Later Mr Fraser returned to the prerogative of the Governor-General. He said:

> He has not said that he would accept the Governor-General's
> decision taken in accordance with his constitutional
> prerogative. There are circumstances, as I have said
> repeatedly, where a Governor-General may have to act as
> the ultimate protector of the Constitution. He ignores that
> prerogative.

In reply, I moved a counter-motion of censure on the Opposition. For the last time, I repeated the arguments and stated the principles at stake:

> The Leader of the Opposition's motion—his first censure
> motion ever against the Government—talks about

unconstitutional conduct. Sure, that is the issue today—but
from what source does it spring? I remind the House that
the Australian Senate cannot originate a taxing Bill or an
appropriation Bill. It cannot amend a taxing Bill, or a Bill
appropriating revenue or moneys for the ordinary annual
services of Government. It cannot amend any Bill so as to
increase any proposed charge or burden on the people. On
the other hand, the Senate may return to the House any Bill
which it cannot amend, with a request for amendment. The
Senate has not done that. It has not complied with the clear
procedures of the Constitution. The Senate has gone on
strike. But without daring to allow senators to vote the clear
rejection or acceptance of the Budget, the Opposition in the
Senate claims authority to nullify a Bill which it cannot even
amend. This means that, if a Government with a clear
majority in the House of Representatives presents its Budget
to Parliament, and then brings into the House of
Representatives financial measures to give effect to that
Budget, and has them passed by the House and sent up to
the Senate, a hostile Senate could effectively reject them—
without even voting on them . . .

Whoever commands a majority in this House forms a
government, and has the right to govern for a normal 3-year
term. The Senate, as a second chamber, plays no part in the
determination of which political party, or group of parties,
shall form the government. The Leader of the Opposition
asserts that my Government is threatening the Constitution
through an attempt to reduce the powers of the Senate. Of
course, the exact reverse is true. The Leader of the
Opposition is seeking to reduce the powers of the House of
Representatives in a way never attempted in Australia. I am

not trying to reduce any legitimate legislative power of the
Senate. I am determined to protect this House and to
prevent usurpation by the Senate.

A curious incident had occurred while I was still speaking.
Mr Fraser left the House—odd conduct indeed on so serious an
occasion and so serious a question, a censure moved on the
Leader of the Opposition as part of the same debate in which he
had moved censure on the Government, the most serious of all
motions a Parliament can ever debate.

I went straight to Government House. Harry Rundle, who
had for many years previously been Mr Barnard's Canberra
driver, had taken Mr Fraser to Government House before I
arrived. Having dropped Mr Fraser at the front door he was
told to park the car around the corner out of sight. Even this
simple manoeuvre was essential to the conspiracy; had I known
Mr Fraser's car was there, I could at once have instructed my
driver, Robert Millar, who had been with me in Sydney and
Canberra for over a decade, to turn round and drive me back to
Parliament House. Had I known Mr Fraser was already there, I
would not have set foot in Yarralumla.

Peter Bowers, the *Sydney Morning Herald*'s political
correspondent who helped prepare the serialisation of Sir John
Kerr's book, has given this account of Mr Fraser's arrival
before me:

> Mr Fraser was already there when Mr Whitlam arrived,
> closeted in a room, blinds drawn, the car round the back out
> of sight, everything planned to the last detail, the dismissal
> documents face-down on the table, out of Mr Whitlam's
> sight but within reach of Sir John Kerr.

There is a simple explanation for Mr Fraser's early arrival at Yarralumla—his office, or rather Mr Tony Eggleton, despatched him too early.

The call from Yarralumla to Mr Fraser's office that morning said the Governor-General wanted to see Mr Fraser after he had seen Mr Whitlam. No time was fixed so Mr Eggleton, the Liberal Party's federal director, who was running the Fraser office that day, posted a look-out to watch for the departure of Mr Whitlam's white Mercedes.

The Whitlam car pulled away, word was passed to Eggleton and Mr Fraser was on his way to Yarralumla within minutes.

No sooner had Mr Fraser left than Mr Whitlam's car returned to Parliament House. It had not had time to go to Yarralumla.

Mr Whitlam apparently was still in his office. Mr Fraser could not be reached by two-way radio in his car.

To the consternation of officials at Yarralumla Mr Fraser arrived before Mr Whitlam. Mr Fraser was immediately escorted to a side-room and the blinds drawn.

The aide poured Mr Fraser a whisky. The aide's hand shook and he spilt some of the whisky. Had he divined that something was up?

I can only say that on the basis of my own olfactory recall, there was a fair whiff of whisky around Yarralumla that day. It certainly exceeded the smell of the newly painted, newly soundproofed office. Nevertheless, to be fair, there were on that day and at significant times occasions of praiseworthy abstinence. As Sir John Kerr himself records, the minute I left Government House he swore in Mr Fraser as my successor.

And Sir John records, they dispensed with the 'customary champagne'.

In their book *Kerr's King Hit* (Cassell Australia, 1976), Clem Lloyd and Andrew Clark write:

> Fraser arrived at Government House before Whitlam. The Governor-General's official secretary, David Smith, met him and briefed him quickly on what was to happen. Fraser and Smith waited in a sitting room for the summons from Kerr.

Whoever arrived first at Government House and whatever happened in Parliament that day, it was essential to the success of the operation that I should leave Government House dismissed and Mr Fraser should leave it as Prime Minister.

I drove to the state entrance. Captain Stephens, the aide, accompanied me to the Governor-General's study. He told me that he was about to end his duty and pointing to one of the closed doors said: 'The successor is being interviewed in there.' I was not correct in saying in a speech the next day that he was referring to *my* successor, Mr Fraser. I was correct in discerning the essence of the conspiracy to trap me into Government House and to have me leave it without any options as Prime Minister.

Sir John asked me to take a seat, as usual on the other side of his desk. I said, 'I have a letter with the advice which I gave you on the telephone this morning.' He said, 'Before we go any further I have to tell you that I have decided to terminate your commission. I have a letter for you giving my reasons.' He passed me a document. After glancing at it I said, 'Have you discussed this with the Palace?' He said, 'I don't have to and it's too late for you. I have terminated your commission.'

I rose to leave. He also rose and added, 'The Chief Justice agrees with this course of action.' He did not tell me that he had a letter from the Chief Justice. I said, 'So that is why you had him to lunch yesterday. I advised you that you should not consult him on this matter.'

He shrugged his shoulders. As he has written, he merely said, 'We shall all have to live with this' and I replied, 'You certainly will.' He wished me luck and extended his hand. I took it. I have never spoken to him since.

Sir John says that I 'rose and looked about for the telephone and said I must get in touch with the Palace'. This is a concoction and an absurd one. I had been in the Governor-General's study at least half a dozen times when Lord Casey was Governor-General and scores of times while Sir Paul Hasluck and Sir John Kerr had been Governors-General. While Sir Paul and Sir John had made telephone calls and received them while I was there, I had no knowledge of the procedure for making calls. I did not know the number of the Palace. I had no staff with me. He had his aides, his secretaries, his telephonists, his police. I was trapped in an ambush; my sole instinct was to escape, to depart at once from the place where the deed had been done and the presence of the man who had done the deed. When he offered his hand and said, 'Anyway, good luck', it was from ordinary habit and simple courtesy that I shook hands.

The portrayal of my starting up wildly to search for the telephone is presumably intended as 'corroborative detail to lend an air of verisimilitude to an otherwise bald and unconvincing narrative'. Nevertheless, it is deeply instructive for the insights it gives into Sir John Kerr's motives and attitudes. He was plainly obsessed by the fear that I would procure his own dismissal by the Queen; and he believed that to prevent this he was justified in practising any deception. It is evident that this was his paramount concern. The extraordinary weight he gave to my remark to Tun Razak is further evidence of this fact. In his book he argues at length that his sole motive was to keep the Crown and the Queen personally out of politics; his real motive was fear for his own job. The strength of his obsession has not diminished after the lapse of three years. This is shown by the interpretation he placed on my reference to the Palace. He could not conceive that anyone would be concerned with the Palace for any reason other than to get him dismissed; he saw every action and statement of mine through the distorted focus of his own fears. To imagine that I could have procured the dismissal of the Governor-General by a telephone call to Buckingham Palace in the middle of the night—it was 2 a.m. in London—is preposterous; to imagine that I would have tried to do so is ludicrous.

At no time during the crisis had the possibility of replacing Sir John Kerr been a significant element in my thinking. I never bothered even to inquire into the legal or practical procedures for so drastic and unprecedented an action. I have not to this day. As to thinking it could be done by a telephone call, had I not, within that very month, had the experience of revoking Sir Colin Hannah's dormant commission as Administrator? That process took ten days. And, as I have stated, it was at Sir John Kerr's own suggestion that I, not he, should make the approach to the Queen. Yet Sir John and commentators who have accepted his account never mention the cashiering of Hannah. From the time of my remark to Tun Razak to the hour I was dismissed, I never gave the possibility of dismissing him before he dismissed me a second's thought or a second thought; Sir John Kerr seems to have thought of little else. His sense of his own danger is shown by one previously unreported action on the morning of 11 November. He telephoned Sir Roden Cutler to warn him of his intentions and of the possibility (in his view) that Sir Roden might have to become Administrator if something went wrong and he ceased to be Governor-General. Sir Roden told Sir John that he thought his proposed action was wrong and would prove damaging to the Crown and the office of the Governor-General.

But the real guide to my intentions is not what I said or did not say in the privacy of the Governor-General's study; it is what I actually did and said after I left it. And for these there are ample witnesses. If my overriding preoccupation had been to contact the Palace, I should have gone back to Parliament House and my staff. Instead I went home to the Lodge for lunch. The Lodge has no switchboard, no office and only domestic staff. I made three telephone calls: to my wife, who was hosting a working lunch at Kirribilli House for the directors of Commonwealth Hostels Ltd, to Mr Menadue and to my principal private secretary, John Mant, to instruct him to ask to the Lodge some of my colleagues who would be involved in carrying out the moves I was planning to take in the only place which had any meaningful role, the House of Representatives.

I then had my lunch. The condemned man ate a hearty meal, although, on this occasion, the normal order was reversed; I had my steak *after* the execution.

My colleagues began to arrive: Mr Daly, Mr Crean, who was due to speak in the censure debate immediately after lunch, Mr Enderby, Mr Scholes, Mr Menadue, the Labor Party's national secretary, Mr Combe, Mr Mant and Mr Freudenberg. The discussion was rather disjointed and fairly desultory. Mr Daly has written that they all felt like 'stunned mullets'. Before we turned to parliamentary tactics, Mr Menadue withdrew.

The resolution I framed at the Lodge, a facsimile of which is included with the illustrations in this book, discloses the true nature of my reference to 'the Palace'. It reads:

> That this House declares that it has confidence in the
> Whitlam Government and that this House informs Her
> Majesty the Queen that, if His Excellency the Governor-
> General purports to commission the honourable member for
> Wannon as Prime Minister, the House does not have
> confidence in him or in any government he forms.

In the event, the motion was not moved in these precise terms. In further discussions at Parliament House, Mr Daly suggested removing the reference to the Queen and resting our case solely on the legitimacy our Government held from the unbroken confidence of the House of Representatives. I agreed.

At 2 p.m. both Houses resumed sitting. At 2.20 p.m. the Budget Bills were passed in the Senate on the voices. At 2.24 p.m. the Senate adjourned. Immediately afterwards in the House of Representatives, Mr Crean sat down and the Government Whip moved that the question—my censure motion—be put.

His motion was opposed. It was carried by 63 votes to 56. My amendment was then put and was also carried by 63 to 56. At 2.34 p.m., Mr Fraser announced that the Governor-General had commissioned him and then he moved that the House adjourn. His motion was lost by 55 to 64. At 2.48 p.m., Mr Daly moved that standing orders should be suspended to permit me to move a motion forthwith. His motion was carried by 64 to 54.

At 3.00 p.m. I made a brief speech:

I move:

That this House expresses its want of confidence in the Prime Minister and requests Mr Speaker forthwith to advise His Excellency the Governor-General to call the honourable member for Werriwa to form a government.

The Governor-General's views have been read at sufficient length to show that the circumstances upon which he relied no longer apply. There is no longer a deadlock on the Budget between the House of Representatives and the Senate. The Budget Bills have been passed. Accordingly, the Government which twice has been elected by the people is able to govern. Furthermore, as has been demonstrated this afternoon, the parties which the Prime Minister leads do not have a majority in the House of Representatives. The party I lead has a majority in the House of Representatives. It has never been defeated in the year and a half since the last election and in those circumstances it is appropriate, I believe, that you, Mr Speaker, should forthwith advise the Governor-General—waiting upon him forthwith to advise him—that the party I lead has the confidence of the House of Representatives, and you should apprise His Excellency of the view of the House that I have the confidence of the House and should be called to form His Excellency's Government.

At 3.03 p.m. Mr Daly seconded the motion and moved that the question be put. His motion was carried by 64 to 54. My motion was then put and was carried by 64 to 54. It will be noticed that six motions had been put and they were all won by Labor by an absolute majority of the House.

The Speaker then said, 'It will be my intention to convey the message of the House to His Excellency at the first opportunity'.

Then, Hansard shows, the two Appropriation Bills were returned from the Senate without amendment or requests, and at 3.15 p.m., the sitting was suspended.

The next day Mr Scholes put his account of the ensuing events in the parliamentary archives. Immediately the standing orders were suspended for me to move the motion against Mr Fraser's appointment, Mr Scholes requested his private secretary, Mary Harris, to contact the Governor-General's official secretary for a tentative appointment so that he could convey the resolution of the House to the Governor-General as soon as the House rose following the passage of the motion. When he returned to his suite following the passage of the motion Mrs Harris told him that the official secretary had been reached and had said that the Governor-General was very busy and might not have time for additional appointments. The Governor-General was clearly making it as difficult for the Speaker to see him in the afternoon as he had made it for me to speak to him in the morning. Mr Scholes then told Mrs Harris to inform the official secretary that unless an audience was granted he would recall the House and inform the members and seek further guidance on subsequent action. The official secretary soon telephoned back with an appointment for the Speaker at 4.45 p.m. Sir John had to arrange with Mr Fraser to dissolve the House before he saw Mr Scholes in the afternoon just as he had to arrange with Mr Fraser to sack me before he saw me in the morning.

At 3.40 p.m. the Budget Bills were taken by Gordon Pike to Government House with the Speaker's request that the Governor-General sign them. Mr Pike reached Government House at 3.50 p.m. Mr Fraser's car was already there. The Governor-General was as prompt in complying with the

Speaker's request for him to sign the Bills as he was being dilatory in complying with the Speaker's request to receive the message from the House. The Speaker arrived at the gates to Government House at 4.25 p.m. He was kept outside the gates until the official secretary drove out. He was then kept waiting until the time of his appointment. It was the very time at which the official secretary took his position at the top of the steps of Parliament House and read the proclamation dissolving both Houses of Parliament.

In his book Sir John describes how Mr Scholes arrived at the appointed time and handed him the letter with the resolution of the House. He then proceeds:

> I informed Mr Scholes that I had already dissolved both
> Houses of Parliament and that there would be an election
> for both on 13 December. There being nothing else of
> relevance to say the interview ended.

Sir John's selective memory and candour are exposed by the contemporary and comprehensive record of his actions and conversations which Mr Scholes lodged with the parliamentary archives. This record shows that a great deal was said and that it was very much to the point. Mr Scholes informed Sir John that the House had carried a resolution of no confidence in Mr Fraser and had requested my reinstatement as Prime Minister. Sir John advised him that he had already signed an order dissolving both Houses, having granted Mr Fraser's request for a double dissolution. Mr Scholes said that he considered it improper for the representative of the Crown to dissolve Parliament without first receiving and hearing from the Speaker who was charged with conveying to the Governor-General a relevant resolution passed by a majority of the House of Representatives.

Sir John informed him that he had been kept informed of the events in the Parliament and was fully aware of the resolution of the House of Representatives, but he had not thought it necessary to observe normal courtesies of waiting for the formal conveyance of the message to the Crown by the Speaker. Mr Scholes protested that it was improper to act without first meeting the obligation implicit in his agreement to receive him at 4.45 p.m. on behalf of the House. He considered the Governor-General had acted in bad faith. Sir John responded that as his mind was made up and Mr Fraser had, as promised prior to being commissioned, delivered Supply, he saw no reason to delay the double dissolution which Mr Fraser had requested.

Mr Scholes said that he considered that the Governor-General had acted to dissolve the House without having first taken all action necessary to resolve the deadlock. He considered the Governor-General's first action should have been to write to the President of the Senate, indicating his concern at the refusal of the Senate to consider the Appropriation Bills and thus its refusal to carry out its constitutional obligation. He suggested that a request from the Governor-General to the Senate to consider the Appropriation Bills and thus indicate its view on the Supply question would have been a proper first step by the Governor-General. Sir John indicated that he had no power to make such a request. Mr Scholes said that he thought it appropriate that the Governor-General should request the Senate to carry out its constitutional function and decide whether it would reject or pass the Appropriation Bills before entering into an agreement with the Leader of the Opposition to hand over government to him without consideration of the fact that he lacked support.

He then raised the resolution of the House about my reinstatement and said that that portion should be complied with irrespective of the dissolution of the Parliament. The Governor-General indicated that he had discussed Supply with both Mr Fraser and me. I had not been able to give an assurance that I could and would get Supply passed by both Houses. Mr Fraser had indicated that he could obtain Supply and on that understanding had been appointed Prime Minister.

On Mr Scholes insisting that the Governor-General should comply with the request of the House to reinstate me, Sir John indicated that for him to comply with the resolution of the House after Mr Fraser had had Supply passed would be viewed as part of a prearranged plan between himself and me. Mr Scholes records that the only other significant remark made during the interview was Sir John's comment that his action in sacking me would result in my re-election as Prime Minister.

On 10 November Sir John had acted on the secret advice of a Chief Justice whom he consulted against the advice of the Prime Minister and without the knowledge of the other members of the High Court. On 11 November he did not wait for the House of Representatives to vote on either of the motions of censure which he knew it was debating. He ignored the vote of the House on those motions. He defied the resolution which he knew the House had passed declaring that it had no confidence in Mr Fraser and wishing me to be reinstated. He refused to see the Speaker to accept the House's message from him until he had dissolved both Houses. He maintained in office a Prime Minister who did not have the confidence of the House and accepted the advice of that Prime Minister in granting a double dissolution.

It will be seen how lightly Sir John Kerr regarded the position of the Parliament and the Government which had and the Government which did not have the confidence of the House of Representatives.

In his book Sir John asserts that I telephoned him after the House had expressed its lack of confidence in Mr Fraser and its wish that I be recommissioned. No such conversation took place. As I have already written, I have never spoken to him since my brief call on him after 1 p.m. that day. I can only suppose that he has a befuddled recollection of his conversation with Mr Scholes. Had such a conversation ever taken place, there would be nothing discreditable to me about it. I should have been merely doing my duty making a last effort to save the elected Labor Government. I would have no reason to conceal such a conversation, had it occurred. But it did not occur.

There is a comment I must make about the position of the Senate and two comments about the House of Representatives in the circumstances of that afternoon. There has been a very great deal of speculation about the steps which my Government could have taken in the Senate to frustrate or delay Sir John's and Mr Fraser's plot. The simplest way would have been to ask the Labor President, Senator O'Byrne, to adjourn the sitting. All the suggestions have involved the proposition that the Labor Party should have acted in a way contrary to all that it had said and done up to that stage. What humbugs we would have been if, after condemning the Liberals for refusing to vote on the Budget, we ourselves had delayed a vote on the Budget. We had fought a great fight by the rules. We stuck by the rules to the bitter end.

With the wisdom of hindsight we can all see that it would have been wiser if Mr Scholes had taken the Appropriation Bills together with the resolution of the House to his appointment with the Governor-General, instead of sending the Bills ahead with the usual written message. This would have been a legitimate and, even against Sir John Kerr, an effective tactic. Mr Scholes and I discussed maintaining or resuming the sittings of the House. It was in this context that I said to him that in those circumstances Sir John would call out the troops. Many people still think it incredible that Sir John could have done that. If, however, a man can interpret the Constitution, where it is silent, in a way which entitled him to perpetrate his actions of that day, how much more certain is it that he would have thought himself entitled to act when, as the Constitution expressly states, 'The command in chief of the naval and military forces of the Commonwealth is vested in the Governor-General as the Queen's representative.'

Despite the Chief Justice's fiat that the issues of the coup were not justiciable, Sir John himself on *This Day Tonight* on 1 December 1978 admitted that in some circumstances the courts could have been involved. If Mr Scholes and I and my colleagues had purported to keep the House in session and our Government in office there would have been the most fruitful grounds for court cases of all kinds and at all levels. There would have been conflicts between the parliamentary staff and the public service, conflicts about broadcasts and reports of proceedings, conflicts about staff and transport for ministers and members. If Sir John Kerr believed that all his powers rested on the most literal interpretation of the Constitution, regardless of the accepted practices, precedents, customs and conventions of two hundred years, why is it unbelievable that he would have acted on his 'powers' as commander-in-chief; why is it, in his words, 'complete nonsense' to believe that he would not have made an exception even in this case?

When I spoke to the Caucus and in talks with Party officials, I stressed and they all completely agreed that we should not depart from the accepted processes. We had won the 1972 and 1974 elections in accordance with the rules. We should strive to win again in accordance with the rules. The Liberals in the State Parliaments, in the Senate, in Government House, on the High Court had done enough damage to Australia's institutions and principles: we would not compound that damage.

At 4.40 p.m. the Governor-General's official secretary arrived at Parliament House to read the proclamation dissolving the Parliament. A large and angry crowd had gathered in the forecourt. Mr Smith was spirited in through a side entrance. There is no legal requirement for the public reading of the proclamation, and certainly nothing in law which says it must be read from the front steps of Parliament House; public posting and publication in the *Gazette* are sufficient. This performance itself was an act of provocation.

Mr Smith concluded his reading of the proclamation with the traditional flourish: 'God Save The Queen!' I then spoke to the people:

Well may we say 'God Save the Queen', because nothing will save the Governor-General. The proclamation which you have just heard read by the Governor-General's official secretary was countersigned 'Malcolm Fraser' who will undoubtedly go down in Australian history from Remembrance Day 1975 as Kerr's cur. They won't silence the outskirts of Parliament House, even if the inside has been silenced for the next few weeks. The Governor-General's proclamation was signed after he had already made an appointment to meet the Speaker at a quarter to five. The House of Representatives had requested the Speaker to give the Governor-General its decision that Mr Fraser did not have the confidence of the House and that the Governor-General should call me to form the Government.

I concluded: 'Maintain your rage and your enthusiasm through the campaign for the election now to be held and until polling day.'

Sir John makes much of this little speech. He emphasises the 'rage' and ignores the 'enthusiasm'. He quotes with portentous pretentiousness the Oxford definition of 'rage'! I must confess that before making my off-the-cuff remarks on the steps of Parliament House it did not occur to me to look up Oxford and I am sure that no one in the crowd needed to do so afterwards. Given the mood that the crowd was in, I daresay I could have stirred them up a lot more than I did; it was a delightful Canberra late spring evening, just the night for a pleasant walk to Yarralumla. This was no exercise in demagoguery; in the astonishing circumstance in which my colleagues and I so suddenly and unceremoniously found ourselves, I am entitled to claim it as a remarkable exercise in restraint and moderation.

After the drama of the day I telephoned a good friend in London, Sir Martin Charteris, soldier, diplomat, sculptor and private secretary to the Queen. It is a fact that the Queen's representative in Australia had kept the Queen in the same total ignorance of his actions as he had the Prime Minister of Australia.

9

VERDICT ON THE VICEROY

'HE [THE GOVERNOR-GENERAL] MUST NOT TRY TO
MANIPULATE THE POLITICAL PROCESS.'
Sir John Kerr, 28 February 1975

Why the *eleventh*? In May Parliament had granted Supply to my
Government until 30 November. Early in the crisis Sir John
Kerr had commented to Senator Jim McClelland that he saw no
need for intervention of the kind being mooted in sections of the
press until Supply actually ran out. The chances of a political
settlement were increasing daily. Sir John simply ignored all this
and deprived the House of Representatives of a full three sitting
weeks in which to resolve the deadlock with the Senate.

Sir Garfield Barwick was the luncheon guest of the National
Press Club in Canberra on 10 June 1976. This exchange occurred:

QUESTION: . . . you refer to the confidence of both
Houses. After 1 p.m. on November 11 Mr Fraser did not
have the confidence of the House of Representatives.

ANSWER: No, but he could get Supply.

QUESTION: What criteria did you have in mind in the last sentence of that letter of November 10 when you said that provided the Governor-General was satisfied that the Government of the day could not obtain Supply he could go ahead and sack it? Given that no vote had been taken on Supply in the Senate; given that journalists were frequently being told by the then Opposition members that they might well have to back down; given that Supply still had nineteen days to run, what meaningful criteria could possibly have existed then to justify the claim that the Governor-General could be satisfied that the Government could not obtain Supply?

ANSWER: I thought that what I wrote was crystal clear. It was a matter for him to be satisfied that there was no chance of getting Supply. It rested with him.

I wasn't asked to determine this. He had to use his own judgement on the facts as he knew them.

What facts were before Sir John Kerr for him to be satisfied that there was no chance of getting Supply? This was a purely political judgement. Whose advice did he take on this political matter? He accepted the advice of the Leader of the Opposition against that of his Prime Minister. He sounded out certain of my ministers, Senator Wheeldon for instance, to find out whether I was correct in asserting that there was no possibility of the Government cracking. He made no attempt to sound out Opposition senators or front-benchers to find out whether Mr Fraser was correct in asserting that there was no possibility of the Opposition cracking in the next three weeks. There was only one way Mr Fraser could make that assertion with confidence.

His confidence could come from one source only, Sir John Kerr himself. Only if he knew that Sir John would act, and act quickly, could he have confidently asserted that not a single senator—and only one was needed—would have a change of heart before 30 November. That is why 11 November was the critical date.

Sir John gives one reason for choosing that day. He claims that the timetable of the election processes required a decision before 13 November, if an election were not to run over into the Christmas holiday period. This accords with the advice I had given him from the Chief Electoral Officer, regarding a normal election. What was normal about the election Sir John brought about? We are asked to believe that a great constitutional up-heaval, a deeply and enduringly divisive action, was preferable to disturbing the great Australian summer torpor! In any case, Sir John himself acknowledges that the thirteenth would have been within the margin of the electoral timetable. That is three full sitting days—a political age in those tumultuous days. Above all, these considerations were political; Sir John made his judgement on them without consulting his Prime Minister. He accepted the advice of the Leader of the Opposition; he by-passed the Prime Minister. And he did this because secrecy and deception were essential if the enterprise were to come off.

At the seminar held at the University of Melbourne in August 1976 to commemorate the 75th anniversary of Australian Federation, Mr Ellicott said:

> We do not know what passed between him and the
> Governor-General except that the Governor-General in his
> letter said: 'You have previously told me that you would
> never resign or advise an election of the House of

Representatives or a double dissolution . . .' I could not
believe that Sir John Kerr would have written that had it
not been true.

This of course gets to the core of the deception. As Sir John
Kerr acknowledges, there was no discussion about elections.
The letter had been written. The copies of Sir John's
explanatory statement were prepared, ready for release to the
press within the hour! It was all cut and dried. Sir John was
determined that I would not leave Government House as Prime
Minister, because he believed—falsely—that it would be fatal to
him if I did.

The very terms of Sir John's letter are misleading and
deliberately provocative. The use of the phrase '*never* resign or
advise an election' is calculated. It is clearly designed to reinforce
the impression of more than simple intransigence, rather of
dictatorship. I had gone to Government House precisely to
advise an election. For three hours Sir John had known that was
the purpose of my call. Yet he refused to discuss it. In his
explanatory statement, he asserted, almost as an afterthought:

> There is one other point. There has been discussion of the
> possibility that a half-Senate election might be held under
> circumstances in which the Government has not obtained
> supply. If such advice were given to me I should feel
> constrained to reject it because a half-Senate election held
> whilst supply continues to be denied does not guarantee a
> prompt or sufficiently clear prospect of the deadlock being
> resolved in accordance with proper principles. When I refer
> to rejection of such advice I mean that, as I would find it
> necessary in the circumstances I have envisaged to determine

Mr Whitlam's commission and, as things have turned out
have done so, he would not be Prime Minister and not able
to give or persist with such advice.

In other words, he had made up his mind to dismiss me
whatever I said to him that day. I had in fact had a definite
timetable for elections in 1976. After the election in May 1974,
following the dissolution of both Houses the previous month,
the term of service of senators was taken to begin on 1 July
preceding the date of the election, i.e. 1 July 1973, while the
House of Representatives could continue for three years from
the first meeting of the House, i.e. 9 July 1974. Thus there had
to be an election for half the senators before 1 July 1976 and
there had to be an election of the House before 9 July 1977.

My intention had been to advise the Governor-General to
have an election for half the senators close to the expiry of their
term in May 1976, as I had originally advised Sir Paul Hasluck
two years earlier. I then intended that the twenty-one Bills
which had been twice rejected by the Senate should be again put
before the new Senate in August 1976 and the following months.
If significant Bills were again rejected by the new Senate it was
my purpose to seek a double dissolution before the end of the year.
The Constitution provides that such a dissolution shall not take
place within six months before the date of the expiry of the House
of Representatives by effluxion of time. Accordingly a double
dissolution could take place at any time before 9 January 1977.

I had thus proposed to act according to the Constitution and
its conventions. Mr Fraser and Sir John Kerr could not afford to
wait.

My Government was arranging for advances to be made by
the banks to public servants, servicemen and sundry contractors,

if the Senate had not passed the Appropriation Bills by the end of November 1975. The Reserve Bank, the Commonwealth Bank and the State Bank of South Australia had already agreed to the arrangements and the other banks would certainly have agreed to them for fear of alienating such public servants, servicemen and contractors as were customers of theirs. The arrangements were authorised by statutory provisions introduced by the Menzies Governments and left unchanged by the Fraser Governments. They are still available.[1]

In his book, Sir John Kerr now claims that there would have been illegalities involved after 30 November and purports to give this as another reason for dismissing my Government on 11 November. He never expressed such doubts to me, the Treasurer, the Attorney-General, the Solicitor-General or the Secretary of my Department. If he was concerned, why did he not say so, and demand full legal advice from us? He kept his counsel, in this as in all things. He raised no such concern on the day. In his explanatory statement, he merely stated, in the very last paragraph: 'The announced proposals about financing public servants, suppliers, contractors and others do not amount to a satisfactory alternative to supply.'

Who so advised him?

If there were legal problems, he had the law officers to advise him. If there were political problems, he had the Prime Minister and the Treasurer to advise him. He raised no queries with any of us. In this, as in every other aspect of the dismissal, he kept his doubts to himself or discovered them retrospectively.

The whole tenor of Sir John Kerr's book implies that the

---

1   The arrangements authorised by the statutory provisions had lapsed when Parliament passed the Budget on 11 November 1975.

crisis was of my Government's making and that my intransigence was the justification for his action. This turns the facts on their head. The Opposition precipitated the crisis; Mr Fraser's intransigence sustained it. And he could have maintained his attitude only if he had knowledge that Sir John Kerr would act as he did. Otherwise, he could not have kept his followers in line until 30 November. Sir John Kerr got Mr Fraser off the hook.

Sir John Kerr's action and book have had rough treatment at the hands of the lawyers. For instance, Geoffrey Sawer, the Emeritus Professor of Law at the Australian National University, has said that 'his Statement explaining his dismissal of Mr Whitlam is not a well drafted document'. It is now acknowledged that Sir John had been one of those judges whose judgments read best in the head-notes. He purports to support a royal prerogative in Australia to dismiss governments and to dissolve parliaments without mentioning founding fathers such as Deakin, Barton and Isaacs at all and by quoting Griffith in part and at second-hand. He feels free to quote some and ignore other statements by Menzies and Evatt among the last generation of lawyers and to follow Ellicott and ignore Byers among the present generation.

The seminar held at the University of Melbourne in August 1976 was attended by judges, including two justices of the High Court, and leading lawyers, academics and political scientists. The papers were published in *Labor and the Constitution*, edited by Gareth Evans and published by Heinemann (1977).

In their paper Professor Colin Howard, Hearn Professor of Law, and Cheryl Saunders, Lecturer in Law at the University, told the seminar:

In the events which happened it is possible to argue that by his intervention the Governor-General, far from giving effect to the intention of the Constitution, positively frustrated its express provisions.

The Chief Justice and the Governor-General, they said,

both adopt the proposition that a supply deadlock should be resolved by the resignation of the Prime Minister. If this is the correct position, it needs to be emphasized that it rests entirely on an unwritten convention which, so far as the present writers can discover, was invented for the purpose in hand in 1975. There is no precedent for it.

They condemned the Governor-General's 'unprecedented break with the well-established constitutional principle that the Crown acts on the advice of the representatives of the majority of the people (and has retained its nominal authority to act only because it habitually does so)'.

Professor Leslie Zines, Professor of Law at the Australian National University, told the seminar:

Section 57 was, of course, aimed at enabling the government, that is those who had the confidence of the House of Representatives, to go to the people where there was obstruction by the Senate . . . Neither the Governor-General nor Mr Fraser sought a double dissolution to resolve the deadlock between the Houses in relation to the specified twenty-one Bills. The Governor-General's only concern was with supply and Mr Fraser and his Party had in fact desired and obtained the defeat of the twenty-one Bills in the Senate

. . . the Governor-General's statement and his 'Detailed
Statement of Decisions' are most unsatisfactory in this regard.
Throughout both statements he concentrated on the particular
deadlock over supply. The Governor-General, therefore, did
not anywhere adequately explain the reason for his view that
only a double dissolution could promptly resolve the situation.

In 1977 Melbourne University Press published Professor
Sawer's book *Federation Under Strain*. The professor criticised
Sir John because:

he did not give Mr Whitlam a fair hearing, as he might have
been required to do by law and needed to do as a matter of
neutral and honourable dealing between the Crown and
ministers . . . If Sir John Kerr's dismissal of Mr Whitlam had
been judicially challenged . . . his action might have been
declared invalid on the ground of lack of fair hearing.

Secondly, Professor Sawer claims that the reason Sir John gave
for his action—the denial of Supply by the Senate:

was not by itself a sufficient conventional reason for such
action . . . the Governor-General's action was completely
without precedent. It is clear from the documents that he
acted for one reason only—because Mr Whitlam was unable
to get supply from the Senate. On no previous occasion in
Britain, Australia or any British-derived parliamentary
system has the Monarch or a Governor-General dismissed a
ministry having a majority in the Commons, Representatives
or similar House, because that ministry has been denied
supply by the Lords, Senate or similar House.

The professor went on:

> One might expect so grave a decision, obviously so
> prejudicial to the elected government in a parliament not yet
> eighteen months old, and in circumstances imperilling the
> reputation of the Governor-General's office, should not be
> taken until it was virtually certain that no change in the
> Senate's attitude would take place. This was not at all certain
> on 11 November 1975.
>
>   The proper ground for gubernatorial action in such
> circumstances, it is suggested, is the ground of illegality . . .
> On this view, the action on 11 November was even more
> plainly premature . . . It is sufficient to say here that there is
> a strong *prima facie* case for believing that the scheme
> proposed—advances by banks against certificates of
> government indebtedness, the banks to be reimbursed with
> interest when an Appropriation Act could be obtained—
> was legal . . . at 11 November 1975 the Governor-General
> had insufficient information as to either legality or
> practicality to justify a summary dismissal of the whole
> proposal.
>
>   Similarly with the Whitlam proposal for a half-Senate
> election on 13 December following . . . the Governor-
> General might at least have waited until the effect of the
> proposal on the opposition attitude, both officially and
> unofficially, was better known. A Governor-General more
> bent on conciliation would have been assisted by the definite
> decision on the half-election question.
>
>   . . . in the circumstances which actually existed on 11
> November 1975, and having regard to the way in which he
> acted, Sir John Kerr is open to the criticism of having

adopted a wrong procedure, based his decision on a
mistaken principle, and intervened prematurely.

He sums up:

. . . a majority in the House of Representatives elected
eighteen months previously, should not easily be overridden
by a Senate majority which in party terms represented the
opposition in the House of Representatives; that the
ministers holding the confidence of the House of
Representatives should not seem to be removed at the behest
of a Senate majority, with the Governor-General acting as
their executioner; and that the alternative ways of meeting
the obligations of the Commonwealth proposed by the
government should be investigated and even given some
trial.

It follows that the Governor-General's action was
premature. On 11 November 1975 he could not be
certain that his proper concern for the meeting of the
Commonwealth's legal obligations would fail to be satisfied
in any other way than by the action he then took, nor that
serious illegalities would occur unless he acted then. There
were three possibilities which were substantial enough to
warrant delay. The Senate half-election proposal might have
produced an electoral solution in sufficient although not
comfortably sufficient time, or before that a change in
political attitudes; political solutions were still possible, such
as fresh compromise proposals or changes in the attitude of
the Senate or of some of its Liberal members; the alternative
schemes for meeting at least the bulk of the government's
financial obligations when existing supply ran out in another

fortnight needed further consideration as to both legality and practicability and a short period of trial.

In his book Professor Sawer said that his 'procedural objection is to some extent conjectural because Sir John's account of the history is not available'. When, however, Sir John's book was published Professor Sawer was no less scathing in the review he wrote for the *Sydney Morning Herald* and the *Age*:

. . . The ground on which Sir John dismissed Mr Whitlam was failure to obtain Supply from the Senate and nothing else.

Sir John did not rely either on existing illegality or a future probability of illegality in the conduct of the Whitlam ministry.

His book does not depart from the reasoning in his letter of dismissal, but it does add at considerable length a further justification based on the obvious grounds of possible illegality and social breakdown if the appropriation crisis had continued.

He puts very strongly the view that the Governor-General can and should seek to act in good time to prevent such consequences—a clear theory of preventive justice.

My objection to all this is that the consequence is to elevate preservation of order to the status of an absolute and to demote the value of responsible government to the point of ignoring it.

Nothing in the book suggests that Sir John weighed the risks to responsible government of allowing the Senate to achieve its purely political objectives against the undoubted risks of allowing the crisis to continue.

By this course he gave effect to the interests of the
Senate, the Parliamentary Opposition and its leader as
against the interests of the Representatives, the
parliamentary majority and the Prime Minister.

Sir John himself relies largely on Menzies and Evatt. He
quotes Menzies' indignant press statement on 21 October 1975:

I think it would be a singular piece of impertinence on the
part of the Prime Minister to go to the Governor-General . . .
and ask him for a premature 'half-Senate' election . . . To
offer advice to the Governor-General on the lines that have
been hinted at would, I think, be both improper and
insulting.

Sir John apparently sees nothing ironic in relying on the
arguments of the great architect of premature half-Senate
elections. Menzies advised successive Governors-General, on 26
October 1955, 20 August 1958, 12 September 1961 and 1 October
1964, to ask the State Governors to issue writs for the election of
senators who were to begin their terms on 1 July following. Sir
John himself was not to find it impertinent, improper or
insulting of Mr Fraser to advise him on 26 October 1977 to
request the issue of writs for an election of senators on 10
December 1977 to begin their term on 1 July 1978.

Sir John Kerr devotes one of his chapters to 'Evatt and
Outside Advice'. He relies on an article, 'The Discretionary
Authority of Dominion Governors', which Evatt wrote for the
Canadian Bar Review in January 1940 to amplify the views he
had expressed in 1936 in *The King and His Dominion Governors*
(Oxford University Press).

Sir John learnt of this article when Mr Ellicott mentioned and tabled it in the House of Representatives in answer to a question by arrangement, but ostensibly without notice, on 13 October 1976. Sir John mentions that in his article Evatt had examined the 1914 double dissolution 'in the light of the contents of the background documents to which he had meantime gained access' and that Evatt had quoted the opinion which Sir Samuel Griffith had given as Chief Justice to the Governor-General at that time. Sir John quotes only from those parts of the Griffith memorandum which Evatt quoted and which Mr Ellicott tabled. The full memorandum is available at the National Library.

The Chief Justice's advice on that occasion was in respect to the Prime Minister's application for a double dissolution; Sir Garfield Barwick's advice was not on a double dissolution but on the termination of a Prime Minister's commission. Sir John can derive no comfort from Chief Justice Griffith for his action in dismissing me as Prime Minister. Evatt's article draws a distinction between 'cases where Ministers remain in full possession of the confidence of the Lower House and cases where they face, or have met with, defeat in that House'. The opening paragraph of the Griffith memorandum states:

> Under the Australian Constitution the Senate and the House
> of Representatives have equal authority, except as to one
> matter of procedure. But a working rule has for the present
> been adopted, based upon what is called the theory of
> Constitutional Government, which lays down that the
> continued life of an Administration is practically dependent
> solely upon its enjoying the confidence of a majority of the
> House of Representatives, and that it is sufficient if it enjoys

that confidence without regard to the views of the Senate. It
may be that in the future some modification of this working
rule will be found necessary, but for the present it must be
taken as we find it.

Griffith had been involved in the constitutional conflict on
money Bills in the mid-1880s between the Queensland
Legislative Assembly and Legislative Council which had gone
to the Privy Council; he had referred to this case at the 1890
Federal Convention and again in a judgment in 1907.

Sir Isaac Isaacs, who had had the most extensive and
distinguished experience as Victorian and Federal Attorney-
General and as a justice and Chief Justice of the High Court
before he was appointed Governor-General, was asked by the
Senate in June 1931, a time when there was an earlier recession
and Labor had a majority in the House of Representatives but
not in the Senate, to disregard the advice of his ministers and he
wrote back:

> If, as you request me to do, I should reject my ministers'
> advice, supported as it is by the considered opinion of the
> House of Representatives, and act upon the equally
> considered contrary opinion of the Senate, my conduct
> would, I fear, even on ordinary constitutional grounds,
> amount to an open personal preference of one House against
> the other, in other words an act of partisanship.

Sir Paul Hasluck in the Queale Lecture on which Sir John
drew in his speeches more than once said that a Prime Minister
occupies 'office only so long as a majority of the members of the
House of Representatives support him'; that 'The Government

is formed by the party which has the support of a majority of members in the popular House of Parliament'; and that 'The Governor-General's only advisers are his Ministers'. In the Queale Lecture Sir Paul discussed a Governor-General's power to refuse a dissolution when the Prime Minister seeks it; Sir John is putting this argument on its head when he tries to establish that a Governor-General has power to order a dissolution when a Prime Minister objects.

One State Governor, who had been, like Sir John, a Chief Justice of the Supreme Court of his State, has since expressed the view that the only time a Governor-General could use his reserve powers to dismiss a Prime Minister is when the Prime Minister, having secured Supply, proposes to continue in office without holding an election for the House of Representatives after the term of the House has expired. Mr Yeend, who is now the Secretary of the Department of the Prime Minister and Cabinet,[2] has expressed the views of all the departmental heads in Canberra when, as the *National Times* reported in November 1978, he 'privately told friends he believes Kerr was guilty of a severe error' in the way he moved without warning and sacked the Whitlam Government.

One of the disturbing aspects of Sir John's and Mr Fraser's co-operation on 11 November 1975 is that the documents which they subsequently exchanged on the double dissolution have not yet been tabled.[3] The correspondence between the Prime Minister and the Governor-General before the double dissolution on 30 July 1914 was tabled on 8 October of that year;

---

2   Sir Geoffrey Yeend, Secretary of the Department of Prime Minister and Cabinet, 1978–86.

3   The documents were tabled by Mr Fraser on 20 February 1979.

the correspondence on the double dissolution of 19 March 1951 was tabled on 24 May 1956; the correspondence on the double dissolution of 11 April 1974 was tabled on 29 October 1975, immediately after the High Court had handed down all its judgments on the Bills passed at the joint sitting which followed the dissolution. Mr Fraser and his latest Attorney-General have refused requests to table such letters as passed between Mr Fraser and Sir John.

Sir Robert Menzies' view on a Governor-General's discretion to grant a double dissolution was demonstrated when Sir William Slim was chosen to succeed Sir William McKell. Churchill asked Menzies to allow Slim to head an Anglo-US mission to Nasser. Menzies agreed, but reluctantly. He let Churchill know by cable on 20 February 1953 that he might have to seek another double dissolution and, since he had had the greatest difficulty in getting one in 1951, he wanted a new Governor-General as soon as possible. In March, the month after I was sworn in as a member of Parliament, Mr Menzies, as he still was, was asked a question without notice concerning the delay in Sir William Slim assuming the office of Governor-General to which he had been appointed four months before. He replied, 'I have read the cabled story about the possibility of Sir William Slim going to some foreign country. I know of no foundation for it.' This was scarcely an honest answer.

In the upshot, the Americans refused to co-sponsor the Slim mission and Slim was installed as Governor-General in time for any eventuality in Australia. Menzies had appeared to go along with Britain in the hope of securing America's support against Egypt. This experience in 1953 should have alerted him against his humiliation over Suez in 1956 at the hands of another patronising British Prime Minister and the same devious Dulles.

Sir Howard Beale has written that Menzies' 'self-esteem . . . did militate sometimes against his success on the international scene . . . he overestimated his own influence and allowed himself to be used'.

Sir John has quoted many documents in his book where, presumably, he has thought it would suit his case to do so. It is remarkable that he has not included the correspondence between Mr Fraser and himself on the double dissolution.

Nothing more clearly shows that his ordering of a double dissolution was a mere device than his failure to order a referendum to alter the Constitution to provide for simultaneous elections and synchronised terms for the Senate and the House of Representatives. Where either House twice passes and the other House twice rejects a proposed law for the alteration of the Constitution, the Governor-General may submit that law to the electors. Whatever doubts there may be about a Governor-General's right to intervene in other cases of dispute between the two Houses, there can be no doubt about his powers to hold a referendum on his own initiative at a time of his own choosing in the circumstances which obtained at that time.

Mr Fraser had incited the Senate to reject twice the Constitution Alteration (Simultaneous Elections) Bill passed by the House. I had told Sir John that I was going to advise him to put this referendum to the electors himself on the same date which I was advising him to propose to the State Governors for the election of half the Senate.

Sir John has written in his book (p. 365):

I next made the point [to Mr Fraser on 11 November 1975] that in my understanding the Parliament was deadlocked not only on supply but on twenty-one bills which the

previous Government had passed and his parties had
rejected in the Senate. It seemed to me that all deadlocks
should be dealt with and should go to the people.

If Sir John had been sincere in wanting to let the people
decide all outstanding issues between the Labor Party and the
Liberal–Country Party coalition he would have ordered not
only a double dissolution on the spurious ground of the other
twenty-one Bills, but also a referendum on the disputed
Constitution Alteration (Simultaneous Elections) Bill. He could
not have a double dissolution without seeking Mr Fraser's
advice; he was able to hold this referendum without the advice
of any Prime Minister.

A similar Bill was approved in May 1974 by a majority of the
electors in New South Wales but was rejected, although only
narrowly, by the electors in the other five States and by the
electors of the six States as a whole. The Bill was again passed
twice by the House of Representatives and rejected by the
Senate in 1975. It was available for submission to the people in
December 1975. The referendum would also have solved a new
problem which had just emerged. Until 1974 Governors of the
States had always issued writs for Senate elections in their States
on a date requested of them by the Governor-General on the
advice of the Prime Minister. There was every justification and
every precedent for an election for half the Senate at the end of
1975. The Federal Council of the Liberal Party, however, passed
a resolution on 12 October 1975 calling on the Federal and State
parliamentary parties and Liberals everywhere to do all in their
power to prevent the Whitlam Government gaining control of
the Senate. This was an instruction to non-Labor Premiers to
advise their State Governors not to issue writs for an election of

half the Senate if they were requested by the Governor-General to do so.

In Melbourne Cup week Sir John Kerr and Sir Roden Cutler were guests of Sir Henry Winneke at Government House. The two Governors discussed with Sir John the Liberal Federal Council's instruction that their Premiers should ignore any request which he made to them to issue writs for a half-Senate election. Both Governors felt they would have to take the advice of their Premiers. It would have been an outrage for Premier Lewis and for Premier Bjelke-Petersen to prevent the people of their States from choosing successors to Senators Field and Bunton.[4] Each would have been capable of such an outrage. Premier Hamer was at least reluctant but had nevertheless told his Governor that there were occasions when one had to go along with one's Party. Sir John Kerr had been mortified by the High Court's review of Sir Paul Hasluck's discretion in granting a double dissolution in April 1974 on the Petroleum and Minerals Authority Bill among others. He was most apprehensive at the possibility of a further unprecedented rebuff to a Governor-General.

After going back to Canberra he decided on 6 November that he would terminate my commission and seek Mr Fraser's advice for a double dissolution. He saw Mr Fraser that morning and he saw me and Mr Enderby that afternoon. He knew that I was still considering advising him to set in train the process for a half-Senate election and also for a referendum on the Constitution Alteration (Simultaneous Elections) Bill. Over the next few days he prepared all the documents for service on me and signature by Mr Fraser. It is hard to understand why he did

4   See Extended Biographies.

not prepare the documents for a referendum which would not only have minimised the chances of future conflicts between the Senate and the House of Representatives but would also have obviated any further rebuffs to Governors-General making requests to State Governors to issue Senate election writs.

The only explanation of his conduct is that he wanted to save Mr Fraser and his colleagues the humiliation of a referendum which they had opposed in and outside the Parliament since it was first recommended by the Constitution Review Committee in 1958.

By 1976 Mr Fraser, Senator Withers and the Liberals had come to realise that under their policies Australia's economic position was declining at home and abroad and that their political situation would deteriorate greatly by the time of the next Senate elections, which had to be held before July 1978. They therefore saw advantage in synchronising those elections with the elections for the House of Representatives, which did not have to be held until February 1979, the third anniversary of the first meeting of the House. At a meeting of the Constitutional Convention in Hobart in October 1976 they supported a motion by Mr Bowen for another referendum on the 1974 Constitution Alteration (Simultaneous Elections) Bill. After two decades of inaction and rejection the Liberals themselves introduced a Constitution Alteration (Simultaneous Elections) Bill.

The referendum was submitted to the electors in May 1977 and this time was approved by 62.2 per cent of them. In New South Wales, Victoria and South Australia there were 70.7, 64.4 and 65.9 per cent majorities. The Premiers of Queensland and Western Australia had not opposed the motion in Hobart but had no compunction in campaigning against their Federal colleagues and were able to reduce the support for the referendum in their States to 47.5 and 48.4 per cent respectively. (Tasmania, as often in constitutional referendums, trailed the field with 34.2 per cent support.) Therefore, although a great majority of Australians wanted this reform to come about, it did not do so because it did not have the support of a majority of the States as required by the Constitution. If Sir John Kerr had put this referendum to the people in December 1975 the Premiers of Queensland and Western Australia would not have opposed it. It would have been carried by no smaller an overall vote throughout the country and Sir John might have made one constructive contribution to Australian public life.

Sir Garfield Barwick's intrusion has had as harsh things said about it as has Sir John Kerr's conduct. At the August 1976 seminar Professor Colin Howard and Cheryl Saunders said:

> Despite Sir Garfield Barwick's unargued assertion to the contrary, it was far from inconceivable that the matters upon which his advice was given would be challenged before the High Court at some future time . . . had the Australian Labor Party won the election and the twenty-one double dissolution Bills been passed at a joint sitting, it would have been perfectly possible for the procedural passage of any one of those twenty-one Bills to have been challenged before the High Court, directly raising some of the issues canvassed in the Chief Justice's opinion. It should not have been the part either of the Chief Justice or of the Governor-General to make assumptions about the result of the election.

In his book Professor Sawer sums up on the Chief Justice's 'injudicious advice':

In 1975, it was particularly unwise of the Governor-General
to seek the advice of the Chief Justice, and of the Chief
Justice to give it. The Governor-General did not have the
consent of the Prime Minister . . . In the list of undecided
cases before the High Court at that time was one in which a
declaration and injunction were sought to prevent the
holding of any further federal elections until an electoral
redistribution should take place . . . as the situation stood on
10 November 1975 the Chief Justice was not entitled to
presume any particular outcome for that case.

The advice given to the Governor-General was
questionable in four respects. First, he said he was free to
give advice because the situation 'was unlikely to come
before the [High] court'. This, however, was an unwarranted
assumption.

. . . Secondly, the Chief Justice asserts a rigid correlation
between inability to obtain supply and necessity to advise
election, resign or be dismissed. He gives no authority
whatever for his assertion.

. . . Thirdly, the Chief Justice confuses the law and the
conventions of the Constitution so as to produce a fallacious
statement of the relevant convention. He does this by
asserting an analogy between the United Kingdom position
of a government in relation to the House of Commons, and
the position of an Australian government in relation to
both Houses . . . The 'responsibility' of an Australian
Commonwealth government is solely to the House of
Representatives.

Fourthly, the Chief Justice keeps introducing the notion
of a 'duty' cast on the Governor-General . . . This was all
thoroughly misleading. In none of these complex political

situations can there be said to be legal duties . . . the Chief
Justice carefully abstained from saying plainly how far he
was dealing with legal duties and how far moral duties, just
as he abstained from saying how far his statements as to
authority, duty and responsibility were based on law and
how far on convention.

Sir John Kerr makes the astonishing admission that on 10
November Sir Garfield Barwick and he 'agreed that the text of
his letter would not at that stage be released, future release being
left for future decision'. Sir John condescended to let the public
see Sir Garfield's letter on 18 November, but only because
portions of Mr Byers' opinion had in the meantime appeared in
the press.

Sir Garfield Barwick did nothing to retrieve his reputation
by his appearance and answers at the National Press Club on 10
June 1976. On this occasion he revealed that Sir John Kerr had
said 'he was troubled in his mind' about the course of political
events as early as 20 September—nearly a month before the
blocking of Supply. This exchange of confidences took place at
the annual dinner of members of the Order of St Michael and St
George (NSW and ACT Groups) at the Union Club in Sydney.
In May 1977 the Constitution Alteration (Retirement of Judges)
referendum—setting a retirement age of seventy years for
future High Court justices—was supported by 80.1 per cent of
the electors and was carried not only in every State but in every
electorate in the country. Sir Garfield Barwick, born 22 June
1903, remains Chief Justice.[5]

---

5   Sir Garfield Barwick, Chief Justice of the High Court, 1964–81.
     See Extended Biographies.

Nothing in Sir John Kerr's book and nothing which has been revealed since 11 November 1975 calls for modification of the assessment made by Donald Horne in his passionate polemic *Death of the Lucky Country* (Penguin Books Australia, 1976), published within weeks of the dismissal:

What happened?

This: The Governor-General secretly made a decision, the effect of which was to support the political plans of the Liberal and National Country Parties.

Against all contemporary practice he did not discuss that decision with the government that was then in power. But having contemplated the decision secretly he secretly got for it the support of the Chief Justice, a person of no more constitutional significance in this matter than you or me, but one whose respected office could seem to give extra authority to what the Governor-General had decided. The Governor-General then mounted a time-tabled operation, for which the phrase 'constitutional *coup d'état*' seems a useful description. It was an operation which had the general effect of leaving the Prime Minister with a false sense of security, then, without discussing any alternatives, kicking him out of office, installing the minority leader as Prime Minister, then dissolving Parliament. It all happened so quickly that no preventive action could be taken.

10

BREACH OF FAITH

'OR BY PRONOUNCING OF SOME DOUBTFUL PHRASE,
AS "WELL, WELL, WE KNOW," OR "WE COULD AN IF WE WOULD,"
OR "IF WE LIST TO SPEAK," OR "THERE BE
AN IF THEY MIGHT,"
OR SUCH AMBIGUOUS GIVING OUT . . .'

Shakespeare, *Hamlet*, I, v

In his letter of 11 November to the Governor-General, in which he accepted the commission to form a 'caretaker' government on the terms specified by Sir John Kerr, Mr Fraser undertook that: 'There will be no royal commissions or inquiries into the activities of the previous government throughout the period of the election campaign.' This undertaking was not honoured by Mr Fraser nor enforced by Sir John Kerr. The insertion of this condition was gratuitous. It had no relevance to the constitutional or legal questions surrounding the dismissal of my Government. It was a veiled reference to the loan affair—the political justification which Mr Fraser and the Senate had claimed from the outset of the crisis. The reference in Mr Fraser's letter was clearly intended to revive the issue and set it squarely in place as part of the denouement of 11 November.

There was, of course, no such reference in Sir John Kerr's statement of his reasons for his action or in his letter to me withdrawing my commission. By including it in Mr Fraser's terms of acceptance Sir John Kerr and Mr Fraser clearly intended that the matter should form part of the underlying justification for the constitutional upheaval they had brought about.

The abruptness of my dismissal and the secrecy through which it had been achieved caused deep shock and bewilderment throughout the nation, not least among Liberal supporters who believed in the conventions behind the Constitution and the traditions of the Westminster system. Their unease and concern at the conduct of the Senate in October and November was reflected in the opinion polls in those weeks and explained in large measure the rapid turnaround in public opinion in favour of my Government. Such people found it difficult to accept that the reasons published by Sir John Kerr were the sole reasons for his action. It was to them incredible that a twice-elected government in unchallengeable possession of the confidence of the House of Representatives, a government whose political position was manifestly strengthened day by day, should be unceremoniously sacked just when the crisis seemed on the point of resolution, if the formal grounds given by the Governor-General were the real grounds and the sole grounds. For such people, there had to be another reason, 'the real reason', the hidden reason, the reason why the Queen's representative had to act in the way he did, when he did— some scandal, some illegality, the missing link which when known would explain all. There is no doubt that such people, still uneasy about what happened on 11 November 1975, three years later keenly anticipated that Sir John Kerr's book would give the answer and provide the real clue; he has let them down too.

For the immediate purposes of November 1975, however, the reference in Mr Fraser's letter, the gratuitous undertaking against 'royal commissions or inquiries' served a necessary purpose. It was a hint and a not very subtle one at that. Those who had never read the Constitution could at least read between the lines. The purpose of the undertaking was to place the imprimatur of the Governor-General, the Queen's representative, on the Opposition's wildest assertions (for there were never and have never been any specific allegations) of improper conduct by my Government particularly in the matter of our loan raising proposal; it achieved that purpose. Yet as I have said and as I shall show, even that undertaking was not honoured by Mr Fraser nor enforced by Sir John Kerr. Indeed, Mr Fraser's conduct was not unlike that of Mr Menzies in the election campaign of 1954. He had undertaken that the defection of the Soviet agent Vladimir Petrov would not be raised during the campaign. He personally did not mention it. The Leader of the Country Party, Arthur Fadden, did the dirty work, airing a range of allegations, subsequently disproved, about Dr Evatt and his staff. In 1975 the dirty work was again left to the Country Party.

In Chapter 4 I dealt with the loan matter, Sir John Kerr's involvement in it and his attitude towards it, up to the special sitting on 9 July. That is a critical date; every matter of substance surrounding the circumstances of our proposal from its origins in October 1974 to its aborted end on 20 May 1975 were raised and answered in the House of Representatives and the Senate. Paradoxically the debate that should have brought the affair to an end marked the beginning of Sir John Kerr's concern about it. It was the public controversy which created retrospectively his private doubts. I shall now take my account as far towards its end as a private prosecution, still pending after three years, permits.[1]

In October Mr Khemlani arrived back in Australia but not a solitary senator was found to suggest that evidence should be called from him. In the House of Representatives, Fred Daly, its most accomplished leader in the quarter of a century of my service in it, delivered this *coup de grâce* to him and the Liberals who now sponsored him:

> I am in a position to give the honourable member a full and complete answer to that question. I understand that yesterday [27 October 1975] afternoon a Commonwealth ministerial car was booked by the Deputy Leader of the Opposition to meet Ansett flight 361, 2.10 p.m. from Sydney, and that of course commenced a drama in Canberra yesterday that has rarely been equalled. The car was to meet a person named Mr Khemlani. I understand that the gentleman approached the Commonwealth car dressed in a safari suit and wearing dark glasses. He was met by bearded investigators who hustled him into the VIP room while the Commonwealth car backed into the normally restricted luggage area and his 8 bulging briefcases were loaded into it.
>
> Mr Khemlani was then pushed into the Commonwealth car along with 2 sinister bearded staff members and taken on a high speed car chase through the back streets of Fyshwick reaching speeds of 100 kilometres per hour, turning down side streets and doing sudden U turns before coming to a

---

1   This matter was concluded. See Extended Biographies.

sudden stop at his destination—a $23 a night room at the Hotel Wellington. Mr Khemlani, still using the car, and the men then disappeared into room 49—the room adjoining the motel shoe-shine box. Lemonade, potato chips and 2 Sydney afternoon papers were pushed through the breakfast hatch. He stayed locked in his room while the staff members stayed huddled in a corner sifting through his 8 suitcases of documents. Later in the afternoon Mr Khemlani was taken on another high speed car chase. This time, as a taxi pulled up at the front of the motel, Mr Khemlani disappeared out the back door and sped off in a late model gold Torana with the manager of the Wellington Hotel at the wheel. That is service. It raced through the peak hour traffic, went one and a half times round State Circle, and reached speeds of up to 120 km along Commonwealth Avenue before swinging around and returning to the hotel. Then Mr Khemlani disappeared.

An hour later his brief cases were lugged into a lift at the $33 a night Lakeside Hotel where Mr Khemlani usually stays. But he was not booked in there last night. Last night Mr Khemlani was locked up with 2 Opposition front benchers, Mr Bob Ellicott and Mr John Howard, going through suitcases full of documents. As if he were not in enough trouble without being locked up with them! I come back again to the Commonwealth car. Poor Mr Khemlani: he had come all the way from Singapore, at his own cost and without a visa, to clear his name and he had all that excess baggage with him. What must he think of Australia—his life was endangered by high speed car chases in Commonwealth cars; his bags were searched by bearded investigators, and as far as we know they were not false

beards; he was booked into a $23 a night room next to a
shoe-shine box yet his bags were booked into a $33 a night
international hotel; he was locked up all afternoon with
bearded men and then all night with 2 members of the
Opposition . . . And then fed with peanuts. He must also be
wondering why the Opposition would pay out all that
money for his bags but was too lousy to pay for a taxi fare
for him to go from the airport to the hotel. That brings me
back to the original point about the misuse of a
Commonwealth car.

The Khemlani documents had been inspected in the
presence of his solicitor, John Francis Licardy, by Mr Ellicott
and John Howard, MP, a Sydney solicitor. Mr Ellicott told the
press that in the eight suitcases of documents he had seen nothing
which involved me. His statement touched off an urgent meeting
of the Liberal parliamentary hierarchy. Mr Ellicott then had to
issue an amplification—the first of many I shall have to record—
that he couldn't imagine I wasn't involved.

In Parliament the Liberals had spent an immense amount of
time making allegations or insinuations against me or my
ministers and had turned up nothing illegal or improper on our
part. They never moved to call Mr Khemlani before either
House. The scene now passed outside the Federal Parliament.

On 21 October 1975 Mr Ellicott had presented a petition
from one of his constituents, Danny Sankey, a Sydney solicitor
in private practice, stating that he wanted to prosecute me, Mr
Connor, Dr Cairns and Mr Justice Murphy under the
Commonwealth Crimes Act and asking leave to serve
'subpoenae' (sic) for the documents tabled and the Hansard
transcripts taken in the House on 9 July 1975.

On Sunday 2 November Mr Fraser called a summit conference of conservative chieftains in his Melbourne office. From the Federal Parliament there were Mr Lynch, the Deputy Leader of the Opposition, Senators Withers and Greenwood, the Leader and Deputy Leaders of the Opposition in the Senate, Messrs Anthony and Sinclair, Leader and Deputy Leader of the Country Party, Senator Cotton and Messrs Nixon and Ellicott. From the State Parliaments there were Premiers Hamer, Lewis and Bjelke-Petersen and Dr Tonkin and Mr Bingham, the Leaders of the Opposition in South Australia and Tasmania. The Liberal leaders in the Queensland and Western Australian Parliaments, Sir Charles Court and Sir Gordon Chalk, did not attend.

According to Mr Ellicott's ministerial statement of 6 May 1976 the meeting discussed rumours of improper dealings in relation to overseas loans. The name of Wiley Fancher was mentioned to the Premier of Queensland as a person who was understood to have information in connection with these rumours. The Premier was asked if he would be prepared to have the matters referred to in the rumours investigated. He said he would. A month later Mr Ellicott in an amplification said that Mr Fancher's name had been mentioned by Mr Anthony and Mr Lynch. Mr Anthony put it more bluntly:

> A gentleman by the name of Mr Wiley Fancher was known to have information which could lead to the exposure of some of the facts. When this was told to the Premier of Queensland he quite willingly said: I will investigate this matter, I will get to the bottom of it.

Mr Fancher and Queensland Police Inspector Keen were sent overseas by the Premier in the first week of November.

On 14 November the Premier wrote to Mr Richard Bradburn Todd, a New York investment banker, in these terms:

> I hereby appoint you as my financial adviser concerning loan raising efforts by the Australian Government that was dismissed on 11 November 1975. . . In acting as my personal adviser, you are requested to co-operate with Mr W. A. R. Rae, Agent-General for Queensland.

Mr Anthony saw nothing wrong with the Premier continuing his investigation during the election campaign:

> But one of the conditions of dismissal was that there would be no further investigation by the Commonwealth Government into the overseas borrowing affair. That did not have any bearing on the Premier of Queensland. He had every right to continue to seek whatever information he could, and thank goodness he had the courage and the determination to find out the facts . . . Maybe the Premier of Queensland has not succeeded but, my word, he did his best to get to the bottom of it. What he did, he did of his own accord. He did it without the help of the Commonwealth . . . But I do say that the Premier of Queensland ought to be commended and not ridiculed for his actions.

On 3 December a statement issued by Mr Bjelke-Petersen confirmed that Mr Rae and Inspector Keen had been undertaking investigations into loans in London, Zurich and Geneva for about four weeks. The same day the Deputy Premier, Sir Gordon Chalk, told Parliament:

> I have some knowledge of a visit outside Britain by the
> Agent-General. The matter was handled by the Premier and
> has not been discussed at Cabinet level. Because of that, I
> have no personal knowledge of the nature of the visit.
> However, I could not deny that I understand that the visit
> has taken place.

The next day the Premier told the press that at no time had he authorised any statement about an investigation. The Police Minister, Mr Hodges, however, told Parliament:

> I am unaware of the episode other than that a police officer
> was requested by the Premier to do a certain job for him
> overseas. Other than that I am not aware of any other
> circumstances associated with the duty he had to perform.

On 5 December the *Courier Mail* stated that the Prime Minister had been 'informed' of the mission. The *Courier Mail*'s article raised a number of questions about the investigation. It asked whether the Premier had consulted his deputy, the Liberal leader, Sir Gordon Chalk, or the Cabinet as a whole, about Mr Rae's secret expedition in Switzerland. The article continued:

> Was Mr Rae, assisted by a Queensland police inspector, sent
> to Switzerland only to gather loans information which might
> be damaging to the former Prime Minister (Mr Whitlam)?
> Was Inspector Keen sent overseas as a bodyguard for Mr

Rae or as an investigator? It is extraordinary that the Police
Minister (Mr Hodges) was not informed of the purpose of
Inspector Keen's mission . . . The Prime Minister (Mr
Fraser) is said to have been informed of the mission. But
when? It would be strange if he had been told before Sir
Gordon Chalk or Mr Hodges.

It would not have been strange at all. The Prime Minister
was the man who stood to gain from the investigation. It had
been planned in his Melbourne office. Its whole purpose was to
assist the Fraser campaign. Sir Gordon Chalk was not at the
meeting in Mr Fraser's office in Melbourne on 2 November, nor
was Mr Hodges.

Does anyone seriously believe that Mr Fraser was not told of
the inquiries? Does anyone seriously believe that he was not
aware of them? On 3 December he had revealed in Launceston
that the Australian Ambassador in Switzerland had sought
advice on whether he should assist the Queensland Government's investigation. The Ambassador was promptly and
properly told that he should have no part of it.

On 8 December, the Monday before polling day, Mr
Sankey's prosecution came on at Queanbeyan Court. We
defendants were not present but were represented by counsel.
Mr Sankey's counsel demanded that bench warrants be issued
for our arrests.

The following day, the last day the Queensland Parliament
sat that year, the Premier made a ministerial statement in these
terms:

Some weeks ago certain information came to my knowledge
concerning the loan-raising activities of the Whitlam

Government and the involvement of secret commissions—
and, I reiterate, the involvement of secret commissions. That
information was of such a nature and was attributable to
such sources that it appeared to me to concern matters of
substance that warranted verification through prudent
inquiry . . . I saw it as my duty to have such inquiries made
on my behalf. Those inquiries have now been made. As a
result, l am in possession of considerably more material
which satisfied me that I was completely justified in having
those inquiries carried out. In one deal alone, it is now clear
that two Ministers of the Whitlam Government together
with a number of other people, were due to receive
staggering sums of money as a consequence of secret
commissions and kick-backs . . . In anticipation that a royal
commission will be held, l do not propose to disclose at this
time any details of the material or of the persons implicated
and so prejudice the conduct of that inquiry.

The Premier was astute enough not to specify the ministers.
On the same day Sir Gordon Chalk said, 'I met Fancher for
the first time on Sunday afternoon for 30 to 40 minutes. I do not
know where he is at the present time.'

As I have since twice stated in the Parliament, the Fraser
Government got others to do its dirty work during the election
campaign. I repeat, Mr Fraser did not honour his undertaking
to the Governor-General and the Governor-General did not
enforce Mr Fraser's undertaking to him. One assumes that His
Excellency had ceased to read and cut out the daily papers
throughout this period.

One would have thought that after the election Mr Sankey's
and Mr Bjelke-Petersen's activities would have served their

purpose. Those activities, however, continued. I shall now give some of the further uncontested facts which have emerged in the last three years in the House of Representatives concerning the Sankey and Bjelke-Petersen initiatives.

Mr Ellicott displaced Mr Fraser's first Attorney-General, Senator Ivor Greenwood, before Christmas 1975. We who were being prosecuted by Mr Sankey wrote on 20 January 1976 through our solicitors to Mr Ellicott seeking legal aid. He wrote back refusing it. In March Mr Fraser had a question asked about the case and showed by his reply that he was most interested that it should proceed and would be discussing it with Mr Ellicott.

Mr Ellicott decided to obtain statements from Mr Byers, Mr Harders, Mr Rose and another officer of his Department and from a former secretary and an officer of the Executive Council. He asked the Crown Solicitor to submit the statements to Counsel. The Counsel chosen comprised Mr D. G. McGregor, QC, now a judge of the ACT Supreme Court,[2] and Mr W. H. Denton, QC. In August 1976 they advised against the success of the prosecution. By this time Mr Ellicott knew Mr Byers' advice, which on 9 July 1975 he had said 'might satisfy a lot of us'. He was still not satisfied.

The proceedings were becoming expensive for us defendants. Mr Connor and I had taken the matter to the Supreme Court of New South Wales where it was heard by Mr Justice Lee; he had, incidentally, been the Liberal candidate against me in 1954. We appealed to the Court of Appeal (Street CJ, Moffitt P. and Reynolds JA). The hearing took six days in June 1976. The judgment was delivered in October. In 1977 it was Mr Sankey's turn to appeal. The hearing before the Court

---

2   See Extended Biographies.

of Appeal (Moffitt P. and Reynolds and Hutley JJA) took place on 13, 14 and 15 April. On 20 April Dr Cairns, Mr Connor and I again sought legal aid from Mr Ellicott. On 9 May the Court of Appeal delivered judgment. We were advised that we should apply for special leave to appeal to the High Court.

Later that month Mr Ellicott took our application for legal aid to Cabinet, which decided that our costs should be paid. Mr Ellicott did not convey that decision to us. In June Mr Connor and I called on him and then our solicitors wrote to him to ask him to take over the proceedings. He did not reply until 17 June and even then did not mention the question of costs. We did not think we could proceed without legal aid and on 29 June we had to advise the High Court that we would not proceed with our application to it.

The decision about costs was not communicated to us until 13 August. For three months we had been left in the dark and our interests had been prejudiced by the financial limitations we thought we were enduring. If we had known that our costs would be paid we would have proceeded with the High Court appeal. The Court could quite conceivably have overturned the decision of the Court of Appeal; in November 1978 the High Court rejected the views expressed by the Chief Justice and the President in the earlier Court of Appeal case. Where does that leave Mr Ellicott's opinion?

For some time now Mr Fraser had been convinced that no good could come of the Sankey prosecution. He realised that there was no prospect of a conviction and that the mere giving of evidence was certain to blow up in his face. He was particularly exasperated with Mr Ellicott, who he thought had a fixation in persecuting me and my ministers. In May Cabinet had not only decided to pay our costs but also decided to claim privilege in respect of documents which had been subpoenaed not only by Mr Sankey but by us. Mr Ellicott took strong exception to the decision and resigned. After discussion with Mr Fraser, however, it was agreed that the question of privilege would be resubmitted to the Cabinet and he would abide by its decision. The matter came before Cabinet again on 26 July 1977.

Mr Ellicott had asked Sir Frederick Wheeler for a statement at the same time as he had sought statements from the Solicitor-General and from officers of his Department and the Executive Council. Sir Frederick refused, taking the view that he was not entitled to know what took place during my Administration or to see any relevant file.

On 26 July Mr Ellicott sought permission from Cabinet to interview and obtain statements from Sir Frederick and other persons who were in the employ of the Commonwealth or its instrumentalities. Cabinet refused. Proceedings became very heated. Mr Ellicott was asked to produce Mr Byers' opinion. Cabinet made it plain to him that in its view he should take over the proceedings and terminate them but left it to him to decide whether he should take over the case. Mr Ellicott then again approached Sir Frederick Wheeler and other departmental heads. They would not oblige him.

On 2 August he informed Mr Fraser that he proposed to take over the proceedings. On 3 August Mr Fraser saw him at the Lodge and reiterated his view that the proceedings ought to be taken over and terminated. On 4 August he again saw Mr Fraser and offered to resign. Since the Prime Minister was going overseas they agreed to consider the matter the following week.

On 5 August Mr Ellicott received the following letter from Mr Justice Murphy:

I wish to make it clear that I have not joined in any application to you to take over the conduct of the prosecution of the proceedings brought by Mr Sankey. If the proceedings were taken over in order to put an end to them I could not object but if they were taken over with the intention of continuing them I would strongly object as they are in my opinion malicious. In any case you should not be involved in any official decision which adversely affects the defendants. Your personal involvement in this affair including certain statements in Parliament should as a matter of simple justice preclude you from acting as Attorney-General in any way against the defendants. As you are well aware there are ways in which any necessary decision can be made without your participation.

On 13 August Mr Ellicott wrote to my solicitors that he had decided not to take over the proceedings. He then went overseas for three weeks. During his absence he was upset by some adverse press stories which he regarded as having been planted by the Prime Minister's press secretary. On 6 September 1977 he resigned.

In the debate on his resignation I summed up:

I believe that the whole core of this matter is that the former Attorney-General has had an obsession about it extending over more than two years. He has taken an excessively vain attitude about his legal opinions. We all know the attitude he took concerning the right of the Viceroy to dismiss a government if it did not have a majority in both federal Houses, an opinion on which the Governor-General acted on 11 November 1975, but he has also had this obsession to defend the opinion he expressed on 9 July 1975, and he has expressed it again and again . . .

These proceedings were conceived notionally as a private prosecution. They were initiated with the incitement of the New South Wales branch of the Liberal Party. They were timed in such a way as to conflict with the undertaking which the caretaker Prime Minister gave the Governor-General . . . They were conceived in breach of an undertaking. They have been promoted and prolonged to this stage through the various methods which Mr Ellicott has now disclosed . . . All I must say now is that we see how flimsy the whole of this thing has been. It has absorbed the time of the New South Wales Courts, it has absorbed the time of the Federal Ministry, it has even absorbed some of the time of this Parliament—all to no good purpose whatever. It has all been done to serve the vanity of a man who has now resigned.

I have said no more about this case than what emerges uncontested from Hansard; I can say no more, because it is still before the court—at Queanbeyan![3]

It did not take so long for Mr Bjelke-Petersen's initiative to miscarry.

On the Wednesday after the elections Mr Fraser's first Attorney-General, Senator Greenwood, conferred in Melbourne with Mr Fancher and Mr Spann, the Under-Secretary of the Premier's Department. Mr Harders was also present. It took almost two years for these facts to come out. They were admitted by Mr Fraser's third Attorney-General, Senator Durack, on 2 November 1977.

---

3   See Extended Biographies.

On 18 March 1976 Mr Ellicott, who had become Mr Fraser's second Attorney-General, made a 'carefully worded statement' in answer to a question by a Liberal backbencher:

> Last year and early this year the Premier of Queensland, Mr Bjelke-Petersen, supplied to the Federal Government certain information which suggested that two Ministers of the Labor Government and a senior official still in the Commonwealth Public Service might have been involved in attempts to obtain for themselves kick-back commissions on proposed loan borrowings by the Labor Government. The information included notarised statements and other documents which pointed to the possible existence overseas of a mandate signed by the Ministers and of an associated document implicating the official, which mandate and associated document evidenced the attempts to obtain the kick-backs.
>
> The information was discussed with the Solicitor-General, the Secretary of the Attorney-General's Department, the Permanent Head of the official's Department and the Chairman of the Public Service Board. With their concurrence it was decided that in view of the fact that the information implicated a senior public servant the Government was bound to institute inquiries to ascertain whether there was any substance in it. Thorough inquiries have since taken place overseas. As a result of these inquiries the Government is completely satisfied that there is no substance in the suggestion that either the official or the two Ministers were involved in the wrongful conduct.

On 23 March the Premier told the Queensland Parliament that expenditure on his investigations incurred to date and charged to departmental votes was $10 456.64; this included an amount of $939.40 in respect of air fares to and from Melbourne and Canberra for discussions with and at the request of Commonwealth authorities and did not include costs of overseas telephone calls not expected to exceed $1000.

On 17 March Mr Fraser had received a letter and a number of documents from Mr Todd. Mr Todd told Mr Fraser:

> Mr Fancher stated that he was in daily direct contact with
> you through Mr Douglas Anthony and Mr Phillip Lynch.
> Mr Fancher stated that you had a gentlemen's agreement
> with Governor-General Sir John Kerr not to pursue the
> Whitlam situation until after the general election on
> 13 December 1975. If I had known this while in the
> United States I would not have accepted the appointment
> by the Premier.

I received copies from Mr Todd on 5 May. At Question Time the next day I asked Mr Fraser if he had received the correspondence and replied to it. He replied that he thought it unnecessary to reply because it did not in any sense, shape or form involve the Commonwealth Government. In answer to another question, Mr Ellicott said he had not kept any statistics about the number of times he had conferred with the Premier since becoming Attorney-General and could not answer how often Mr Fancher had accompanied the Premier.

Thereupon I held a press conference to release Mr Todd's correspondence. That night Mr Ellicott made an amplification by way of a ministerial statement. His memory had now improved sufficiently for him to say that he had conferred with the Premier in Canberra on 15 January in the presence of Mr

Harders, Mr Spann, Professor O'Connell and Mr Fancher. He repeated his answer of 18 March. He tabled Mr Todd's correspondence and said that the only action taken was to advise the Premier of it.

On 19 May I was given leave to incorporate in Hansard a notarised statement which Mr Todd made on 11 May. I shall summarise it.

Mr Todd was contacted by Mr Fancher on 20 October 1975 by telephone and on several occasions between then and 7 November. He spoke with Mr Anthony by telephone on 31 October, 1 November and 3 November. He met Mr Fancher in California on 9 November. Mr Fancher had in his possession several large rolls of notes of Australian currency, which Mr Spann had acquired from hotel bars, because normal sources of funds were closed at the time of his departure.

On 15 November he left with Mr Fancher for Zurich. There they were met by Mr Rae. He secured an appointment for Mr Rae, Mr Fancher and himself to meet the Director of the Swiss National Bank. Mr Fancher raised questions about access to information regarding Australian Government loan raising. The Director told him that such matters ought to be raised by the Australian Foreign Ministry through the Swiss Foreign Ministry.

Between 18 and 21 November Mr Fancher told him that he had telephoned Mr Anthony in Australia who in turn would speak to Mr Peacock about access to the Foreign Ministry. On or about 21 November the three travelled to Berne and met Mr Keith Brennan, the Australian Ambassador. The question of access to information about loan raising attempts by the Australian Government was discussed. The three returned to Zurich.

On 26 or 27 November Mr Brennan visited the three at their hotel in Zurich and warned Mr Fancher and Mr Rae about activities which might amount to a breach of Swiss law. Throughout the stay in Zurich Mr Fancher made repeated telephone calls to persons in Australia, among them Mr Bjelke-Petersen, Mr Anthony, Mr Lynch, Mr Andrew Hay, Mr Lynch's principal private secretary, and Mr Spann.

On or about 14 November Mr Todd received US$13 488 for services rendered to the Premier. As a result of inquiries made by him he believed that sum was paid from the account of Tancred Bros at the 110 Plaza Branch of the Bankers Trust Bank, New York City, on the authorisation of Mr B. J. Tancred. He was still owed the sum of US$17 572.

On 27 April 1976 he received a telephone call from Mr Fancher who informed him that both he and the Queensland Premier wished to pay him the outstanding fee for his services but that Mr Ellicott had blocked exchange control clearance.

In his notarised statement Mr Todd also swore that on 10 November 1975 he had received a telephone call from a person who said he was John Maddison, the New South Wales Attorney-General. Mr Maddison told him that Mr John Bracey who was known to him had been detained in connection with the manipulation of stocks in natural resources companies. Mr Maddison asked him whether Mr Bracey could obtain certain information on Australian Government loan raising if he travelled to Switzerland. He told Mr Maddison that in his belief no person, particularly not Mr Bracey, could obtain such information. Mr Bracey was also mentioned in the Queensland Parliament on 9 December.

On 10 May 1976 Mr Maddison, who had just become Deputy Leader of the New South Wales Opposition, said in a press release:

It is true that I did speak to Mr Todd to seek confirmation of
certain information which came into my possession about
the so-called loans affair. Mr Todd was unable to provide
confirmation but indicated that he was acting for the
Queensland Government and was in a better position than
my informant to assess the information.

In the debate on Mr Todd's statement nine days later I said:

The former N.S.W Attorney-General was apparently anxious
for Mr Bracey to go to Switzerland if necessary. Mr Bracey's
passport, which had been taken from him after he was
apprehended at Sydney airport, was subsequently restored to
him ... Mr Todd has sworn that although Mr Bracey had
been charged with an offence under the company laws of
New South Wales, the N.S.W Attorney-General wanted to
know whether Mr Bracey could help the loans investigation.

In October and November 1977 it emerged that Mr Anthony
had spoken by telephone to Mr Bracey during the time he was in
Opposition in 1975 and that Mr Lynch and Mr Hay met him in
Sydney on 4 June 1975 and that Mr Hay had a number of
telephone conversations with him prior to 11 November 1975.
There is, however, no evidence that Mr Fraser or Sir John Kerr
knew of the activities of Mr Maddison and Mr Bracey.

None of those mentioned in Mr Todd's statement spoke
when it was debated; the only speaker on the Government side
was Mr Sinclair. Mr Todd had exposed the whole shabby
business by May 1976. It was two and a half years before it
became public knowledge through Hansard that the senior
Federal official whom Mr Bjelke-Petersen had so disgracefully

sought to implicate was the Australian Ambassador to Switzerland, Mr Brennan. In January 1976 Mr Brennan was sent to Law of the Sea consultations in New York. Mr J. T. Howard, a principal legal officer in Mr Ellicott's Department, was immediately sent to make inquiries in Switzerland during his absence.

There is some piquancy in following the subsequent fortunes of those who pursued inquiries into overseas loans inside and outside the Parliament.

Mr Licardy had on or before 6 June 1975 failed to comply with the requirements of the Legal Practitioners Act and the Solicitors Trust Fund Regulations and had appropriated very large sums of clients' money for his own use. By 27 October 1975, when Mr Lynch received a letter from him, he had again misappropriated a very considerable amount from his clients. My colleague, Mr Peter Morris, alleged in the House that Mr Lynch's staff had dictated the letter to Mr Licardy's staff. Mr Lynch, in a written answer on 31 March 1977, denied that he had received communications from Mr Licardy. On 2 June, however, he admitted that he in fact had received the letter and had sent copies of it to the President of the Senate, the Leaders of the Labor, Liberal and Country Parties in the Senate and the two Independent senators. Later the Solicitors' Statutory Committee found that Mr Licardy was unfit to be a solicitor or to be employed in a solicitor's office and ordered his name to be struck off the Roll of Solicitors.

In the light of evidence given to Sir Gregory Gowans' inquiry into some of the Victorian land scandals Mr Lynch had to resign from the Fraser Ministry. He was succeeded by Mr Howard, who had to admit that he had met Mr Licardy not only in Canberra but once or twice in Sydney in about October 1975.

Mr Ellicott, who had met Mr Licardy in Canberra, had to resign as Attorney-General on becoming, as he put it, 'another victim' of 'the loans affair'. Liberal leaders can be no more fortunate in their contacts with solicitors than Mr Sinclair, the Deputy Leader of the Country Party, whose long-time professional and personal friend, a Tamworth solicitor, was struck off the Roll by the Court of Appeal in December 1978 for misleading a widow into leaving him her half-million-dollar estate.

Mr Fancher and his wife have been declared bankrupt. They owed $17 000 to Telecom on two telephone services in Atherton. In proceedings in May 1977 they swore that the calls were made and accepted on behalf of the Federal Government late in 1975 and early in 1976 and that one of the services—an unlisted one—was installed for that purpose. Before 11 November 1975 he had, so Mr Lynch admitted, made a number of communications by telephone with members of Mr Lynch's staff. On 31 March 1977 Mr Lynch admitted that Mr Fancher had put loan proposals to the Federal Government early in 1976 through third parties. On 2 June 1977 he disclosed that Mr Fancher had offered an overseas loan of 'two to three billion dollars' on 6 January 1976 and a supplementary loan of $800 million six days later but he would not disclose who were the third parties. He should not have been so coy. Mr Sinclair had disclosed a year earlier—on 19 May 1976—that Mr Bjelke-Petersen had himself spoken to Mr Lynch about Mr Fancher's offer.

Mr Bracey also presumed on his acquaintance with Mr Lynch to offer overseas loans in January and May 1976.

The strange associations which the Liberals formed in 1975 and which they pursued in ostensible defiance of Sir John Kerr in November and December of that year have returned to haunt them in the following years.

11

NEGRESCO TO UNESCO

PEERS: OUR LORDLY STYLE
           YOU SHALL NOT QUENCH
           WITH BASE *CANAILLE*!
FAIRIES: (THAT WORD IS FRENCH.)
           W. S. Gilbert, *Iolanthe*

After the elections on 13 December, Sir John Kerr was eager to resume an overseas tour which the crisis had aborted. Before he left, however, Sir John had to help Mr Fraser with his ministry. Mr Fraser wanted to be rid of Don Chipp and Tom Drake-Brockman. Mr Chipp had been a minister under Prime Ministers Holt, Gorton and McMahon, a shadow minister under Mr Snedden and Mr Fraser himself and was in the caretaker ministry appointed on 12 November 1975. Senator Drake-Brockman DFC had been a minister under Prime Ministers Gorton and McMahon, Leader of the Country Party in the Senate for six years, a shadow minister under Mr Snedden and Mr Fraser himself and also a member of the caretaker ministry. To save Mr Fraser the embarrassment of having their commissions terminated, Sir John accepted the resignation of

Mr Fraser as Prime Minister on 22 December, which entailed the termination of all other ministerial commissions, and immediately swore in an augmented ministry from which Mr Chipp and Senator Drake-Brockman were omitted.

Sir John and Lady Kerr left for Europe the following day. In his book Sir John Kerr is at pains to assert that his 1975–76 tour was a delayed version of one which I had approved and helped him arrange. In fact the itinerary, nature and purpose of the two were markedly different.

After his remarriage, Sir John had been pressing me to let him take his wife to London and Paris as soon as possible. I stressed that, on his first visit to London after being installed as Governor-General, he should also visit Ireland. For too long Governors-General had had regard to three-quarters of the original European settlers in Australia who had come from the United Kingdom and had overlooked the quarter who had come from Ireland. I took his point about visiting Paris but urged him also to visit Belgium and the Netherlands. I reminded him that two years earlier I had told him of the visit of the Governor-General of Canada to all three countries. In the meantime the French had applied the Persepolis rules when Sir Paul Hasluck had, in the absence of the Queen, represented Australia at the funeral of President Pompidou in April 1974 and I had in January 1975 raised the question of a visit with the Dutch Court because of the great number of Dutch settlers in Australia. Overall I was sure that Ireland, France, Belgium and the Netherlands were sufficiently familiar with the notion of constitutional monarchy to understand the position of the Governor-General in Australia. He agreed with these proposals and suggested that he might combine his visit to Western Europe with a visit to Japan and Canada. Prince Hiro, the elder son of the Crown Prince of Japan had been his guest in August 1974; I was against his visiting Japan because in Japanese eyes the Governor-General was seen as having neither the power of a Prime Minister nor the mystique of a monarch. (This view was borne out in 1977 when he had the Department of Foreign Affairs sound out whether he might visit Japan as a Head of State; he was rebuffed.) He had taken part in our consultations with Canada on the composition of the vice-regal salute and the establishment of the Order of Australia, each of which took a form parallel to those developed by Canada; in this case I warmly endorsed his suggestion. We were arranging for the visits to Canada and Western Europe to be made in November and December but suspended the arrangements when the Senate went on strike in October.

The resumed visit agreed to by Mr Fraser was vastly different from the one agreed to by me.

The Governor-General could travel by commercial aircraft and not, as previously, by RAAF aircraft, because, although the visit was to take somewhat longer than had originally been planned, it was to be much simpler. None of his intended hosts were now willing to entertain him. (He had already aroused controversy in Canada about the possible role of her Governor-General and *fainéant* Senate. His name was similarly anathema in all the Commonwealth countries in the Caribbean, where there was now an accelerating movement to follow Guyana which was already a republic with a President and unicameral legislature. His *ancien régime* pretensions were no more acceptable anywhere in Europe. President Tito had already cancelled an intended visit and President Makarios only resumed negotiations for his intended visit after Sir John announced his retirement in July 1977.)

Sir John and Lady Kerr spent eighteen days in Britain, seventeen days in France, four days in Hong Kong and three days in Italy. The Governor-General did not publish his engagements and Mr Fraser has, when asked, been unable to specify their place and nature. Five officials, unnamed, accompanied Their Excellencies throughout—an aide-de-camp, a valet, a maid and two security agents—and the official secretary joined them on 22 January. The press reported that the accommodation at the Connaught Hotel in London cost $300 a day, that the party moved from one hotel to another in Paris and that the time in Italy was spent touring Tuscany. By the time the party returned on 3 February, Sir John had spent 103 days overseas at public expense since his appointment had been announced two years before.

In his book, Sir John Kerr claims that the protests and demonstrations against him at home were organised and orchestrated by the Labor Party and that they expressed the feelings of a fraction—the work of the *enragés,* as he describes them. They were in fact spontaneous and nationwide.

Sir John first tested the climate at home by making another visit to Tasmania. It was not thought prudent for him to attend a public function like a race meeting, as he had done on his first visit to Tasmania a year earlier. Official functions were precluded because ministers of the Tasmanian Labor Government would not attend them with him. He was limited to functions at Government House and Hadley's Hotel.

On Sunday afternoon 8 February Sir John and Lady Kerr visited the late Professor Jim McAuley and his wife. They had all known each other at the Australian School of Pacific Administration thirty years before. Sir John related how he had told his wife that he intended to discuss with me proposals to dismiss my Government and order an election but she had told him not to do that because I would have the Queen sack him. He also told the McAuleys that he had wanted to resign after the election but his wife dissuaded him. One of those present during this conversation recounted it to a friend who related it to me when I was in Hobart the following Saturday. I referred to the visit in a speech to the conference of the Tasmanian branch of the Labor Party a week later. Sir John refers to it in his book and Professor McAuley in the June 1976 issue of *Quadrant*. As the professor states, we had been contemporaries at the University of Sydney. In August 1958 I had spoken in the House about unrest in Rabaul on the basis of articles and information he gave me. He was one of the great poets in our language and was the only intellectual in the DLP, although his political writings, like Milton's, are only memorable in having distracted him from his poetry. In *Quadrant* he corrected me by saying that he had not discussed Brian Harradine's candidature for the Senate with Bob Santamaria in his house but in hospital. He did not deny the conversation I have recounted; he knew who my informant was and could not deny it.

Sir John opened the new Parliament on 17 February. He proposed to appoint only one deputy to swear in the members of both Houses. The Father of the Parliament, Kim Beazley, exposed this 'act of very great discourtesy':

Had there been only one deputy to swear in both Houses we would have been cooling our heels in this chamber waiting for the process to be finished in the Senate. I would like to know why such a discourtesy, never offered to this House in my 30 years in this Parliament, took place. But it is consistent with the attitudes shown towards the rights of the House by the holder of that office.

The first business of the House was to elect a Speaker. The opportunity was taken in nominating Mr Scholes to point out that he had striven to carry out the House's directions and to assert its rights against the Governor-General on 11 November. When the Governor-General entered the Senate chamber to deliver his address opening the Parliament, the Labor senators left the chamber. When he invited members of the House of Representatives to attend in the Senate chamber to hear his address the Labor members declined the invitation.

The next State Sir John visited was South Australia. Whereas his reception in Tasmania had been frosty, in South Australia it was torrid. As in Tasmania, ministers of the State Labor Government would not attend any functions which he attended. He opened the Torrens College of Advanced Education on 19 March. The rowdy crowd limited his speech to one and a half minutes. His reactions were shown on television around the whole country.

On 1 April 1976, Claude Forell wrote in the *Age*:

> It is becoming increasingly more difficult to escape the conclusion that Sir John Kerr ought to retire as Governor-General as soon as he can decently do so.
>
> Sir John Kerr should go for the sake of the nation, the Government and the Opposition, as well as for his own peace of mind.
>
> I believe Sir John Kerr ought to go for the simple conservative reason that he is no longer capable of fulfilling the supreme requirement of his high office.
>
> The Governor-General is the surrogate Head of State of the Australian Commonwealth, the resident representative of the Queen of Australia.

He is—or ought to be—the paramount symbol of
national unity, a vigilant guardian of the Constitution, and
the embodiment of continuity and consensus above the
muddy fray of politics.

It is essential that he should command the respect and
confidence, if not necessarily the admiration and affection, of
his Ministers, the Parliament and the great majority of people.

Sir John Kerr no longer qualifies for this vital symbolic
role. On the contrary, he has become the focus of
controversy, a target of recrimination, an object of partisan
passion, a symbol of disunity.

Sir John and Lady Kerr's position was certainly jeopardised
by the public manifestations against them. Their standing, however, was more seriously undermined among sections of the
community disposed to support them, particularly in New South
Wales where the personalities were well known, when her speedy
and secret divorce and their marriage a year earlier came under
questioning to State Attorney-General Maddison and Federal
Attorney-General Ellicott. The marriage was solemnised six
weeks and a day after her divorce petition was filed. Mr Justice
Larkins made the decree absolute forthwith because of
engagements she had as an interpreter in Paris. In the Legislative
Assembly the climax came when Rex Jackson gave notice of
motion to call Mr Justice Larkins before the bar; this was a factor
in the decision a few days later by Sir Eric Willis—Liberals had
installed him in place of Mr Lewis—to call an election a year
early. In the House of Representatives Mr Ellicott admitted that
the Chief Justice, Sir Laurence Street, had telephoned him to
correct the answer he had given Parliament about the divorce
hearing, which had been unlisted and after hours.

The ground of the petition was two years' desertion. Judge Robson had left the matrimonial home scarcely a year before. Senator Jim McClelland, who had not previously known of Mrs Robson, learned of the Governor-General's intense interest in the progress of the Family Law Bill through the Senate in October and November 1974. Sir John himself used his direct line to telephone the Senator constantly, sometimes on successive days. He was particularly interested in what is now section 49(2) of the Act: 'The parties to a marriage may be held to have separated and to have lived separately and apart notwithstanding that they have continued to reside in the same residence.'

Senator McClelland repulsed an attack by the shadow Attorney-General, Senator Greenwood, on this 'farcical' provision.

On 3 June 1976 Mr Ellicott introduced legislation to extend the minimum period for giving notice of intended marriage from seven days to one month. It was irreverently dubbed 'the Kerr amendment'.

Sir John and Lady Kerr continued their round of public engagements in April 1976. In Canberra itself they were continuously jeered at the Australian National University and repeatedly hissed at the theatre. Until they left the country they continued to encounter more overt resentment at theatres and concerts than any other vice-regal couple since Lord Stonehaven walked out of a concert by Paderewski in Sydney in March 1927.

Later in April the Labor councillors of the Melbourne City Council resolved not to boycott but to attend the Quarter-Day Luncheon at which Sir John was to be a guest. They published their letter to him:

> We are totally opposed to you retaining the office of
> Governor-General, and we consider that you have disgraced

your office and politically alienated more than 43% of the
Australian population.

The Governor-General of Australia should most
properly be seen as the Queen's representative, an impartial
figure, above party politics.

We write to inform you in advance that we intend to
attend the Melbourne City Council Quarter-Day Luncheon
in order to make our views known to you personally.

We are not interested in dissuading you from attending,
as I am sure you are already aware that you are not welcome
anywhere in Australia so long as you retain the office of
Governor-General.

Sir John did not attend.

In May New South Wales also gained a Labor Government.
The new Premier, Neville Wran, had known the Governor-
General well at the Bar and on the Bench. (He had appeared
before him in *Moore v. Doyle*.) He did not hide his views of his
conduct in 1975. In consequence Sir John and Lady Kerr could
not attend any official engagements in the largest State. Their
visits were increasingly confined to private clubs and country
towns. For the first time in history the vice-regal Rolls-Royces
were seen on dusty roads. One was actually transported from
Sydney to Melbourne and back for the VFL Grand Final in
September 1976. The vice-regal couple did not neglect even our
remotest islands. They were accompanied on a visit to Lizard
Island by a naval aide, a butler, a Commonwealth police officer,
the head of Queensland's police special branch and a Queensland
constable. An RAAF Caribou went up to Cairns to convey them
to Lizard Island and back to Cairns. Security problems on
Lizard Island are assessed as minimal.

Parliamentary and public interest was now being shown in the way the National Gallery was lending works of art to the official establishments in a profusion and with a speed which would have satiated even Catherine the Great. Official residences under the British Crown had never acquired so many works of art since the days of the Prince Regent, although his consort never saw them. Art lovers and taxpayers will find it interesting to have a consolidated catalogue of the paintings which were lent to Government House in the first two years of Sir John Kerr's second marriage, together with the dates of acquisition.

Artist	Artwork title	Date of acquisition
Ralph Balson	Untitled	August 1971
Jean Bellette	*Non-objective*	October 1976
	Figure Group	February 1972
	Greek Sketch	April 1976
Arthur Boyd	*The Valley*	March 1974
	Unicorn and Figure in a Tree	February 1975
	Rosebud Landscape	February 1975
	Landscape	February 1975
	Figure with Black Can	February 1975
Rupert Bunny	*The Fortune Teller*	1950
	Fons Veneris	1975
	Landscape in the Pyrenees	September 1963
	Study for Summertime	February 1976
	Nocturne	March 1976
	Le Chant Lointain I	March 1976
	The Rape of Persephone	March 1976
Nicholas Chevalier and other artists:		
24 historic lithographic prints		October 1975

Artist	Artwork title	Date of acquisition
Roy de Maistre	*King George V and Queen Mary Receiving the Freedom of the City of Melbourne*	November 1972
Russell Drysdale	*Burnt Out Country*	October 1967
John Firth-Smith	*Peanut Time*	February 1976
Haughton Forrest	*Ship at Sea in a Storm*	February 1976
E. Phillips Fox	*Promenade*	December 1974
	On the Sand	December 1974
	Venice	September 1975
Leonard French	*The Burial*	March 1976
Donald Friend	*Rushcutters' Bay*	November 1962
Sam Fullbrook	*Plane Over Dunlop*	February 1965
James R. Jackson	*Woman with a Parasol*	July 1971
Frank McNamara	*Long Reef in a Storm*	February 1976
	Heat Wave, Mt St Vincent	February 1976
Max Meldrum	*The Merry-go-round*	November 1964
Godfrey Miller	Untitled JH376	August 1970
Sidney Nolan	*Death of Sgt. Kennedy at Stringybark Creek*	June 1972
Justin O'Brien	*Interior with Flowers*	March 1967
	Still Life with Fresco	February 1976
Margaret Olley	*Pomegranate I*	October 1976
Margaret Preston	*Banksias*	August 1975
	Still Life	February 1976
John Peter Russell	*Vue D'Antibes*	September 1976
Jeffrey Smart	*Antibes*	May 1976
Margaret Stones	*Botanical Study*	June 1962
Tim Storrier	*North Queensland Landscape (Descent to the Plains of Circa)*	August 1975

Michael Taylor	*Late Hour Monaro*	February 1976
	Flying Insects	February 1976
Hayward Veal	*Casino, Dieppe*	December 1973
Douglas Watson	*Low Tide Geraldtown*	April 1972
Brett Whiteley	*Inside an Avocado Tree*	October 1976

Government House was also adorned with two of Robert Klippel's sculptures acquired in February 1976, three ceramic pieces by Peter Rushforth acquired in September 1972 and three others by Hiroe Swen acquired in August 1975 and two Arthur Boyd tapestries of St Francis acquired in February 1972. Admiralty House received the Sidney Nolan tapestry *The Trial*—it was Sir John's favourite backdrop on television—and the following paintings:

Artist	Artwork title	Date of acquisition
Charles Blackman	*Charlie Chaplin*	February 1976
Sidney Nolan	*Ned Kelly*	August 1970
	Ned Kelly Writing His Will	April 1976
Fred Williams	*Triptych Landscape*	January 1970
	Grey and Silver Landscape	March 1976

Mr Cobden, an officer of the Gallery, became a great favourite of both the Governor-General and his lady. The court circular recorded his appearances at Government House and Admiralty House. He must have helped to take their minds off affairs of state during the Supply crisis and election campaign, because he was their guest on VIP flights on 24 and 26 October, 6, 9 and 10 November and 6 and 8 December 1975. Sir John writes, 'I knew on 6 November that I would have a weekend of very serious private deliberations which I intended to undertake alone.' One wonders what happened to that particular weekend.

My colleague Les Johnson showed a sad lapse of taste in December 1976 by suggesting that it would have been more in keeping with the Gallery's role to put this unique collection on circuit. He proceeded to put the preposterous proposition that 'the collection should be put into universities of Australia, into the colleges of advanced education, into the art galleries in the great cities, the country towns and the provincial cities and in civic centres and art galleries all around Australia to let the people who paid for them draw some inspiration from them'.

The vice-regal court was becoming truly regal. While women had not been required to curtsy to the first Lady Kerr, they now did so to the second. The Australian vice-regal salute gave way to 'God Save the Queen'. Under my Government both Sir Paul Hasluck and Sir John Kerr had used stationery headed with the words 'Government House, Canberra', surmounted by a crown; under the Fraser Government, Sir John came to use stationery headed by the Lion and the Unicorn. It should not be concluded that the second Lady Kerr could not unbend and in fact be positively gracious. Madame du Barry could not have been more gracious to Choiseul than Lady Kerr always was to me. It was not long before she told Mrs Fraser that she might call her Anne, when they were alone. (We contemporaries had come to sense that she had ceased to fancy Nancy.)

In his book Sir John gives loving details of the honours with which he was showered. First there was the CMG[1] in the 1966 New Year's Honours on the recommendation of the Australian Government, and next the KCMG[2] in the 1974 New Year's

---

1   CMG: Companion of the Order of St Michael and St George.

2   KCMG: Knight Commander of the Order of St Michael and St George.

Honours on the recommendation of the British Secretary of State for Foreign and Commonwealth Affairs at the request of the Premier of New South Wales.

When he had been appointed Chief Justice of New South Wales he had not been created a KCMG, as is usual, because his predecessor, Sir Leslie Herron, was still Lieutenant-Governor and only a KBE.[3] When Sir Leslie died the New South Wales quota of knights allowed by the Foreign and Commonwealth Office was exhausted. So the Liberal Premier, Sir Robert Askin, asked the Liberal Prime Minister, Mr McMahon, to recommend the Chief Justice for a KCMG, which he could do directly to the Queen. Mr McMahon made this recommendation for the 1973 New Year's Honours. Sir Paul Hasluck, however, knowing the Labor Party's attitude towards the award of Imperial Honours, held this and other recommendations until after the elections on 2 December 1972. He asked me whether I advised him to forward the recommendations to the Queen. I said that the policy of my Party was against it. He asked me to put the advice in writing, which I did. Sir John had to wait a further year for his KCMG from the New South Wales Liberal Government.

As Prime Minister, Mr Fraser was able to oblige Sir John in a way I could not. Sir John records his apotheosis:

In Canberra I was sworn in as a member of Her Majesty's Privy Council at a meeting presided over by the Queen at Yarralumla. During an audience on board the *Britannia* in Fremantle harbour Her Majesty invested me as a Knight Grand Cross of the Royal Victorian Order. (I had previously, in 1975 when the Queen established the Order of Australia

---

3   KBE: Knight Commander of the Order of the British Empire.

of which she is Sovereign, become the first Chancellor and a Companion of the Order and later, when the rank of knighthood was introduced, the first Knight of the Order of Australia. In 1976 Her Majesty had promoted me to the rank of Knight Grand Cross in the Order of St Michael and St George. Throughout my governor-generalship I was Prior in Australia and a Knight of the Order of St John of Jerusalem and in April 1977 was awarded the Grand Cross of Merit of the Sovereign and Military Order of Malta, the Catholic Order which exists in brotherly relationship with the Order of St John.)

Such a *cursus honorum* clearly gave the greatest gratification to a *novus homo*. He was loaden with honours, if not, like Coriolanus, with honour.

The explanation of Sir John's priorities and preoccupations lies in the complex hierarchy of Imperial Honours. The Order of the Garter, the oldest order of chivalry in the world, the Order of the Thistle and the Royal Victorian Order (1896) are the only Orders awarded by the Queen herself without the recommendation of any of her governments. She made Lord Casey Australia's only Knight of the Garter when he retired as Governor-General and in 1963 she made Prime Minister Menzies Australia's only Knight of the Thistle. During the terms of her Governors-General Slim, De L'Isle and Hasluck, she paid visits to Australia and made them GCVOs and the State Governors KCVOs.[4] Her Governors-General McKell,

---

4   GCVO: Knight/Dame Grand Cross of the Royal Victorian Order;
     KCVO: Knight Commander of the Royal Victorian Order.

Dunrossil and Casey did not become GCVOs because the Queen did not visit Australia during their terms. She did not award any knighthoods in this Order during her two visits while I was Prime Minister out of consideration for my Government's policy on Imperial Honours.

Sir John's honours all indicate his standing with Liberal governments and not his standing with the Queen. In the case of Australians the Orders of the Bath (1725), St Michael and St George (1818) and the British Empire (1917) are awarded by the Queen either on the recommendation of the Prime Minister or on the recommendation of the British Secretary of State for Foreign and Commonwealth Affairs at the request of a State Premier. The last three Orders and the Royal Victorian Order have two classes of knights: Knights Grand Cross and Knights Commanders. Knights in these Orders take precedence according to the date of the creation of the Order but all Knights Grand Cross take precedence over all Knights Commanders. Thus the Imperial order of precedence is KG, KT, GCB, GCMG, GCVO, GBE, KCB, KCMG, KCVO and KBE.[5] Knights Bachelor do not constitute an Order of Chivalry. Since 1950 Liberal Prime Ministers have recommended seven

---

5   KG: Knight of the Garter; KT: Knight of the Thistle; GCB: Knight Grand Cross of the Order of the Bath; GCMG: Knight/Dame Grand Cross of the Order of St Michael and St George; GCVO: Knight/Dame Grand Cross of the Royal Victorian Order; GBE: Knight/Dame Grand Cross of the Order of the British Empire; KCB: Knight Commander of the Order of the Bath; KCMG: Knight Commander of the Order of St Michael and St George; KCVO: Knight Commander of the Royal Victorian Order; KBE: Knight Commander of the Order of the British Empire.

GCMGs, one GBE, eighteen KCMGs, 118 KBEs and 268 Knights Bachelor. Any Australian Prime Minister can, if so minded, secure a GCB or any lesser Order for himself by making a direct recommendation to the Queen.

When I approached Sir John in September 1973 about the governor-generalship, he was the Hon. J. R. Kerr, CMG. When I nominated him he was the Hon. Sir John Kerr, KCMG. Thanks to Mr Fraser, he had become in a single *annus mirabilis* the Rt. Hon. Sir John Kerr, AK, GCMG, GCVO, K St J.[6]

Stunned by Mr Fraser's largesse, my sceptical colleague Dr Klugman put questions to Mr Fraser about the status of the Order of St John of Jerusalem. Mr Fraser had to admit that the Order was a private organisation and its awards have no official recognition. Nevertheless, Sir John Kerr used the vice-regal notices to make announcements about this 'Order'.

Sir John's ambition was to be created a viscount, like Slim at the end of his term as Governor-General and Dunrossil at the outset of his term. Mr Jim Callaghan had been unable to resist Mr Fraser's request to recommend Sir John as a member of the British Privy Council, because such appointments have been customarily accorded to Governors-General and Federal political leaders in Australia; it was too much for Mr Callaghan to recommend that the Queen of Britain grant Sir John a peerage.[7]

On 30 November 1977, however, Sir John was granted a Coat of Arms. Aficionados will be interested in the full armorial bearings:

---

6   AK: Knight of the Order of Australia; K St J: Knight of the Order of
    St John.

7   See Extended Biographies.

Arms—ermine, a Mimosa flower ensigned with the
Royal Crown proper on a chief gules a heart or between
two pierced mullets of seven points argent.

Crest—a wedge-tailed eagle and a bird of paradise
respectant proper supporting a sword point upward argent
hilt and pommel or.

Supporters—on the dexter side a unicorn argent crined
and unguled or and on the sinister side a griffin also or each
supporting a sword point downwards argent hilt and
pommel gold.

The motto is 'Independence Under Law'. In his book Sir
John proclaims that 'by this I have lived'. Such a man could not
blot an escutcheon before he had acquired it. One can forgive
him a retrospective aspiration to live up to it even if to quote it
is somewhat like producing one's own character reference.

At the Lodge in February–March 1977, Senator Withers
told the press in August 1978, Mr Fraser and some of his senior
ministers decided that Sir John Kerr had to be replaced as
Governor-General and a suitable position had to be found to
entice him out.

Sir John and Lady Kerr had to go overseas again, this time to
the Queen's Silver Jubilee Thanksgiving Service in London on 7
June 1977. They set out in good time on 25 April. Senator James
McClelland asked why their itinerary included stays in Teheran,
Nice, Paris, Rome and Bangkok, where one presumed there were
to be no Silver Jubilee festivities. He had to wait till the Senate
rose on 3 June to receive a written answer from Mr Anthony, the
Acting Prime Minister, who told him: 'The Governor-General
will take a period of mid-term leave abroad as is the normal
practice. The visit is at official expense, also as is normal practice.'

Sir John's book shows that this was a fallacious answer. He had told the Queen and Mr Fraser in March that he was proposing to resign; he writes, 'My decision was already being fully acted upon in April'. Thus the Governor-General was not in mid-term; he was about to resign. The ministerial answer was circulated too late to be included in the daily Hansard which appears the following day, where it would have attracted attention; like all late answers on the last day of a session it was to be found only in the weekly Hansard which is published a month later. (This technique accorded with the notorious answer by Prime Minister Holt that no records were kept by the RAAF VIP Squadron of the names of passengers and the places to which they were taken. That answer was circulated too late to be included in the daily Hansard for the last day of the Easter session 1966 and appeared only in the weekly Hansard.)

Mr Fraser, however, let it be known that this time the vice-regal entourage was on an austerity basis. To quote the *Canberra Times* of 18 May 1977:

> Sir John and Lady Kerr, with a personal assistant each and a security officer, agreed to reduce their staff by half and stay away only 7½ weeks in the interests of Australia's economy.
>
> Government sources said yesterday Sir John had originally asked to be away about nine weeks with a staff of six, but had agreed to the reductions after discussions with Mr Fraser.

From the same paper it was learnt that Sir John had again been the guest of the Shah. It was next learnt from the Adelaide *Advertiser*, one of Australia's most tasteful papers, under the uncharacteristic headline 'The Suite Life', that Sir John and

Lady Kerr 'have been occupying a suite at the Negresco Hotel in Nice on the French Riviera, which, according to the Michelin Guide, has period suites of "rare luxury and tradition". About $140 a night, says the guide.' Their last port of call was in Bangkok, where, so the *West Australian* reported, they were accommodated in a suite at the Oriental Hotel at a cost of $350 a day.

Australian television recorded their visit to Nice and their reception at the Negresco. A contemporary observer with the insight of a Samuel Johnson might have commenced *The Vanity of Human Wishes* (1749):

> Let Governors-General with extensive view
> Survey mankind from Nice to Katmandu.

By 12 May Sir John and Lady Kerr were in Paris and visited the Executive Board of UNESCO. It will be recalled that on 21 April 1975 Sir John had told me of his prospective wife's interest in that organisation. When Amadou-Mahtar M'Bow, the Director-General, visited Australia in July 1975, the Kerrs had entertained him at morning tea at Government House. In welcoming the vice-regal couple to UNESCO Mr M'Bow paid tribute to my Government for arranging for him to meet our Aboriginal critics and for its total support of the organisation. He thanked Lady Kerr for coming as she had promised to do when they had met in Canberra.

Sir John and Lady Kerr took the opportunity to visit the great new Australian Embassy building in Paris for which the McMahon Government had acquired the site and I had laid the foundation stone. The architect, Harry Seidler, who was in Paris at the time, was struck by the detailed interest the Kerrs took in the accommodation in the Embassy which he had designed and even in the furniture which he had specified.

For Sir John the road ended in Rome. In June, while he was giving an audience at the Hotel Hassler-Villa Medici to the Foreign Minister, not of the Italian Republic but the Sovereign and Military Order of Malta, a courier from London brought him a message that the Queen had approved the procedure for his resignation. In Canberra on Bastille Day he announced that he would be going before the end of the year.

Before his departure from Yarralumla and Australia, Sir John performed one last service for Mr Fraser. On 27 October 1977 he granted Mr Fraser's request for a premature election of the House of Representatives.

On 24 October 1972, two days before the House of Representatives rose for the elections, Sir Paul Hasluck said in his Queale Lecture:

> If a Prime Minister were to advise a mid-term dissolution simply because 'he would like to have an election', a Governor-General would quite reasonably ask for additional reasons to support a general argument that Parliament had become unworkable or that some exceptional and unforeseen situation had arisen which could not be resolved by Parliament itself.
>
> There is precedent, too, that in the event of a mid-term dissolution, Parliament may subsequently ask for the publication of the correspondence between the Governor-General and Prime Minister. Hence there is need for both of them to set out their views in writing, and to take care that what they say and do will stand the test of historical and political scrutiny. They should know that they should have good and sufficient reasons for taking an unusual course.

... The key question is whether in fact Parliament has become 'unworkable'. Have all the proper steps been taken to resolve the conflict between the two Chambers; can an alternative Government be found without an election; can the Government party or parties find a new leader behind whom a majority will rally? There are good authorities to support a view that Parliament should not be dissolved and an election held simply to help a party leader or a party get out of their own difficulties but that the electorate should only be asked to overcome difficulties which Parliament itself cannot overcome.

In his speech in New Delhi on 28 February 1975, Sir John Kerr drew on Sir Paul's Queale Lecture and amplified it thus:

There is one other aspect of the Governor-General's role which is important. This has to do with the power to dissolve Parliament. You will all be familiar with the way in which this works under the Westminster system.

One particular point I should like to mention is the Governor-General's role in relation to the dissolution of Parliament in mid-term. Sometimes the situation arises in which a Prime Minister may seek to have Parliament dissolved before its constitutional term has expired. It is of course not sufficient for him to obtain from the Governor-General a dissolution of Parliament simply because he would like to have an election. The basic constitutional issue in such cases is whether or not Parliament has become unworkable.

... Parliament may become unworkable because of the defeat of the government on an important issue in the House or it may be that the Prime Minister is in difficulty with his own supporters. The essential question is whether the Governor-General can be satisfied that Parliament has in fact become unworkable.

He has to consider whether an alternative government can be brought into existence without an election, whether the government parties can find a leader with a majority. Parliament should not be dissolved simply to help a party leader, or a party solve their own difficulties. The country should not be forced to an election merely to help leaders solve internal party questions but only to deal with a situation which Parliament itself cannot solve. The decision to dissolve Parliament in mid-term is one of the matters which the Constitution leaves to the Governor-General to decide on his own. It is not a power exercised by the Governor-General in council.

No portion of Sir John's book is more lame and less convincing than his explanation of his failure to apply the principles enunciated by Sir Paul Hasluck and endorsed and elaborated by himself. The views which Sir John and Mr Fraser may have set out in writing have not been published.[8] There would have been a convincing case for having an election for the House of Representatives before the end of June 1978 because thereby the terms of the two Houses would have been synchronised. Sir John destroyed what was left of his reputation by allowing an election for the House of Representatives to be held fourteen months before the House's term expired and the election of half the Senate to be held seven months before the

8   The letters were tabled on 20 February 1979.

new senators could begin their term. Mr Fraser ruined his reputation by his conduct of the election. He well knew that his electoral stocks would slump in 1978, but even he could not have realised that they would slump as much as they did. Never again will the people believe his promises or his denials in an election campaign.

Sir John was last observed in public when he presented the 1977 Melbourne Cup. As he was seen, like Caligula in the BBC program *I, Claudius*, weaving his way down from the Imperial box and making his merry remarks to the owner, the fascinated crowd and a million viewers may have thought that the horse would have made a better proconsul.

There had long been, and certainly since Bastille Day, much speculation that Sir John would accept another post. The *National Times* recently disclosed that 'just before dinner at Government House, Sir John Kerr, in a note of levity, remarked to Tony Staley, then Minister for the ACT, that as he would soon retire, he would have time to be chairman of the ABC'. All such speculation was stopped in its tracks on 9 February 1978 when Mr Fraser announced that Sir John had been appointed to the revived post of Ambassador to UNESCO.

On no public issue has there been such instant, spontaneous and unanimous outrage. The editorial in the *Australian* was headed 'Ripping the Scab off the Sore', in the Melbourne *Herald* 'Jobs for the Boy', in the Sydney *Sun* 'A Pension in Paris', in the Brisbane *Courier Mail* 'Good Lord, It Can't Be!' and in the *Canberra Times* 'Undiplomatic Posting'.

The *Age* in an editorial headed 'Lazarus In A Top Hat' said:

We are now led to believe that the pressure of diplomatic
work in Paris has built up to such a degree that our

Ambassador to France can no longer attend adequately to
the Unesco responsibilities which he took over in September
1976. We are to believe, moreover, that the person best
qualified for this newly resurrected sinecure is Sir John
Kerr—a man whose departure from public life last
December was almost universally greeted with relief. Let us
say it plainly. We do not accept these propositions.

The *Canberra Times* said:

> . . . future Governors-General might feel if they wish to
> follow Sir John's precedent that to offend in any way the
> feelings of the Government could jeopardise an attractive
> retirement posting.

Even the *Sydney Morning Herald*, which had consistently
been protective of Sir John, said:

> it would be considered a nakedly political appointment by
> half the country and was entirely to be regretted. The
> Government has made a mistake; it should never have set a
> precedent under which a future Governor-General may have
> some new appointment to hope for from the party in power.
> It is not healthy.

The *Bulletin*, which tries hard to cultivate an establishment
readership, was moved to say under the heading 'Fraser's act of
political madness':

> If there is an element of a pay-off in the Paris job, it lies in a
> tacit deal between Fraser and Kerr last winter, when Kerr's

early stepping down from the governor-generalship was
announced. It was 18 months before the scheduled date, and
the Prime Minister said at his press conference last week
that when they discussed that early retirement Kerr had
mentioned his desire to have another government job.
People close to Fraser said last week that he had been under
a commitment to Kerr to find him a plum job. He had no
alternative. The Prime Minister has adamantly denied that
Kerr made this kind of job a condition of going early. But
there does seem to have been some kind of tacit deal
involved. At least an understanding.

Much of the criticism of the appointment turned on the
immense income that Sir John would receive. Mr Hayden
calculated that there would be $140 000 a year gross income
effect before taxation available to Sir John, including a non-
contributory pension of $33 000 a year, which is equivalent to a
gross income effect before taxation of $55 000 a year.

In defending the appointment Mr Fraser attributed this
consequence to the legislation for the Governor-General's
pension which I 'quite specifically and personally introduced
into this Parliament'. On 28 February 1978 I said in the House:

The situation is that judicial pensions and the Governor-
General's pension are non-contributory. The judges know
that while they are in office they will be able to act without
fear or favour because when they retire they will receive a
pension which will be so ample that they will not have to
take jobs in retirement.

. . . The Governor-General was given a pension similar
to that of the Chief Justice so that he could act without fear

> or favour because he knew that in retirement he would have
> an ample pension which would not require him to seek
> other employment.
>
> ... Judges and the Governor-General cannot take jobs
> when they are in office; because of their pensions they are
> not expected to take jobs in retirement.

There may be some excuse for Mr Fraser not understanding the reason for the legislation but there is no possible explanation for Sir John's insensitivity. The best one can say in his defence is that Sir John had not grasped the principle which lay behind my response to his financial problems which he had discussed with me in 1973. The principle is that former Governors and judges should never accept subsequent preferment or appointments from governments or interests to which they have stood in a constitutional or judicial relation; that is the necessary guarantee of their independence and impartiality while in office.

On 2 March Mr Fraser had to come into the House to announce that Sir John had resigned the UNESCO post.

Mr Fraser's fury at Sir John losing the UNESCO appointment cost me—and Australia—a seat on the International Court of Justice (ICJ).

The court has fifteen judges, each of them elected for a nine-year term by the United Nations Security Council and General Assembly and a third of them retiring every three years. Judges who were nationals of the USA, USSR, Spain, Uruguay and Benin were due to retire at the beginning of 1979. The Spaniard would be succeeded by a national from WEOG, the Western European and Others (i.e. Canada, Australia and New Zealand) group in the UN. From this group Britain and France, with their status as permanent members of the Security Council, have always had judges, and judges have also been elected from Belgium, Norway (twice), Canada (twice), Greece, Australia, Italy, Sweden, Spain and West Germany, in that order. Australia could now reasonably expect a second term.

Early in 1978 Canada inquired of Australia whether she would be nominating an Australian for the WEOG vacancy. Our Department of Foreign Affairs saw the advantages of doing so. Because of her geographical location Australia would be very much affected by issues which could come before the Court, such as sea and sea-bed boundaries, fisheries, peaceful passage through and over archipelagos and Antarctica. Australia had suffered in the revulsion against the judgments which Sir Percy Spender had given in the south-west Africa cases and particularly by his casting vote as President in favour of South Africa. The department thought I was the only Australian who could muster a majority of votes among the members of the UN.

Mr Peacock put the suggestion to Mr Fraser. Despite the objections of the Country Party, Mr Fraser was still considering it when he blew up over the UNESCO fiasco. His frustration was compounded by an act of defiance by his senators. He had conveyed his view to them through Senator Withers that it would not be appropriate for them to choose John Knight, who had been secretary to Sir Billy Snedden when he was Liberal leader, as the Government's assistant whip; but they did. Mr Fraser was described by a colleague as being so taut one could have played a tune on him. He declared that an Australian would be nominated for the ICJ vacancy, but not I. As is his custom in foreign affairs where he sees some personal advantage, he briefed the press. The Australian National Group, however, responsible for nominating candidates and comprising Sir Garfield Barwick, Mr Byers, Sir Clarence Harders and Emeritus Professor Shatwell, could suggest no other Australian who could win the position.

The vacancy which Australia could have filled went to an Italian, Professor Roberto Ago, whom my Government had engaged in the French Nuclear Tests case, the first of the environmental issues likely to come before the Court. He was somewhat lucky to be elected; the four other new judges were elected on the first ballots in the Council and the Assembly but he was elected after four ballots in the Assembly and fourteen— a record number—in the Council. At least Australia was able to find another ambassador to UNESCO.

Sir John and Lady Kerr's furniture and effects had already arrived in Paris. They had, however, not yet been taken out of their cases and the Government promptly returned them to England.

For all Sir John's patronage of the arts, the artists proved perceptive critics. The Historic Memorials Committee in bipartisan harmony decided that Sam Fullbrook's painting of him was not suitable to hang in King's Hall in Parliament House. During the crisis over Supply he had been sitting for Clif Pugh, who found him obsessed with his place in history and the potential of his office. Sir John had told another painter, Graeme Inson, that he preferred to be painted in profile; Inson responded that that would be 'just right for a one-eyed justice'. Sir John's book has a dustcover of him in profile.

In his address to the Indian Law Institute in February 1975, Sir John Kerr had said:

The governor-generalship is a developing institution in
Australia and it is coming more and more to symbolize

Australia's independent identity abroad and the nation's
unity and legitimate political system at home.

By his conduct and actions on 11 November 1975 Sir John
Kerr destroyed the governor-generalship as a symbol of the
nation's unity. By his conduct and actions after 11 November
1975, he had become, in the words of the *Age* of 1 April 1976, 'an
embarrassment to the Fraser Government, being to many
Australians a constant reminder of its impugned legitimacy and
a potent stimulus to republican sentiments' and had made the
office a 'symbol of disunity'.

12

TOWARDS THE REPUBLIC

———————————————

'WELL MAY WE SAY "GOD SAVE THE QUEEN", BECAUSE
NOTHING WILL SAVE THE GOVERNOR-GENERAL.'
E. G. Whitlam, 11 November 1975

A major part of Sir John Kerr's defence rests upon his claim that
he wished to protect the monarchy and to ensure that the Queen
was not involved. This is his principal justification for keeping
the Prime Minister of Australia and the Queen of Australia
equally in the dark. The greatest of all ironies is that by his
conduct he has done more damage than any Australian in our
history to those very institutions which he claims that he sought
to protect and preserve.

After his interview with Sir John Kerr, Speaker Scholes
wrote a letter to the Queen:

12 November 1975

Your Majesty,

I am compelled by events involving yourself through your
representative in Australia, His Excellency, the Honourable
Sir John Kerr, A.C., K.C.M.G., K.St.J., Q.C., to communicate
my concern at the maintenance in the office of the Prime
Minister of the Hon. Malcolm Fraser, M.P. despite his lack of
majority support in the House of Representatives.

Immediately following the announcement of the
dismissal of the former Prime Minister, Mr Whitlam, and
Mr Fraser's appointment, the House of Representatives
carried a resolution expressing want of confidence in
the Governor-General's nominee and requesting the
reinstatement of the former Prime Minister in whom the
House expressed confidence.

I am seriously concerned that the failure of the
Governor-General to withdraw Mr Fraser's commission and
his decision to delay seeing me as Speaker of the House of
Representatives until after the dissolution of the Parliament
had been proclaimed were acts contrary to the proper
exercise of the Royal prerogative and constituted an act of
contempt for the House of Representatives. It is improper
that your representative should continue to impose a Prime
Minister on Australia in whom the House of Representatives
has expressed its lack of confidence and who has not on any
substantial resolution been able to command a majority of
votes on the floor of the House of Representatives.

It is my belief that to maintain in office a Prime Minister
imposed on the nation by the Royal prerogative rather than

through parliamentary endorsement constitutes a danger to our parliamentary system and will damage the standing of your representative in Australia and even yourself.

I would ask that you act in order to restore Mr Whitlam to office as Prime Minister in accordance with the expressed resolution of the House of Representatives.

For Your Majesty's information I would point out that Supply was approved by the Senate prior to 2.25 p.m. Mr Fraser announced that he had been commissioned as Prime Minister in the House of Representatives at 2.35 p.m. The House expressed its view at 3.15 p.m. by 64 votes to 54. I sought an audience with the Governor-General immediately following the passage of that resolution. An appointment was made for me to wait on the Governor-General at 4.45 p.m. The Governor-General prorogued the Parliament at 4.30 p.m.

The House expressed its view after the passage of the Supply Bills and was and is entitled to have that view considered.

Yours sincerely,
G. G. D. SCHOLES
Speaker

On 17 November the Queen's private secretary wrote to Mr Scholes:

As we understand the situation here, the Australian Constitution firmly places the prerogative powers of the Crown in the hands of the Governor-General as the representative of The Queen of Australia. The only person

competent to commission an Australian Prime Minister is
the Governor-General, and The Queen has no part in the
decisions which the Governor-General must take in
accordance with the Constitution.

At the same time, in response to the great number of letters
asking that Sir John be overruled or dismissed, the Queen's
assistant secretary used the formula:

The Australian Constitution (written by Australians, and
which can only be changed by Australians) gives to the
Governor-General (who is appointed by The Queen on the
advice of her Australian Prime Minister) certain very specific
constitutional functions and responsibilities.

The written constitution, and accepted constitutional
conventions, preclude The Queen from intervening
personally in those functions once the Governor-General has
been appointed, or from interfering with His Excellency's
tenure of office except upon advice from the Australian
Prime Minister.

In *Majesty* (Hutchinson, 1977) Robert Lacey, noting that 'it
had been the son of a boilermaker 6,000 miles away who had
most spectacularly demonstrated how live a force the royal
prerogative could still represent in late twentieth-century power
politics' raised the question:

So in 1975 Australia set itself the question that all the ten
overseas kingdoms of Elizabeth II will one day have to
face—how far they can maintain a nominally monarchical
government without the personal presence of a monarch to

preside over it. The Queen's symbolic position might—or might not—command sentimental weight, but in her overseas kingdoms she does not herself exercise the powers which make her a working component of government in Britain. Can these powers with a royal origin be credibly exercised by a non-royal nominee? And if Governor-Generals are to exercise presidential powers, what role is left for the monarchy?

No institutions and no constitutions can long survive if indeed they embody the contradictions, paradoxes and absurdities implied by Sir John Kerr's actions and his interpretation of the Australian Constitution. According to the new dispensation these are things a Governor-General can do without his government's advice, irrespective of his government's advice, or against his government's advice:

He can dismiss the government. He can appoint and dismiss individual ministers. He can decide which department each minister is to administer. He can dissolve the House of Representatives. If, for instance, the Senate refuses to vote on a Budget, he can dissolve the House of Representatives and if, after a fresh election for the House of Representatives, the Senate still refuses to vote on the Budget, he can again dissolve the House of Representatives. He can call or prorogue both Houses. He need not grant a double dissolution although the government asks for it. He need not call a joint sitting if the Houses still disagree after a double dissolution. He need not assent to a Bill or to Bills passed at any such joint sitting. He need not submit to the electors a Bill to alter the Constitution which has twice been passed by one House and rejected by the other, even if he is advised to do so by the government. He need not in fact assent to a Bill to alter the Constitution even if it has been approved by the electors. He need not assent to any Bills which are passed by both Houses. He could even refuse to take the advice of his ministers to send a message to the Parliament asking for grants of money.

The actual events of November 1975, the conduct of Mr Fraser and his followers, the Chief Justice and State Premiers, ratified by Sir John Kerr and enshrined in the Kerr interpretation of the Constitution, lead inexorably to the collapse of the system. The foundation of that system is that it has the allegiance and confidence of the overwhelming majority of the people. What chance is there of that if the events of 11 November and the actions of Sir John Kerr, Mr Fraser and Sir Garfield Barwick are allowed to stand as an acceptable method of changing Australian governments?

If those events stand as a precedent, it means that the party which wins a majority in the people's House at the election is not necessarily entitled to govern. It means that a Senate, no member of which may have faced the people for three years and some of whom may not have faced the people for six years, can deny the party with the majority in the Lower House the right to govern and force it to an election without itself facing the people at that election; that elections for the House of Representatives can occur every six months; that no government without control in the Senate can afford to take unpopular measures which may be necessary for good government for fear of being forced to an election at a time when its popularity is low. It means that seventy-four years and literally hundreds of precedents in our own system alone, to the effect that a hostile Senate does not deny Supply, are to be ignored. It means that a Governor-General need no longer act on the advice of his ministers and, indeed, may act contrary to that advice. It means that a Governor-General may keep his intention to so act secret from his ministers and not even give them a chance to dissuade him or propose alternative courses of action. It means that a Governor-General can ignore the advice of the law officers of the Crown and without the knowledge and even against the advice of his Prime Minister seek the advice of the chief justice in secret. It means that a chief justice of a court not entitled to give advisory legal opinions can give advisory political opinions to a Governor-General. It means that whenever the technical provisions of section 57 of the Constitution are satisfied a Governor-General can dissolve both Houses without and even against the advice of the government. It means that a Governor-General can dismiss a Prime Minister who has the confidence of the Lower House and appoint and maintain in office one who does not. It means that a Governor-General, who cannot obtain the Prime Minister's signature on a proclamation of dissolution to validate that proclamation, can dismiss that Prime Minister and appoint one who will sign the proclamation. It means that a Governor-General can impose political conditions on his appointment of a Prime Minister and lay down policies his appointed Prime Minister must follow. It means that whether or not a Senate election can occur will depend on the caprice of State Governments in deciding whether or not to issue the writs for the election. It means that a Governor-General may ignore a request from the Speaker of the House of Representatives to attend on him and may in the meantime act in a manner directly contrary to the request he knows the Speaker to be carrying from the House. It means that a Governor-General, as representative of the Queen, enjoys powers which the Queen has never herself enjoyed and which her forebears have not enjoyed for two centuries.

A constitution riddled with such power for disruption cannot stand. It is true that since the Constitution Alteration (Senate Casual Vacancies) referendum in May 1977, Premiers cannot again change the political composition of the Senate and, since the Constitution Alteration (Retirement of Judges) referendum of that month, new High Court judges cannot hang on to office too long. It is true that senators may well shrink from transgressing again and that future Governors-General and their wives will realise how intolerable their lives will be if there is a repetition.

There are also some simple safeguards that can be taken against a repetition. In her Letters Patent and Instructions to the Governor-General, the Queen could authorise and command him to act with the advice of the Federal Executive Council in exercising the powers and functions which she assigns to him.

The Executive Council could always meet on neutral ground, as it does, for instance, from time to time in the offices in Treasury Place, Melbourne, instead of the Governor-General's premises at Government House, Canberra, or Admiralty House, Sydney.

Money Bills could have a clause: 'This Act shall come into operation on a date to be fixed by resolution of the House of Representatives.' This clause was considered by the Legislation Committee of my Cabinet in August 1975 but rejected as too provocative in a period of speculation on how the Senate might act on the Budget.

In the first year after Sir John Kerr's coup it was suggested that Prince Charles might become Governor-General in order to restore respect for the monarchy. It is certain that, like the Queen, he would scrupulously act on the advice of his ministers who had the confidence of the House of Representatives. He, like his mother, would realise that if the monarch or the heir to the throne were to act as Sir John Kerr did, it would be the end of the monarchy. It came to be realised, however, and it can be confidently asserted that, great as is Prince Charles' knowledge and love of Australia and great as may be his desire to pursue a meaningful career in preparation for his succession, he would not become Governor-General of Australia under the Constitution as it stands.

There is diminishing enthusiasm for the monarchy in Australia. An Australia-wide survey of public opinion by Australia Post in 1975 showed that only 4 per cent of people interviewed were interested in seeing royalty depicted on Australian postage stamps. In the plebiscite for the national anthem in 1977 'God Save the Queen' came third out of the four choices, being supported by 18.6 per cent of the voters and, after the elimination of the fourth choice, by 20 per cent. The census in 1976 showed that, while in the whole country only 10 per cent of the population were not born as subjects of the Queen, this was the case with 18 per cent of the population of Melbourne and 15 per cent of the population of Sydney. In the whole country 17 per cent of the population had fathers and 16 per cent had mothers who had not been born as subjects of the Queen; in Melbourne one-quarter of the population had fathers and one-quarter had mothers and in Sydney one-fifth had fathers and one-fifth had mothers who had not been born as subjects of the Queen.

It is not possible to assess the number of migrants and indeed the number of the Queen's subjects who are offended by the religious discrimination attached to the Head of State by the Act of Settlement of 1701, which, to put it bluntly, says that Prince Charles cannot become or remain King if he marries a Catholic.

As my colleague Ben James has expressed it, 'it is archaic and objectionable that the crown is worn and inherited subject to the Monarch not adhering to a particular religion or not marrying a person who adheres to that religion'.

Whatever may be said and done, however, I am convinced that Australia must sooner or later adopt a republican constitution. By this I mean a constitution with no reference to the Crown or a Governor-General; which provides adequate machinery for the transfer of power from one administration to another when the electorate decrees it; which clearly defines the rights and powers of the Head of State to exclude forever the exercise of reserved or inherited powers in a manner contrary to the will of the elected government; and which enforces certain basic democratic principles for the conduct and timing of elections and the drawing of electoral boundaries. These seem to me the minimum conditions for a genuine framework of Australian democracy.

The case for a republic is not primarily directed against the monarchy but against the faults in the Australian Constitution. The case rests not so much on the need to sever links with the Crown, but on the need to strengthen Australia's own institutions and democratic safeguards. Any worthwhile improvement of the Constitution will require major changes, and since the monarchy is integral to, and virtually inseparable from, the Constitution as it stands, the only realistic course is to replace it altogether. There is really no middle way. Inevitably this will mean cutting some royal ties, though not necessarily all of them. (There is no reason, for example, why Australia should not continue to acknowledge the Queen as head of the Commonwealth; two out of every three Commonwealth countries are not included in her Realms and Territories.)

The standard conservative response to a republic is that the present system is working well enough. It is said that Australia is to all intents and purposes an independent country and a republic would make no useful difference. In fact, to take just one of these points, Australia is not a wholly independent country at all. All State Governors, for example, are British officials appointed by the British Head of State on the recommendation of the British government; all State honours are awarded in the name of a defunct empire and by the British Head of State on the recommendation of British ministers; all State courts operating under State laws are subject to veto by a court in another country appointed by the government of that other country. Even State laws on merchant shipping are circumscribed by laws of the British Parliament, although this position can be rectified by the Federal Government seeking and ratifying international maritime conventions.

Australia's relations with Britain are regulated by the Statute of Westminster, 1931. The compact enshrined by that Statute originally included not only Australia and Canada but South Africa and Ireland, which have gone their own ways; Newfoundland, which has been incorporated into Canada; and New Zealand, a unitary and unicameral state. Of those countries only Australia and Canada are still not yet absolutely independent of Britain. Features of their Federal systems—in Canada's case amendments of the Constitution itself, and in Australia's case the appointment of Governors and appeals to the Privy Council—still involve the British Government and the British Parliament.[1]

---

1   Appeals to the Privy Council ceased after the *Australia Acts 1986*.

The Statute of Westminster is no longer an instrument of Canadian and Australian independence but an impediment to it. It is begging the question to say, as the late British Secretary of State for Foreign and Commonwealth Affairs said in the House of Commons on 21 December 1976, that 'the United Kingdom Government for their part would not stand in the way of any changes that command the agreement of all concerned in Australia.' It is precisely when our Federal and State Governments do not agree that Britain is involved. In 1972 two States, one Labor and one conservative, appealed to Britain over offshore borders. Fortunately the Queen of Britain was given the same advice by the British Government as she was given as Queen of Australia by the Australian Government. Under the present system Britain will be brought into Australian controversies whenever State Governments believe that they can use their colonial status to frustrate their own national government.

None of the countries—monarchies or republics—which Britain has emancipated since the Second World War would tolerate dominion status under the Statute of Westminster. Papua New Guinea would certainly not do so. It is a remarkable irony that Papua New Guinea, which Australia long ruled, is now a completely independent country in a way that Australia is not. Australia should no longer accept the dominion status that other British colonies have cast off. It would suit the dignity of both Britain and Australia if the Statute of Westminster were repealed.

A far greater defect in our present Constitution is its failure to provide safeguards for democratic elections and elected governments. In Australia it is common for governments to be installed with symbolic powers, but no real powers at all. The Queen, although specified in the Constitution as part of the structure of Parliament itself, was not consulted in a situation in which Parliament was dissolved against the advice of the Prime Minister. Whatever arguments there may be for the Queen as Head of State, it is difficult to sustain them if the Queen herself is acknowledged to be powerless. Whatever arguments there may be for the reserve powers of the Crown, it is surely extraordinary if the Crown itself cannot exercise them.

It is usual for conservatives to avoid this question by arguing that the Queen's powers are exercised in her name by her representatives in Australia. But what powers do they mean? They cannot mean the powers of the Queen of Britain, since no such powers have been exercised by a British monarch since George III's day, and in any case they are not specified in Britain's unwritten Constitution. It is absurd to suggest that the Governor-General is exercising in the Queen's name powers which she does not possess and would not presume to invoke. As I wrote in 1977: 'In purporting to exercise such powers the Governor-General in 1975 destroyed the credibility of an institution which three generations of the royal family had striven devotedly and conscientiously to establish.' If it is suggested that the Governor-General is exercising powers in his own name, we find ourselves in deeper trouble. It would mean that the Governor-General had powers in addition to those derived from his status as the Queen's representative. It would mean that the Queen's representative had more powers than the Queen! Where would this leave the Queen as one of the three constituent elements of Parliament? No interpretation of the actions of Sir John Kerr on 11 November can be logically reconciled with the Queen's present status as Queen of Australia and Head of State. In the Melbourne seminar in August 1976 I said:

Sections 2 and 61 of the Constitution make it clear that the
Governor-General is the representative of the Queen, that it
is her power that he exercises. Whatever reserve power the
Governor-General enjoys cannot be wider than the Queen's.
Constitutional lawyers are unanimously of the opinion that
she does not enjoy the power to dismiss a British Prime
Minister in parallel circumstances to those which prevailed
in Australia last year. The Queen of Australia is powerless
once she has appointed her representative. Having appointed
a Governor-General she is *functa officio* until she appoints
his successor.

Conservatives still argue that some sort of Head of State,
with some sort of reserve or inherited or divinely ordained
power, is needed to hold sway over the fate of governments. The
argument runs: 'If we do not have a Queen or a Governor-
General, what will we put in their place? There still has to be a
Head of State.'

The answer is surely that we do not need a Head of State
with any powers at all. The Governor-General was acceptable as
a de facto Head of State when it was assumed that he had no
powers; he is unacceptable as a Head of State when he assumes
powers, or imagines that he derives inherited powers from a
British monarch who is under no such delusion herself.
Experience has shown that a Head of State who is anything
more than an ornament is a menace. One Prime Minister having
been ambushed by a Governor-General, no Prime Minister can
ever afford to trust a Governor-General again. All that is needed
is transitional machinery to hand over government from one
party to another when the electorate so determines. A panel of
certain office holders or the High Court—not, obviously, the

chief justice alone—would probably suffice. The idea that the orderly handing over of government can be guaranteed only by a Head of State is a fallacy. In the United States, the first and greatest of modern democracies, the Head of Government and the Head of State are the same person. The transition from one administration to the next is made by the Electoral College. The great attraction and safeguard of a republican constitution are that a President, or whatever we might call the Head of State, would have no inherited or reserve powers at all; his powers would be defined by the document creating his office. He would have no powers anterior or superior to those specified in the document.

Throughout my public career, I endeavoured to make the Australian Constitution an instrument for reform. Within the Australian Labor Party my whole effort was directed to convincing my fellow members that the Constitution, properly used and properly interpreted, was no barrier against reform. By the time we came to government in 1972, the Labor Party had developed a program of reform fully capable of achievement within the Constitution. The policies which we most promptly and effectively implemented were those we had most thoroughly thought out and thought through in terms of their practicality and their constitutionality. No part of the program was ever invalidated by the High Court. No appeals against our legislation were ever upheld.

The Australian Constitution is a deeply conservative document; the High Court has been deeply conservative, grounded in the traditions of strict and close construction which have dominated the Australian Bench and Bar for generations. For our opponents, however, the Constitution and the High Court were not conservative enough; so the Constitution had to be subverted and the High Court circumvented. My Government was destroyed not because we broke the Constitution but because we were using it all too effectively and successfully in pursuit of reform and equality and in the assertion of the rights of the Australian people over their own resources and their own destiny. If the Constitution itself was not sufficient to thwart our efforts, then the Constitution and its conventions had to be overturned; and so it was done. The basic flaw which has now been exposed in the Constitution is that it enshrines a monarchical system of which the monarch is not a part. The preservation of an Australian democracy and the development of an Australian identity lead inexorably to an Australian republic.

After the disaster of Cannae, the consul Varro was officially thanked for not having despaired of the Roman republic. After the manipulation of the monarchy in 1975, I became committed to the Australian republic.

Appendix A

EXTENDED BIOGRAPHIES

Page 29
Harold Hyam Glass, AO (1988), was appointed to the Supreme
Court of NSW in September 1973 and to the Court of Appeal in
March 1974. He retired in 1987 and died, aged 70, on 29 March
1989.

Pages 82 & 188
Albert Patrick Field, aged 79, died at Caboolture on 1 July 1990.

Pages 66, 197 & 209
Sankey resided in the division of Wentworth, which Ellicott
represented from 18 May 1974. Connor, aged 70, died on 22
August 1977. On 16 February 1979, after hearing Sankey's
witnesses, the magistrate at Queanbeyan found there was no case
for Murphy, Cairns and me to answer and he formally discharged
us. On 4 November 1980 he ordered Sankey to pay costs of
$30 430 to me, $28 500 to Murphy and $16 081 to Cairns within
twenty-one days or, if he failed to do so, to serve twelve months'
hard labour. On 2 December 1980 an undisclosed benefactor,
believed to be William McMahon, paid the amount of the costs
into court. According to evidence before an Estimates Committee

of the Senate on 3 September 1980, the Commonwealth's legal costs amounted to $228 260. Murphy, aged 64, died on 21 October 1986 and Cairns, aged 89, died on 12 October 2003.

Page 205

On 4 November 1977 Attorney-General Durack announced the appointment of Douglas Gordon Patrick McGregor QC (1968) as an additional Judge of the Supreme Court of the ACT and as a judge of the Federal Court of Australia. At that time he was President of the NSW Bar Council and Treasurer of the Law Council of Australia.

Page 208

Ellicott was never a member of a Fraser Cabinet but he was a member of Fraser Ministries as Attorney-General from 22 December 1975 to 6 September 1977, Minister for Home Affairs from 20 December 1977 to 3 November 1980 and Minister for Home Affairs and Environment from 3 November 1980 to 17 February 1981, when he resigned from the House. He was a judge of the Federal Court of Australia from 2 March 1981 to 18 January 1983.

Page 215

Fraser had Lynch appointed to the Privy Council in January 1977. Lynch's vulnerability as the Liberal member for Flinders was revealed in evidence before the Board of Inquiry constituted by Sir Gregory Gowans, a former judge of the Supreme Court of Victoria, into Certain Land Purchases by the Housing Commission Victoria:

> A partnership which included Lynch family interests had recently realised a gross profit in excess of $74 000 from land

dealings in the Mornington Peninsula. The other partner had profited handsomely from earlier transactions with the Housing Commission; one of its principals was a former Chairman of the Liberal Party Electoral Committee for Flinders and a former ministerial aide to Alan Hunt, then under scrutiny by the Gowans Inquiry. (*Wayward governance: illegality and its control in the public sector*, published by Australian Institute of Criminology, 1989)

With elections to be held on 10 December 1977, Fraser required Lynch to resign as Treasurer and appointed John Howard in his place on 19 November. Fraser appointed Lynch as Minister for Industry and Commerce on 20 December 1977. The next elections were held on 18 October 1980 and Fraser had Lynch created a KCMG in January 1981. The Federal Liberal Party elected Howard to replace Lynch as deputy leader on 8 April 1982. Lynch resigned from the Fraser Government on 11 October 1982 and from Flinders on 22 October 1982 and was appointed to the board of the Reserve Bank in January 1983. At the elections on 5 March 1983 Bob Hawke defeated Fraser. Lynch, aged 50, died on 19 June 1984.

Page 216 & passim
On 23 January 1976 the NSW Liberal Party elected Sir Eric Willis to replace Lewis as Premier.

On 25 October 1975 Bracey had been taken from a plane about to depart from Sydney for Germany. Brought by the NSW Police before a magistrate at Redfern, he had to surrender his passport. Maddison had it returned to him. The court papers could not be found. On 16 December 1977 the NSW Liberal Party replaced Maddison as its deputy leader and he resigned as Attorney-General and Minister of Justice. He resigned from Parliament on 4 July 1980 and, aged 60, died on 29 August 1982.

In June 1977 Fraser had Withers appointed to the Privy Council. On 7 August 1978 he was removed as Minister for Administrative Services, Vice-President of the Executive Council and Leader of the Government in the Senate as a result of the finding of impropriety against him by Justice McGregor sitting as the Royal Commission of Inquiry into Matters in Relation to Electoral Redistribution, Queensland 1977. He remained a Senator until the double dissolution in 1987. The 'Toe-Cutter' ended up as the Right Honourable the Lord Mayor of Perth in 1991–93.

On 3 April 1979 Bracey was convicted of conspiracy to cheat and defraud and sentenced to four years' hard labour.

In June 1979 Hay, Lynch's companion and agent in contacts with Bracey, received an OBE.

On 20 July 1979 Keith Compton Gale, whose assistance to Fraser and the Liberal Party was often raised in the House and who had himself presided over the greatest company crash in Australia's history to that time, was convicted on twenty counts of conspiracy to cheat and defraud, appropriating company property ($900 000) and falsifying documents. He was sentenced to thirteen years' penal servitude.

On 5 August 1981 the Victorian Liberal Party elected Lindsay Thompson to replace Hamer as Premier. Hamer, who was born in Kew, Victoria, in the same month as I, died, aged 87, on 23 March 2004.

On 15 April 1984 Fancher died, aged 63. He was buried at Atherton and Bjelke-Petersen gave the address.

On 1 December 1987 the Queensland National Party elected

Mike Ahern to replace Bjelke-Petersen as Premier. Bjelke-Petersen, aged 94, died on 23 April 2005.

On 5 February 1990, Governor-General Hayden received a message from Sir William Heseltine GCVO, Private Secretary to Menzies (1955–59) and to the Queen (1986–90), that 'this seems a good moment to consider whether the time has not arrived for Australia, like Canada, to honour its citizens exclusively within its own system.' Smith, Hayden and Heseltine became aware that the Queen might create Smith a KCVO and the last Australian knight. His investiture took place at Balmoral, Scotland, on Sunday 19 August and the award was announced at the same time in a special *Commonwealth of Australia Gazette* dated Monday 20 August. On 31 August, the *Sydney Morning Herald* reported that Prime Minister Hawke 'was notified that Smith was about to be knighted and is understood to have considered blocking it. But he apparently decided it was a private matter between the Queen and Smith.' In October 1992, after more than two years of negotiations with State Governments, Prime Minister Keating announced that the Queen had agreed that the Federal Government and the State Governments should make no further recommendations for British honours.

Kerr died, aged 76, on 24 March 1991. His wife died on 16 September 1997.

McGregor had to retire when he attained the age of 70 on 15 June 1985 since he was appointed after the act for the Constitution Alteration (Retirement of Judges) referendum received assent on 29 July 1977. He died, aged 77, on 10 July 1992.

Hasluck died, aged 88, on 9 January 1993.

Barwick, unmoved by the 1977 referendum, which is known as the Barwick amendment and was carried in every electorate and by 80 per cent of the electors, remained Chief Justice until 11 February 1981 and died, aged 94, on 13 July 1997.

Page 233
Callaghan, whom I had known since his visit to New Zealand and Australia in 1959, was aware of Prime Minister McMahon's relentless efforts, recorded by Hasluck, to secure peerages for Prime Minister Sir Robert Menzies, Victorian Premier Sir Henry Bolte and High Commissioner Sir Alexander Downer.

Appendix B

Bills Passed Twice by the House in the 29th Parliament and Negatived or Otherwise Not Passed by the Senate.
(See table on the next page.)

Title	Introduced	Reported in Senate	Second reading negatived or otherwise not passed in the Senate
Health Insurance Levy Assessment 1974	10.7.74	31.7.74	1.8.74
Health Insurance Levy Assessment 1974 [No. 2]	27.11.74	10.12.74	11.12.74
Health Insurance Levy 1974	10.7.74	31.7.74	1.8.74
Health Insurance Levy 1974 [No. 2]	27.11.74	10.12.74	11.12.74
Income Tax (International Agreements) 1974	10.7.74	31.7.74	1.8.74
Income Tax (International Agreements) 1974 [No. 3]	27.11.74	10.12.74	11.12.74
Minerals (Submerged Lands) 1974	11.7.74	23.7.74	24.7.74
Minerals (Submerged Lands) 1974 [No. 2]	11.2.75	20.2.75	26.2.75
Minerals (Submerged Lands) (Royalty) 1974	11.7.74	23.7.74	24.7.74
Minerals (Submerged Lands) (Royalty) 1974 [No. 2]	11.2.75	20.2.75	26.2.75
National Investment Fund 1974	16.7.74	30.7.74	13.8.74
National Investment Fund 1974 [No. 2]	11.2.75	25.2.75	4.3.75
National Health 1974	16.7.74	31.7.74	1.8.74
National Health 1974 [No. 2]	11.2.75	20.2.75	27.2.75
Conciliation and Arbitration 1974	25.7.74	13.8.74	24.9.74
Conciliation and Arbitration 1974 [No. 2]	11.2.75	20.2.75	4.3.75
Conciliation and Arbitration (No. 2) 1974	25.7.74	13.8.74	24.9.74
Conciliation and Arbitration (No. 2) 1974 [No. 2]	11.2.75	20.2.75	4.3.75

Title	Introduced	Reported in Senate	Second reading negatived or otherwise not passed in the Senate
Superior Court of Australia 1974	16.7.74	30.7.74	26.2.75
Superior Court of Australia 1974 [No. 2]	28.5.75	5.6.75	11.6.75
Broadcasting and Television (No. 2) 1974	3.10.74	14.11.74	3.12.74
Broadcasting and Television (No. 2) 1974 [No. 2]	5.3.75	23.4.75	11.6.75
Broadcasting Stations Licence Fees 1974	3.10.74	14.11.74	3.12.74
Broadcasting Stations Licence Fees 1974 [No. 2]	5.3.75	23.4.75	11.6.75
Television Stations Licence Fees 1974	3.10.74	14.11.74	3.12.74
Television Stations Licence Fees 1974 [No. 2]	5.3.75	23.4.75	11.6.75
Electoral Laws Amendment 1974	13.11.74	26.11.74	28.11.74
Electoral Laws Amendment 1974 [No. 2]	5.3.75	15.4.75	(a)
Constitution Alteration (Simultaneous Elections) 1975 (b)	11.2.75	19.2.75	25.2.75
Constitution Alteration (Simultaneous Elections) 1975 [No. 2] (b)	27.5.75	3.6.75	10.6.75

cont'd ...

(a) Returned by Senate with amendments, 19.5.75; Senate amendments disagreed to by House, 26.5.75; Senate insisted on amendments, 2.6.75; House insisted on disagreeing to Senate amendments, bill laid aside, 3.6.75.

(b) This bill was not cited in the proclamation dissolving both Houses on 11 November 1975. As a bill proposing to alter the Constitution it does not come within the ambit of s. 57 but s. 128 of the Constitution.

Title	Introduced	Reported in Senate	Second reading negatived or otherwise not passed in the Senate
Electoral 1974 (Year in title changed to 1975)	5.12.74	18.2.75	25.2.75
Electoral 1975	27.5.75	20.8.75	21.8.75
Privy Council Appeals Abolition 1975	11.2.75	19.2.75	25.2.75
Privy Council Appeals Abolition 1975 [No. 2]	27.5.75	20.8.75	21.8.75
Electoral Re-distribution (South Australia) 1975	28.5.75	3.6.75	10.6.75
Electoral Re-distribution (South Australia) 1975 [No. 2]	11.9.75	1.10.75	8.10.75
Electoral Re-distribution (Tasmania) 1975	28.5.75	3.6.75	10.6.75
Electoral Re-distribution (Tasmania) 1975 [No. 2]	11.9.75	1.10.75	8.10.75
Electoral Re-distribution (Queensland) 1975	28.5.75	3.6.75	10.6.75
Electoral Re-distribution (Queensland) 1975 [No. 2]	11.9.75	1.10.75	8.10.75
Electoral Re-distribution (Victoria) 1975	28.5.75	3.6.75	10.6.75
Electoral Re-distribution (Victoria) 1975 [No. 2]	11.9.75	1.10.75	8.10.75
Electoral Re-distribution (New South Wales) 1975	28.5.75	3.6.75	10.6.75
Electoral Re-distribution (New South Wales) 1975 [No. 2]	11.9.75	1.10.75	8.10.75

Source: J. A. Pettifer (ed.), *House of Representatives Practice*, Australian Government Publishing Service, Canberra, 1981, pp. 766–7.

Appendix C

---

19 August	Appropriation Bills (Nos 1 and 2) 1975–76 introduced into House of Representatives.
20 August	Loan Bill 1975 introduced into House.
27 August	Loan Bill 1975 passed House and introduced into Senate.
3 September	Queensland Parliament chose to fill Senate casual vacancy with Albert Patrick Field who was not a nominee of the same political party as former Senator.
9 September	Senator Field sworn in.
8 October	Appropriation Bills (Nos 1 and 2) passed House.
14 October	Appropriation Bills (Nos 1 and 2) introduced into Senate.
15 October	Senate resolved not to proceed with Loan Bill until the Government agreed to submit itself to the judgment of the people, etc. Resolution communicated to House.
16 October	Senate resolved not to proceed with Appropriation Bills (Nos 1 and 2) in the same

terms as adopted in respect of the Loan Bill the previous day. Resolutions communicated to House.

Motion of confidence in the Government and the role of the House of Representatives agreed to by the House.

21 October   House resolved that the Senate's action on the Appropriation Bills was not contemplated within terms of the Constitution and was contrary to established constitutional convention, etc.

House resolved that the Senate's action in delaying the Loan Bill was contrary to the accepted means of financing a major portion of the defence budget, etc.

Resolutions communicated to Senate.

22 October   Senate resolved that its action in delaying the Appropriation Bills was a lawful and proper exercise, within the terms of the Constitution, of the powers of the Senate, etc. Resolution communicated to House.

Bills identical to original Appropriation Bills and entitled Appropriation Bills (Nos 1 and 2) 1975–76 [No. 2] introduced and passed by House and introduced into Senate.

Loan Bill 1975 [No. 2] introduced and passed House.

23 October   Senate resolved not to proceed with Appropriation Bills [No. 2] until the Government agreed to submit itself to the judgment of the people, etc.

28 October	House further denounced the Senate's actions in relation to original Appropriation Bills. Resolution communicated to Senate.
	Senate considered resolution of House relating to original Loan Bill. Further resolution proposed and negatived.
	Loan Bill [No. 2] introduced into Senate.
29 October	Motion of want of confidence in the Government moved in House and negatived.
	Bills identical to original Appropriation Bills and entitled Appropriation Bills (Nos 1 and 2) 1975–76 [No. 3] introduced and passed House.
5 November	Senate rejected House's claims of 28 October in relation to original Appropriation Bills. Resolution communicated to House.
	Appropriation Bills [No. 3] introduced into Senate.
	Senate resolved not to proceed with Loan Bill [No. 2] in the same terms as adopted in respect of original Loan Bill on 15 October. Resolution communicated but not considered by House.
	House considered Senate resolution of 5 November in relation to original Appropriation Bills and again denounced actions of Senate. Resolution communicated to Senate.
6 November	Governor-General provided with an opinion of the Solicitor-General, dated 4 November, concerning the deadlock and the constitutional position.

	Leader of the Opposition gave a notice of motion of censure of the Government. Senate resolved not to proceed with Appropriation Bills [No. 3] in same terms as adopted in respect of original Appropriation Bills. Resolution communicated but not considered by House.
10 November	Chief Justice, by letter, advised Governor-General as to his 'constitutional rights and duties'.
11 November	
9.00 a.m.	Prime Minister, Leader of the Opposition and their senior colleagues met to discuss crisis.
10.00*	Leader of the Opposition telephoned Prime Minister and informed him that Appropriation Bills would not be passed. Opposition parties meeting scheduled for this time delayed while opposition leaders continued talks. Prime Minister telephoned Governor-General to make an appointment for 1 p.m. and informed him that he would then advise a half-Senate election.
10.10	Labor Caucus met and endorsed Prime Minister's decision to ask the Governor-General for a half-Senate election.
10.30	Opposition parties met.
11.45	House met.
11.46	Government allowed precedence to motion of censure of the Government.
12.00 noon	Senate met.
12.10	Prime Minister moved amendment to censure

	motion, censuring Leader of the Opposition.
12.50*	Prime Minister arrived at Government House to advise Governor-General of a half-Senate election.
12.55	House sitting suspended for lunch.
1.00	Senate sitting suspended for lunch.
1.01*	Governor-General determined Mr Whitlam's commission as Prime Minister.
1.30*	Governor-General swore in Mr Fraser as 'caretaker' Prime Minister.
2.00	House and Senate resumed sitting.
2.05*	Government House issued press release announcing Prime Minister had been dismissed.
2.23	Appropriation Bills (Nos 1 and 2) 1975–76 passed Senate.
2.24	Senate sitting suspended until ringing of bells.
2.33	Mr Whitlam's amendment to censure motion agreed to by House.
2.34	Mr Fraser informed House that the Governor-General had commissioned him to form a Government. Mr Fraser unsuccessfully moved adjournment of House.
2.49	Standing orders suspended to enable Mr Whitlam to move a motion without notice forthwith.
3.01	Mr Whitlam moved motion expressing want of confidence in the Prime Minister and requesting Mr Speaker forthwith to advise the Governor-General to call Mr Whitlam to form a Government.

3.14	Mr Whitlam's motion agreed to.
	Speaker stated he would convey resolution of the House to Governor-General at the first opportunity.
3.15	Messages from Senate reported returning Appropriation Bills without amendments or requests.
	House sitting suspended.
*	Speaker made appointment with Governor-General for 4.45 p.m.
3.40*	Mr Fraser, together with Secretary of Attorney-General's Department, met Governor-General and advised that the Appropriation Bills had been passed and were being presented to him for assent, and recommended that the Governor-General dissolve both Houses.
3.50*	Appropriation Bills arrived at Government House and assented to by Governor-General.
4.30*	Governor-General dissolved House and Senate which did not resume sitting.
4.35*	Speaker arrived early at gates of Government House and kept waiting.
4.40*	Speaker met with Governor-General.
4.45*	Dissolution of both Houses proclaimed on steps of Parliament House.
12 November	'Caretaker' Ministry sworn in.
	Mr Fraser provided Governor-General with a formal opinion of the Solicitor-General in respect of 21 bills that satisfied requirements of section 57 of Constitution.

	Speaker communicated House resolution of 11 November to the Queen requesting her to intervene and restore Mr Whitlam to office.
17 November	Writs for elections issued with exception of South Australia and Western Australia Senate elections.
18 November	Chief Justice's advice of 10 November published.
21 November	Writs for South Australia and Western Australia Senate elections issued.
24 November	Reply of Queen's Private Secretary dated 17 November received by Speaker.
13 December	Elections for both Houses held.

* Denotes approximate time.

Source: J. A. Pettifer (ed.), *House of Representatives Practice*, Australian Government Publishing Service, Canberra, 1981, pp. 62–4.

SELECT BIBLIOGRAPHY

Crisp, L. F., *Australian National Government*, Longman, Melbourne, 1978.

Evans, Gareth (ed.), *Labor and the Constitution, 1972–1975: Essays and Commentaries on the Constitutional Controversies of the Whitlam Years*, Heinemann Educational Australia, Richmond, 1977.

Evatt, Herbert Vere, *The King and His Dominion Governors: A Study of the Reserve Powers of the Crown in Great Britain and the Dominions*, Oxford University Press, London, 1936.

Horne, Donald, *Death of the Lucky Country*, Penguin Books Australia, Ringwood, 1976.

Innes, Jane (ed.), *Millennium Dilemma: Constitutional Change in Australia*, University of Wollongong, Wollongong, 2000.

Kelly, Paul, *November 1975: The Inside Story of Australia's Greatest Political Crisis*, Allen & Unwin, St Leonards, 1995.

Kerr, Sir John, *Matters for Judgment: An Autobiography*, Macmillan, South Melbourne, 1978.

Lacey, Robert, *Majesty: Elizabeth II and the House of Windsor*, Hutchinson, London, 1977.

Lloyd, Clem and Clark, Andrew, *Kerr's King Hit*, Cassell
    Australia, Stanmore, 1976.

Menadue, John, *Things You Learn Along the Way*, David Lovell
    Publishing, Melbourne, 1999.

Reid, Alan, *The Whitlam Venture*, Hill of Content, Melbourne,
    1976.

Sawer, Geoffrey, *Federation Under Strain: Australia 1972–1975*,
    Melbourne University Press, Carlton, 1977.

Whitlam, E. G., *Abiding Interests*, University of Queensland
    Press, St Lucia, 1997.

Whitlam, E. G., *On Australia's Constitution*, Widescope
    International Publishers, Camberwell, 1977.

Whitlam, E. G., *A Pacific Community*, Australian Studies
    Endowment in collaboration with the Council on East
    Asian Studies, Harvard University, Cambridge,
    Massachusetts, 1981.

Whitlam, E. G., *The Whitlam Government 1972–1975*, Viking,
    Penguin Books Australia, Ringwood, 1985.

INDEX TO SURNAMES

INDEX TO SUBJECTS